The Political Economy of Edmund Burke

The POLITICAL ECONOMY of EDMUND BURKE

The Role of Property in His Thought

by

FRANCIS CANAVAN

Fordham University Press
New York
1995

Copyright © 1995 by FORDHAM UNIVERSITY PRESS
All rights reserved.
LC 94-30655
ISBN 0-8232-1590-3 (*hardcover*)
ISBN 0-8232-1591-1 (*paperback*)
Printed in the United States of America

Library of Congress Cataloging in Publication Data

Canavan, Francis, 1917–
 The political economy of Edmund Burke : the role of property in his thought / by Francis Canavan.
   p.   cm.
 Includes bibliographical references and index.
 ISBN 0-8232-1590-3 (hardcover) : $30.00. — ISBN 0-8232-1591-1 (paperback) : $ 17.95
  1. Burke, Edmund, 1729–1797—Contributions in economics. 2. Burke, Edmund, 1729–1797—Contributions in political science. 3. Economics—Great Britain—History—18th century. 5. Property. I. Title.
HB103.B87C36   1995
330.1′7—dc20   94-30655
                                                                  CIP

Publication of this book was aided by
a grant from the Earhart Foundation

To
Peter J. Stanlis

CONTENTS

Preface	ix
Short Titles, Primary Sources	xiii
1. Burke's World	1
2. The Soul That Animated	24
3. The Stability of Property	47
4. Property and Government	70
5. True Whigs and True Whiggism	97
6. Burke's Economics	116
7. The French Revolution	147
Works Cited	177
Index	181

PREFACE

In their *Edmund Burke: A Bibliography of Secondary Studies to 1982*, Clara I. Gandy and Peter J. Stanlis state:

> Most scholars have identified his [Burke's] economic theory as similar to or identical with that of Adam Smith in *Wealth of Nations*, a free market, *laissez-faire* system of free trade and natural liberty in economic enterprise, a world removed from modern socialist and Marxist collectivist systems. One of the large unanswered questions is how Burke's economic theory is related to his political theory, and whether they are complementary or contradictory [p. 213].

The question has remained unanswered, because few, if any, have tried fully to answer it. I myself have consciously ducked it in my previous writings on Burke, and I am not sure that I have satisfactorily answered it here. Still, it was the question that first drew my attention to the larger one of Burke's conception of the role of property in society. That led to a consideration of his political economy, because in Burke's mind there was no gulf between economics and politics. Whatever the truth may be, he at least was aware of no contradiction between his political and his economic theories.

My purpose in this book has been neither to praise nor to condemn Burke's views on property and society, but only to elucidate them. Descended as I am from a long line of Irish peasants, I have no nostalgia for the days when a British aristocracy not only ruled but owned the land. But it is the views of Burke, who loved the aristocratic social order of his time, not mine, that are of interest here. I have therefore for the most part avoided expressing my opinions, though I have not been able to forbear all question and comment on Burke's ideas. I have also generally declined to argue with other writers on Burke. In fact, except for the first chapter, I have made little use of secondary literature on Burke, in order to let him express his mind in his own words. The reader will no doubt be able to decide for himself to what extent he agrees or disagrees with Burke.

Some explanation of my use of primary sources is advisable. Since the set of *The Writings and Speeches of Edmund Burke*, under the general editorship of Paul Langford, was not yet complete at the time this book was written, I have preferred to use the first edition of Burke's writings and speeches, published by Rivington of London, in order to be able to refer to a complete set. Langford himself says:

> Many editions have appeared in the course of the last hundred and fifty years, but all derive essentially from the first, which was commenced in Burke's own lifetime and finally completed in 1827. The work of the editors, French Laurence and Walker King, has many virtues, but, not surprisingly, it has proved less than adequate to the requirements of twentieth-century scholars [*W&S* 2: vii].

I can see that for a political historian, to whom it is important to know exactly the date and context of a piece of writing by Burke, the first edition may be inadequate. But where I have compared the first and latest editions, I have found them to vary in no respect that is significant for the analysis of Burke's ideas on property. I have therefore used the new edition only for material that did not appear in the first one.

I have made sparing use of Burke's speeches in the House of Commons as reported in Cobbett's *Parliamentary History of England*, because, as Paul Langford says, they are "based on abstracts from the newspaper reports of parliamentary proceedings," and furnish "the modern reader with no assurance that what was published was the best obtainable account of what Burke said, let alone what Burke himself would have wished to appear in print." But I have felt free to use those reports of speeches which the editors of *Writings and Speeches* have included in their volumes, because they judge them to "represent most accurately what Burke is likely to have said" (*W&S* 2: viii).

Similarly, I have not used the 1844 edition of Burke's *Correspondence* except for some documents that do not appear in the new edition of the *Correspondence* published under the general editorship of Thomas W. Copeland from 1958 on.

My citations of Adam Smith's *The Wealth of Nations* require some explanation. For example, the first reference to that work is I, 11, n. 9; 1: 258, and means Book I, chapter 11, section n, paragraph

9, in volume 1, page 258 of the Liberty Classics edition of that work, published by the Liberty Fund in Indianapolis. For fuller publication data for *The Wealth of Nations*, as for all other works cited in this book, the reader may consult the list of Works Cited in the back of the book. Secondary works referred to in the text are cited in the first instance by the author's name and the book's title, thereafter by the author's name alone if only one book by that author has been used here; if more than one book, by the author's name and a short title.

The sources of Burke's own writings are referred to by short titles, a list of which, with the longer titles of which they are abbreviations, appears after this Preface. Full publication data on those sources in included in Works Cited at the rear.

My work on this book has been greatly aided by a fellowship from the National Endowment for the Humanities, followed by one from the Earhart Foundation, both of which generous benefactors I sincerely thank, and to both of which I am happy to report that the book has appeared.

I also owe a debt of gratitude to Dr. Nancy J. Curtin of the Fordham University History Department for her suggestions and advice on Chapter 1, and to Dr. Mary Beatrice Schulte of Fordham University Press to whose urging and editing this book owes its publication. I am particularly indebted to Dr. Peter J. Stanlis, who read and commented on all the chapters as I wrote them. His advice has improved the work; its remaining defects are due to me alone. Not only gratitude but admiration for his own work on Burke lead me to dedicate the present book to him. No man in this country has done more for the study of Edmund Burke.

SHORT TITLES, PRIMARY SOURCES

Corr.	*The Correspondence of Edmund Burke.* 10 vols. 1958–1978.
Corr. 1844	*Correspondence of the Right Honourable Edmund Burke.* 4 vols. 1844.
Parl. Hist.	*The Parliamentary History of England from the Earliest Period to the Year 1803.* 36 vols. 1806–1820.
W&S	*The Writings and Speeches of Edmund Burke.* 9 vols. to date. 1981—.
Works	*The Works of the Right Honourable Edmund Burke.* 16 vols. 1808–1827.

1
Burke's World

THE GREATER PART OF Edmund Burke's adult life was that of an active—a very active but not very successful—politician. Apart from his early writings, his literary remains are an enormous quantity of speeches, letters, pamphlets, and some books, the greater part of them addressed to the political issues of his day. To understand them, it is necessary to situate them in the place and time in which he wrote them. A brief sketch of the economic and social structure of Burke's world is therefore necessary before we present his conception of the role of property in it. A sketch it will be, derived from secondary literature, and by no means the larger part of the literature that is available. But it will serve to furnish the reader with a general idea of the social context in which Burke wrote and spoke.

First, however, we must give a short account of the man himself. Burke's life fell entirely within the eighteenth century. He was born in Dublin on January 12, 1729. His father, Richard Burke, was a Catholic who had conformed to the Established Church in order to be able to practice law, a profession that the Irish penal laws forbade to Catholics. His mother remained Catholic. According to the custom of the time, the family's boys, Garrett, Richard, and Edmund, were raised in their father's religion, and the one girl, Juliana, was raised in her mother's.

Because as a child Edmund suffered from poor health, he was sent to spend the years 1735–1740 with his mother's Catholic relatives, the Nagles, in the countryside of County Cork. He kept in touch with them throughout his later life through correspondence and visits. This continuing relationship helps to account for the intense sympathy he always showed for the plight of Irish Catholics, and for his desire to relieve them of their economic as well as religious penalties. It probably also explains his constant insistence that the doctrinal differences among Christian denominations were minor and unimportant.

Burke studied from 1741 to 1744 in a school conducted in Ballitore, near Dublin, by a Quaker, Abraham Shackleton; his contact with the Shackleton family, as with the Nagles, was lifelong. From 1744 to early in 1750 he was a student in Trinity College, Dublin, at the entrance to which his statue still stands, along with that of the poet Oliver Goldsmith, his contemporary. After leaving Trinity, he went to London to study law, but tired of it, and (much to his father's annoyance) abandoned it for a literary career. In this he made a splash with two books, *A Vindication of Natural Society* in 1756, and *A Philosophical Enquiry into the Origin of Our Ideas of the Sublime and Beautiful* in 1757.

Since living on the income from one's writings was even more difficult then than now, he took a job as private secretary to William Gerard Hamilton, and accompanied him to Dublin in 1761, when Hamilton became Chief Secretary to the Lord-Lieutenant of Ireland. After returning to London in 1764, Burke had a unpleasant break with Hamilton, and took a post as private secretary to the Marquis of Rockingham. The Marquis was one of the richest men in both England and Ireland, the leader of a faction of the Whigs, and twice, after Burke joined him, for brief periods the First Lord of the Treasury or, as we would say today, Prime Minister of Great Britain.

In 1765 Burke was elected to the House of Commons from the "nomination borough" of Wendover (where Lord Verney's nomination guaranteed his election), and so began his career of nearly thirty years as a Member of Parliament. The details of that career need not be recounted here but will be mentioned, when they are relevant, in the course of this book. He retired from the Commons in 1794, and died three years later.

Eric Hobsbawm has remarked, "If the eighteenth century was a glorious age for aristocracy, the era of George IV (as regent and king) was paradise" (*Industry and Empire*, p. 80). Burke did not live to see that paradise, but he saw and rejoiced in the glorious age of the British aristocracy, and died mourning what he saw as its coming doom. "In the long series of ages which have furnished the matter of history," he wrote, "never was so beautiful and so august a spectacle presented to the moral eye, as Europe afforded the day before the revolution in France" (*Works* 7: 362–363). He feared, almost to the point of despair, that the French Revolution would destroy that aristocratic world, not only in France but in

Britain and elsewhere in Europe as well, and its foreseen passing broke his heart.

What was the aristocracy whose cause Burke made his own? It did not consist of the nobility alone, although certain authors—for example, John Cannon in his *Aristocratic Century: The Peerage of Eighteenth-Century England*—so use the term. More broadly, the aristocracy was composed of both the nobility and the gentry with whom the nobles were closely interwoven, often by blood and marriage, in a single ruling class. The rest of the population belonged to several status groups, but only the nobles and the gentry constituted the class that will be called the aristocracy here.

In the seventeenth century, aristocracy so understood consisted of about four, at most five, per cent of the people. This proportion did not change significantly in the eighteenth century. In *The World We Have Lost*, Peter Laslett says, "This tiny minority owned a third, or even up to a half of all the land in the country, and an even greater proportion of all the wealth. They wielded the power and made all the decisions, political, economic and social for the national whole" (p. 27). G. E. Mingay gives the gentry alone "a half, or nearly as much of all the land, leaving the other half to be shared among the great lords, the yeomen freeholders, the Crown, and the Church; and land was more than income, it was power" (*The Gentry: The Rise and Fall of a Ruling Class*, p. 16; cf. M. L. Bush, *The English Aristocracy*, p. 38). Elsewhere, Mingay says that "it would seem that landlords owned altogether about three-quarters of the cultivated land [of England] at the end of the eighteenth century" (*English Landed Society in the Eighteenth Century*, p. 24; cf. Hobsbawm, pp. 29, 98).

Within this landed aristocracy of nobles and gentry there were gradations of wealth and rank. The noble ranks are well known even in republican America: what American girl would not like to be a duchess? Below them there were four ranks of gentry. The highest, smallest, and richest rank was that of the baronets, holders of an inheritable but not noble title created by James I in 1611. Next in order were the knights, the esquires or squires, and, finally, the lowest level of gentry, who were known simply as gentlemen, a name that could also refer collectively to the gentry as a whole. The qualifications for being considered a gentleman were, as Mingay says, "elusive," but were "acquired principally by birth, education, and the wealth and leisure to follow gentlemen's pursuits" (*The Gentry*, p. 3). These pursuits included those of members of the professions—lawyers, doctors, some clergy, military and naval officers, for example—as well as the landed gentleman's administration of his own estate. Some professional persons and some well-off landowners might also be what were called "the middling sort," whom Dorothy Marshall describes in her *Eighteenth Century England* as "all those families whose income came from some non-manual occupation but who, by their way of life and attitude of mind, had no claims to be ranked with the gentry" (p. 33). Manual labor or engaging in trade were incompatible with gentility (Laslett, pp. 35, 44; cf. Mingay, *The Gentry*, p. 7).

Among people farming the land, the highest grade below the aristocracy belonged to yeomen. One definition of a yeoman is a farmer-owner with a holding sufficient to occupy his whole time, as opposed to a man whose holding was so small that he was forced also to labor for others (J. D. Chambers, in E. L. Jones, ed., *Agriculture and Economic Growth in England, 1650–1815*, p. 100). A yeoman was, therefore, a freeholder, and if his property was worth forty shillings a year, he could vote for a Member of Parliament. Mingay warns, however, that the term "yeoman" could refer also to "a copyholder or leaseholder whose interest in the land was more than an annual tenancy but less than a freehold" (*Landed Society*, p. 88). Freehold itself was a tenancy that had become lifelong and could be passed on to heirs, so that freehold was virtually ownership of land (Bush, p. 33).

Farther down the social scale were lesser freeholders and farmers who rented their land and were therefore tenants rather than freeholders, yet who, if they rented large farms, could be as wealthy as freeholders. Below the tenants were laborers who had little or no land of their own, and so did not work land on their own account, but lived on wages earned by working for other people. A laborer might also be a cottager, occupying a cottage that might or might not have a bit of land attached to it. At the bottom of the scale were paupers, who had nothing.

Many of the poor families furnished servants to the houses of those better-off than they were (but not necessarily much better-off), where they lived and were fed as well as worked. In an age in which labor-saving devices were primitive and economic production much lower than now, households needed servants, and the poor needed work for their children. A married day-laborer had to pay rent for his cottage and provide for himself and his dependents out of his wages. When his children were old enough to work, they augmented the family income, either as servants in richer homes or by becoming laborers themselves (Mingay, *Landed Society*, p. 241). The day-laborers and cottagers thus constituted a rural proletariat.

In London and the provincial towns there were merchants, craftsmen, and artificers of all sorts. The merchants could and sometimes did become rich, even very rich, in London especially (Laslett, p. 49). But only in London, some large port cities, and the eighteenth-century's few predominantly industrial districts did merchants and manufacturers hold important offices of local government. Nor did they greatly resent the aristocratic monopoly of power, because "the interconnexion between landed and mercantile wealth inclined the governing class towards a broad view of what constituted the national interest" (Mingay, *Landed Society*, p. 11).

Social lines, though certainly drawn and insisted on in that stratified society, were not rigid. Upward mobility was difficult but possible. Downward mobility was inevitable for many. Only an eldest son could inherit a noble title or an entailed estate. If a family was gentry and intent on keeping the estate in the family, they entailed it, so that it had to be passed on largely intact to the eldest son. Daughters got dowries, but younger sons, though not unprovided for, went into the army or the Church, or were sent out to make their way in the world. Although gentlemen did not engage in trade, "there can be no doubt that gentlemen did become apprentices in very considerable numbers to the more profitable trades" (Laslett, p. 48; cf. Bush, pp. 74–75; Mingay, *The Gentry*, p. 116). Conversely, the daughter of a city merchant might marry the son of a manor house, and the son of a successful merchant or tradesman might win the hand of the daughter of a country gentleman (Laslett, p. 48).

At the top of the pyramid there was, as Cannon puts it, "a considerable narrowing of the commanding social heights" (p. 33). According to Laslett, "a majority of all marriages made by the English nobility from the sixteenth century until the twentieth were made with commoners, mainly with the gentry" (p. 40). But the gentry they married were often themselves relatives of peers and, in any case, were members of that wider aristocracy that was the ruling class. Furthermore, though merchants could buy country estates, both the price of land and the practice of entailment, which kept the larger estates off the market, made upward mobility, particularly into the nobility, difficult (Cannon, pp. 6–9; Mingay, *Landed Society*, pp. 19–27).

The ruling class was a landed class, because, until the nineteenth century, the British economy was fundamentally an agricultural economy. Agriculture employed the largest number of workers and produced the greatest part of the national wealth. Even in 1776 Adam Smith declared in *The Wealth of Nations*: "The land constitutes by far the greatest, the most important, and the most durable part of the wealth of every extensive country" (I, 11, n, 9; 1: 258). "Food not only constitutes the principal part of the riches of the world, but it is the abundance of food which gives the principal part of their value to many other sorts of riches" (I, 11, c, 36; 1: 192). It was only toward the end of the eighteenth century that large-scale industrial activities began, and the relative importance of agriculture in the national economy began to decline. To the ruling class (and to Edmund Burke), property meant primarily landed property, with its qualities of permanence and stability (Mingay, *The Gentry*, pp. 107–108, and *Landed Society*, p. 12; Laslett, p. 190).

England was the beneficiary of a "revolution" in farming techniques from the middle of the seventeenth century to the middle of the eighteenth (E. L. Jones, in Jones, ed., pp. 7, 12, 152; D. Marshall, p. 8). The improvement in farming practices fitted into a longer and slower trend toward consolidation of farms and large-scale production for the market. The agricultural revolution was in part the result of a "commercial revolution," that is, a rapid expansion of England's export and re-export trade in the late seventeenth century, which enabled successful merchants to invest much of their new wealth in land (Jones, p. 6). "Whatever the source of his wealth," says Dorothy Marshall, "as soon as he could, a man bought land" (p. 29).

The increased food supply that resulted led to lower prices for food, a release, among a widening sector of the population, of purchasing power for manufactured goods, and a consequent rise in the standard of living. The level of wages also rose, internal transportation facilities improved, and England's foreign trade continued to grow. England in the eighteenth century was a prosperous agricultural and incipiently industrial country (A. H. John, in Jones, ed., pp. 178–186). So strong was the position of agriculture in the nation's life that, even though "the nineteenth century revealed the superior quality of other forms of capital for infinite multiplication and endless variety of application, and so spelt the end of the domination of land," nonetheless for much of that century, "the force of tradition and deep-rooted respect for landed property, together with the vast strength of old-established political leadership, enabled the forms of the old social structure to be maintained almost intact" (Mingay, *Landed Society*, p. 4).

"To the eighteenth-century Whig," says Carl Cone, "nothing was more sacred than the rights of property, because English constitutional liberties depended upon their preservation" (*Burke and the Nature of Politics: The Age of the American Revolution*, p. 153; henceforth Cone 1). We may presume that attachment to the rights of property was felt most keenly by those who had the most property. But enough people had some property to make its rights respected well down the social scale.

Differentials in income, however, were marked among the several levels of society. In the late eighteenth century, Cannon remarks, "the inequalities in society were probably greater than at any time before or since" (p. 148). With a warning that "the figures are guesswork," Hobsbawm reports contemporary estimates of income around the year 1760 as follows: ten noble families received £20,000 a year, twenty such families £10,000, and another 120 families £6000–8,000 a year, "more than ten times what the richest class of merchants was supposed to earn." Among merchants, average incomes ranged from £600 a year for the rich few to £200 for the many; among tradesmen, from £400 a year to £40; among master manufacturers, from £200 a year to £40. The average income of lawyers and innkeepers was estimated at £100 a year; that of the wealthiest farmers at £150. Laborers in the provinces got five or six shillings a week (pp. 30–32). Mingay offers somewhat similar figures, again with a warning that the "figures are merely guesses, and are based on the calculations of contemporaries who themselves had no very accurate means of arriving at their estimates" (*Landed Society*, pp. 9–10, 24–25; cf. Cannon, pp. 129–133). That a man taking in £100 a year was making a respectable living suggests how enormous the wealth of the upper crust of aristocracy was in comparison.

"Nominally," says Hobsbawm, "England was not a 'bourgeois' state. It was an oligarchy of landed aristocrats, headed by a tight, self-perpetuating peerage of some two hundred persons, a system of powerful rich cousinages under the aegis of ducal heads of the great Whig families—Russells, Cavendishes, Fitzwilliams, Pelhams, and the rest." Yet, according to Hobsbawm, they were really a bourgeoisie. What struck visitors to mid-eighteenth-century Britain was "the essentially 'bourgeois', commercial, nature, of the country" (pp. 31–32).

C. B. Macpherson has argued in similar vein:

> There is plenty of evidence that England approximated closely to a possessive market society in the seventeenth century. Very nearly half the men were full-time wage-earners; if the cottagers are counted in as part-time wage-earners, the proportion is over two-thirds. And while the wage relationship was not as completely impersonal as it was to become in the following century, it was already ... essentially a market relationship. The tendency for land to be exploited as capital was already well advanced, to the detriment of such paternal relations between landlord and tenant as had survived the changes of the sixteenth century [*The Political Theory of Possessive Individualism*, p. 61].

By a "possessive market society" in this context Macpherson means one whose defining characteristic is "that man's labour is a commodity, i.e., that a man's energy and skill are his own, yet are regarded not as integral parts of his personality, but as possessions, the use and disposal of which he is free to hand over to others for a price" (ibid., p. 48; cf. 53–61).

We touch here on a controversial point. Hobsbawm, Macpherson, and Christopher Hill, whom we shall cite later, are Marxists. They see in, or impose on, history a scheme in which bourgeois capitalism follows and replaces the feudal system. Other writers—Cannon, Laslett, Mingay—disagree. John Cannon, for example, says:

> The identification of a 'bourgeois revolution' in the mid-seventeenth century has, in my view, caused Marxists to postulate a vast chronological misplacement, anticipating developments by two hundred years or so, and ignoring the nature of the eighteenth-century political regime. . . . More than a century of Marxist influence leads us to expect to find class conflict and disposes us to believe that class loyalties are the most potent. But, in fact, religious, family, or national loyalties may well be more decisive, possibly today and certainly in the eighteenth century.

Besides, he adds, too many people of the middling orders identified their interests with those of the landed aristocracy for there to have been an urban bourgeois revolt against it (pp. 177–178).

Even the Marxists are now ready to agree, according to Laslett, that "the capitalists as a group of persons capable of coming into conflict with other groups of persons are unlikely ever to be identified in England under pre-industrial conditions." Their present view, he says, is "that the whole of the English gentry, in our own terminology the whole of the ruling segment, was imbued with bourgeois values by the middle years of the seventeenth century." Conflicts, therefore, must presumably have been due to the internal contradictions of capitalism rather than the clash of bourgeoisie and aristocrats (pp. 36–37; cf. 184–187, and J. G. A. Pocock, *Virtue, Commerce and History,* pp. 67–71, 109).

A wider view now traces the beginnings of capitalism far back into the High Middle Ages, and sees it as developing within, not against, feudalism. Harold J. Berman, for example, who writes of Western Christendom generally, and not of England alone, argues that "western Europe during the period from the late eleventh to the early sixteenth century was a traditional society that underwent rapid and dynamic expansion and development in the economic as well as in many other aspects of social life." Many social historians are mistaken in holding "that the feudal economy of medieval Europe remained static until it received an exogenous shock from the urban and commercial expansion of the sixteenth century." On the contrary, in the internal development of the feudal economy new "forms of property relations were used to create what much later was called 'agricultural capitalism'" (*Law and Revolution,* p. 544).

Part of this development was a tendency, for reasons that served the interests of lords and peasants alike, "to substitute fixed cash payments for labor services and rents in kind." It was accompanied by a change in the way in which a manor was conceived of. "As early as the thirteenth century in many if not most parts of Europe, manors came to be considered income-producing enterprises," and "the gradual conversion of peasants into lessees (or, alternatively, hired laborers) was connected with the gradual transformation of the manor itself from a community into a business" (ibid., pp. 329–330; cf. Bush, pp. 33, 61–63, Mingay, *The Gentry*, pp. 22–25).

In short, a money-and market economy emerged within feudalism. It led to an expansion of agricultural production, which was a precondition for a commercial revolution and the growth of cities. And so, says Berman, "in the eleventh and twelfth centuries (and for some time thereafter) capitalism and feudalism were essentially compatible with each other, and indeed utterly dependent on each other" (pp. 333–338; quotation on p. 338).

If Berman is right in this, we may agree that Macpherson is also right in holding that Edmund Burke "venerated the traditional order. But his traditional order was already a capitalist order" (*Burke*, p. 5). We need only add that it had been becoming capitalist for centuries and was not yet the roaring capitalism of the Industrial Revolution, of which Hobsbawm has said, "No change in human life since the invention of agriculture, metallurgy, and towns in the New Stone Age has been so profound as the coming of industrialization" (pp. 21–22).

In the Middle Ages, the tenures by which free tenants held land were often inheritable and at fixed rents. For the free tenant the land he held was virtually his property, subject to feudal dues and exactions, but otherwise not under the lord's control. The lords therefore moved steadily toward turning the customary tenures into leaseholds, preferably on short-term leases, and toward replacing the fixed rents with revisable ones (Mingay, *The Gentry*, p. 96). "By the eighteenth century," says Bush, "the typical tenancy was the leasehold," and by 1780 "ninety per cent of the rented land was leased" (pp. 63, 181). Most leases, moreover, were annual ones. "The majority of tenants of English estates held their farms on this apparently insecure basis," according to Mingay. But in practice they enjoyed considerable security because "landlords in England commonly allowed farms let at will to pass to widows, sons, or daughters, and usually no major alteration in the rent was made until the sitting tenant gave up the farm or died" (*Landed Society*, p. 45; cf. 60, 170).

Tenants generally lacked this security in "the cruel caricature of a rural economy which was Ireland" (Hobsbawm, p. 81). The reason is that Ireland was a conquered country, owned and governed by men who had little fellow-feeling with the despised natives. "Three quarters of Irish land," says J. H. Plumb, "belonged to Englishmen or to Anglo-Irish Protestant families" (*England in the Eighteenth Century*, p. 179). In Ireland, Mingay reports, "when a farm was re-let no preference was customarily shown to the old tenant, and for political reasons Catholic tenants were often turned out in favour of Protestants" (*Landed Society*, p. 45). These facts account for Burke's contrasting attitudes toward the economic and political systems of England and Ireland.

"Accompanying the destruction of the customary tenures," says Bush, "was the engrossment of holdings [i.e., the consolidation of farms into larger rental units]. In the course of the sixteenth and seventeenth centuries the number of farms fell dramatically as large farmers swallowed up the smaller ones" (p. 63). Agricultural productivity was also increased by the enclosure movement, which reached its peak in the eighteenth century. Enclosure meant dividing common lands into fenced-off plots to be farmed by individual holders or tenants. It could also mean fencing-in waste lands for cultivation. The lord's purpose in engrossing and enclosing was that of "letting them out as large units to capitalist farmers producing on a big scale for the market, or even to farm himself [using hired laborers, of course, since gentlemen did not do manual work]" (Mingay, *The Gentry*, p. 41; cf. D. Marshall, p. 11).

Landlords thus became a mainly rentier class who managed their estates with a view to improving their rentals (Bush, p. 62; Mingay, *Landed Society*, p. 172). They enhanced their income in a number of ways, "by revising tenancies, farming their desmesnes [those parts of their estates that they did not rent out], enclosing waste lands, by manufacturing, and by selling timber and minerals" (Mingay, *The Gentry*, p. 44). But the chief source of their wealth and power was the rents they collected from tenants. As Sir Lewis Namier has said, "Primarily on the rental of England, whilst agriculture still paid, were raised her political system and lore, and her civilization" (*England in the Age of the American Revolution*, p. 17). Landed property was the material base on which it all stood.

In farming, the role of the landlord was to provide the fixed capital; that of the tenant, to provide the working capital (Bush, p. 184; cf. Jones, p. 14). There was thus, says Mingay, "an enduring common bond of interest which permeated the landlord–tenant relationship. . . . The landlord looked after a good tenant because he wanted to keep his land well tenanted; equally, the tenant performed his part because he valued a good bargain and wanted to continue in occupation" (*The Gentry*, p. 190).

Such an agrarian society can be called capitalistic; certainly, it had evolved a long way from feudalism. But it was not the bourgeois society whose only bond was the "callous 'cash payment'" that Marx denounced. The dominant ideals of the eighteenth century were those of an aristocracy that felt itself born to rule and "stressed that rootedness and ancient lineage were superior as measures of success to the acquisition of wealth or social promotion." Far though it fell in practice from living up to them, its professed ideals were those of leisure, honor, hospitality, generosity, paternalism, public responsibility, and concern for the common good. The bourgeoisie, on its part, strove to emulate the aristocracy and, if possible, to join it (Bush, pp. 74–77; cf. Cannon, pp. viii–ix; Laslett, p. 78; Mingay, *The Gentry*, pp. 108–109, 121–124, 134, 140, 163–164, 192–193, and *Landed Society*, pp. 53–60).

The aristocratic family's concern with status necessitated concern with the wealth that supported that status. Keeping wealth in the family required maintaining the integrity of the estate as it passed from one generation to the next. By the late thirteenth century primogeniture had emerged as the usual, and eventually the sole, form of inheritance among the wealthier landowners: the estate and the title, if there was one, was passed on to the eldest son (Mingay, *The Gentry*, p. 109). From the mid-seventeenth century on, another legal device to keep spendthrift heirs from dissipating the estate came into increasing use: namely, the entail or strict family settlement. Probably half or more of the country was under strict settlement in the eighteenth century (Mingay, *Landed Society*, pp. 32–34). The effect of this legal arrangement was to make the titular owner of an estate only a life-tenant, bound to pass on the estate largely intact to his eldest son, who would be similarly obliged to his eldest son (see ibid. for fuller details).

Naturally, the strict settlement tended to keep the great estates off the market and, in Hill's opinion, "led on to the great consolidations of landed property which made the Whig oligarchy of the eighteenth century" (*Reformation to Industrial Revolution*, pp. 115–116, but see Cannon, pp. 132–137, for some qualification of this view). But because primogeniture and entail were not the universal rule among the lesser landowners, there was "an active market in small estates and country houses, particularly noticeable in the home counties" (Mingay, *The Gentry*, pp. 7, 115–116; cf. Namier, p. 12), and Edmund Burke bought one such estate.

Division of property and its salability were the more capitalistic way of running an agrarian economy. Adam Smith recognized the reasons for the rise of primogeniture and the strict settlement in the circumstances of their origins, and "the pride of family distinctions" that kept them in use. "But in the present state of Europe," he thought," . . . nothing can be more completely absurd." They were an obstacle to economic progress: "It seldom happens that a great proprietor is a great improver" (III, 2, 3–7; 1: 382–386). To this extent aristocracy was a check on capitalist development. Agricultural experts such as Arthur Young, Smith's and Burke's contemporary, complained that landlords kept rents low in order to court popularity and political support, to the detriment of the most efficient cultivation of the land (Mingay, *Landed Society*, p. 53; cf. Cannon, pp. 138–139). Hill also faults landowners for impeding industrial development (pp. 196–197; cf. Hobsbawm, pp. 226–228).

The century in which Burke lived, and particularly the decades from 1760 on, in which he spent his political life, was a period in which population grew significantly because of the greater supply of food and rising standard of living already mentioned (see also Hill, pp. 208–209). Agricultural prices rose, and rents nearly tripled from 1760 to the end of the Napoleonic wars, so that most proprietors got richer. General prosperity also increased, but with unequal benefits to different parts of the population (Mingay, *The Gentry*, pp. 90, 94, 113–114; *Landed Society*, pp. 49, 52, 56–57).

Adam Smith claimed that "the real recompence of labour, . . .

the real quantities of the necessaries and conveniences of life which are given to the labourer, has increased considerably during the course of the present century" (I, 11, g, 20; 1: 219). Hill, however, asserts that pauperism grew along with prosperity, and that the rising cost of poor relief was a subsidy, at taxpayers' expense, to the meager wages paid by employers (pp. 212–213; cf. Hobsbawm, pp. 104–105). Mingay agrees to this extent: that, although the wages of laborers increased in the later eighteenth century, "the social distance between labourers and the middling farmers grew steadily" (*Landed Society*, p. 241). He concludes:

> It is difficult to say where the balance of advantage lay. Probably all those country-dwellers of and above the rank of small farmer and skilled artisan benefited from the expanding economy of the later eighteenth century, and maintained or improved their living standards, but very likely those below this level found life harder and more uncertain, particularly in the occasional years of great scarcity [ibid., pp. 244–245].

Partly as a result of this concentration of wealth, no doubt, "circumstances tended to favour the aggrandisement of estates in the hands of the great landlords at the expence of the lesser gentry and owner-occupiers," and "the countryside moved gradually towards that aristocratic monopoly of land which gave rise to such heartburning among later nineteenth-century radicals" (ibid., p. 15).

The aristocratic monopoly, however, did not produce or perpetuate a two-tiered society of lords and peasants but a three-tiered one of aristocratic landlords, tenants who ran large commercial farms, and a rural proletariat of landless farmhands (Bush, pp. 174–178; cf. 66, 140, and Hobsbawm, pp. 29, 38). Laslett, who rejects the "division of history into the ancient, feudal, and bourgeois eras or stages," nonetheless adds that the paupers ("anyone who was in receipt of charity for his upkeep, or who had ever been in such a position") were "surely as much a proletariat as ever there has been in the age of industrialism. Growing in the sixteenth and seventeenth centuries, a great mass by the year 1800, such persons had nevertheless existed at all times" (p. 20). Authors disagree, however, on whether enclosures and the engrossment of farms are to be condemned as dispossessing small farmers and cottagers, and thereby increasing the number of the landless, or praised as aiding the progress of agriculture, and thereby increasing the food supply (Hill, pp. 222–225; Mingay, *The Gentry*, pp. 91–94, and *Landed Society*, pp. 268–269; and several of the contributors in Jones, ed., pp. 21–25, 49, 94–95, 102–107, 117–129, 132–133, 142–144).

As has already been noted, until the nineteenth century England was a primarily agricultural country governed by the landed interest. The great landlords did not confine their interest to the land, however, or draw their income from it alone. "The breadth of the landowners' interests and the diversity of their investments," says Mingay, "help to explain not only the growth of their incomes and the permanence of their way of life, but also their extraordinary grip on the government of the country, and the long acquiescence of the commercial and industrial interests in their rule" (*Landed Society*, p. 58). Among the ways in which the very rich got richer still, or at least maintained their wealth, he ventures the surmise that inheriting or marrying great wealth was the most important. "Access to the wealth of mercantile families played a significant role here, of course." The most lucrative government offices were also very largely a monopoly of the upper aristocracy, as were the best pensions. With the expansion of industry and cities in the late eighteenth century, the possession of capital to invest and the ownership of property for urban development became sources of additional income, as the names of Cavendish, Russell, and Grovesnor Squares in London testify (ibid., pp. 71–80; cf. *The Gentry*, pp. 99, 106–107; Cannon, p. 140).

The commercial revolution produced an increasingly important part of Great Britain's wealth in the eighteenth century. The colonial trade was a growing part of this commerce, amounting to 15 per cent of it around 1700, but to as much as a third of it by 1775 (Hobsbawm, p. 53; cf. D. Marshall, pp. 12–18). This in turn affected British policy: "The aggressive foreign policy waged after 1688," says Hill, "was largely economic in motivation, and contributed . . . in the long run (conquest of India, West Indies, Canada) to the dominant position in the world economy which England attained" (p. 200). Adam Smith was of the opinion that the British Empire existed in order to maintain a monopoly of the colonial trade for the benefit of British merchants, not of the British people

(IV, 7, c, 56–66; 2: 610–617), but it was in any case a major object of Great Britain's policy. Hill adds: "The Commercial Revolution not only created an expanding colonial market for English manufacturers: it also helped to cheapen, diversify and expand the production of manufactured goods, to stimulate new industries," and to develop the infrastructure of transportation and communications within England (pp. 201, 204–205).

That revolution antedated the better-known Industrial Revolution, about which Laslett states: "We can say with confidence that large-scale undertakings for the purpose of manufacturing goods are conspicuously lacking in all descriptions of life in England before the late eighteenth century," although there certainly were "approaches to that peculiarly industrial form of social and economic organization . . . before the great industrial revolution." Capitalism existed, "but industrial capitalism, our sort of industrial capitalism, was absent," and "when industry had scarcely begun to transform society, . . . the scale of life was virtually unchanged" (pp. 190, 193, 180; cf. p. 297, n. 22. Cf. Mingay, *The Gentry*, pp. 192–193, and *Landed Society*, pp. 12–13, 189, 190, 195). Hobsbawm agrees that "the British [industrial] revolution was preceded by at least two hundred years of fairly continuous economic development, which laid its foundations." But this development did not initiate "the characteristic modern phase of history, self-sustained economic growth by means of perpetual technological revolution and social transformation" (pp. 34–35; cf. p. 56).

This mighty change in British society began during Burke's political lifetime, but did not hit its full stride until the nineteenth century, after his death. Hobsbawm regards the years between 1750 and 1770 "as the runway for the industrial 'takeoff'" (p. 48). Gertrude Himmelfarb, in *The Idea of Poverty*, suggests that "the timing of the [industrial] revolution . . . has been somewhat changed, the preferred date today being 1780 rather than 1760" (p. 44). Dorothy Marshall has the Industrial Revolution "starting to take effect" by the close of the eighteenth century (p. 29). On any reading, it is understandable that Burke did not recognize what it was doing and would do to British society.

In addition to the agricultural and commercial revolutions of the seventeenth century, there was also a financial one. Pocock describes it in these terms:

I am alluding . . . to what we now call the Financial Revolution of the middle 1690's, which saw the foundation of the Bank of England and the successful and lasting creation of a system of public credit whereby individuals and companies could invest money in the stability of government and expect a return varying in proportion to the success of the government's operations. Over the quarter-century that followed, contemporaries came to hold that this had led to the creation of what they called a 'monied interest,' and that this new class of creditors and speculators was tending to dominate politics [p. 108].

Hill comments that "the National Debt was the first *safe* long-term investment other than land" (p. 200). Useful though it was in keeping capital employed, however, it created a new kind of property which, in contrast to land and trade goods, was not only mobile but unreal, consisting as it did in government promises to repay at a future date that it was known would never be reached, because the government would only float new loans to pay off the old ones. But, as Pocock says, "the tokens of repayment are exchangeable at a market price in the present," and so constitute a kind of property which "has ceased to be real and has become not merely mobile but imaginary" (p. 112).

Mingay believes that there was little real disharmony between the aristocracy and the commercial and financial interest until the nineteenth century (*Landed Society*, pp. 12–13). But Pocock's thesis is that out of the financial revolution there emerged "a confrontation between real and mobile property," because "mobile property presented itself in the guise not of a marketable commodity, so much as of a new and enlarged mode of dependence upon government patronage." Land was seen as real property and the basis of civic virtue and independence from government. The threat to that independence was "property in government office, government stock, and government expectations to which the National Debt has mortgaged futurity." But, while the advent of eighteenth-century capitalism "somehow destroyed" the classical ideal of man as a political being, nonetheless "the classical ideal quite simply did not die, . . . it was reborn with the great recovery of aristocracy which marks the later seventeenth and early eighteenth centuries" (pp. 68–70; cf. pp. 107–123). Without unreservedly subscribing to Pocock's thesis, we may bear it in mind when analyzing Burke's understanding of the nature and role of property, and ask what was the property he so highly valued, and why did he value it.

Writing from his anti-capitalist, anti-bourgeois point of view, Hill says: "The monied men were quite happy to leave the details of administration to those whose traditional function it was, secure in their ultimate control through the Bank of England and the great companies which advanced money to the government" (pp. 176–177). The majority view among scholars, however, is that Great Britain in the eighteenth century was governed by an aristocratic, landholding ruling class, because the kind of property it held was the country's major source of production and employment.

In the eighteenth century, Namier says, the connection between the ownership of land and a share in the state was acknowledged and upheld by Whigs and Tories alike (p. 21). In Mingay's words, "it was regarded as the natural order of things that the property-owners should be represented in Parliament by other property-owners" (*The Gentry*, p. 119). Nor is this at all surprising. Parliament had come into being in the thirteenth century in order to grant financial "aids" to the king, which aids could be given only by those who owned substantial property (see, e.g., C. H. McIlwain, "Medieval Estates," *Cambridge Medieval History* 7: 674–679).

Kings succeeded in becoming absolute monarchs elsewhere in Europe because they were eventually able to tax without the consent of their Estates-General, Cortes, or other parliamentary assemblies. In England they failed finally and definitively in the seventeenth century. The Whig aristocracy of the eighteenth century consequently was able to present its dominance in Parliament as the bulwark of English liberties. This claim was generally accepted: "For the most part men conceived the alternative to aristocratic rule to be some form of royal absolutism" (Cannon, pp. 178-179).

Where royal absolutism triumphed, it eventually worked its own downfall, according to Bush. Kings broke the power of their nobles and created a "service elite" of professional people who in time became the spearhead of bourgeois opposition to the absolute monarchy. But in England the aristocracy's effective resistance to royal absolutism made the state subordinate to the landed interest, prevented the alienation of the aristocracy, and kept the bureaucracy in a primitive condition. This limitation of royal power "preserved for the aristocracy until the late nineteenth century an indispensable role in the administration as unpaid, amateur JPs responsible for local government" (p. 12; cf. 57, 203).

The rule of the aristocrats depended "upon a managed parliament and the absence of an extensive, independent bureaucracy. In the cabinet, [the aristocrats] exercised executive authority through actual membership; in parliament they exercised legislative control through the Lords and a manipulated Commons; in the country, they exercised administrative control through the office of lord lieutenant" (ibid., p. 124).

Below that level, the most important work of local government was done by virtually unpaid members of the gentry, the Justices of the Peace, whom the Lords-Lieutenant had the exclusive right of nominating. Mingay describes their functions:

> The primary duty of the Justices was to maintain the King's Peace and hold the Quarter and Petty Sessions, but numerous other responsibilities fell on them. They supervised weights and measures, repairs of roads and bridges, police, gaols and houses of correction, markets, prices and qualities of certain commodities, and the licensing of higglers, drovers and alehouses. For good measure the Justices also had authority over the Poor Law and all its ramifications, together with wages, labour conditions, and even pension funds for maimed soldiers [*Landed Society*, p. 118].

The most basic duty of government was to maintain the supply of food. "The disorder which might break out if food shortage threatened the poor was a signal to the authorities to intervene in the operations of the market in grain. . . . Those likely to suffer expected action, and they usually got it" (Laslett, p. 139; cf. 134–135, 138–139, 148–151).

Bush remarks that "the aristocracy had everything to gain from a form of government in which the state was ruled by a noble-dominated parliament." Nonetheless, he says, the aristocracy thereby made an indispensable contribution to constitutional, representative government in England (pp. 198–200). We must qualify the notion of aristocratic rule, however, by adding that, although the landed aristocracy was an effective check on the power of the monarchy, it by no means rendered the monarch the figurehead he later became. Cabinet ministers were well aware that they were the king's ministers, and

> it was a commonplace of politicians in both houses [of Parliament] to insist that their allegiance was personal to the king. Not only did any rumour about the king's doubts toward his ministers pluck at the political conscience of members, it also advertised to time-servers that the days of the administration were almost certainly numbered [Cannon, pp. 103–104; cf. 4–5].

As Carl Cone says, "No ministry could stand without the king's favor, and royal backing alone could attract the support of about one-third of the members of the Commons" (*Burke and the Nature of Politics: The Age of the French Revolution*, p. 217; henceforth Cone 2; cf. Mingay, *Landed Society*, p. 114). But if the aristocratic politicians could not govern without the king, neither could he govern without them.

The political hegemony of the great Whig lords grew during the eighteenth century. They "dominated the House of Lords, and for the most part were able successfully to 'manage' the House of Commons." A few leading families, whose tenants formed the majority of the freeholder electorate, so strongly influenced the election of county representatives that in some counties contested elections became a rarity (Mingay, *The Gentry*, pp. 72–74; cf. *Landed Society*, pp. 120–121). By the year 1700, according to Laslett, "the gentry had taken over the representation of the boroughs from their retained, wage-earning MPs" (p. 41; cf. Bush, p. 164; Namier, p. 34), as the boroughs came to prefer being represented by independently wealthy gentlemen (Mingay, *Landed Society*, p. 112). Although the peers themselves could not sit in the Commons, their influence in elections and their control of the "nomination boroughs" left them little to fear from the House of Commons.

They did have reason to fear extensions of the franchise, which would threaten to bring into being a House of Commons that they could not control. "The aristocracy," says Bush, "instinctively feared two tyrannies: on the one hand, royal despotism; on the other, the tyranny of the multitude." Therefore, both the size and the character of the electorate must be restricted, so that power would remain in the hands of the men of property, who could act responsibly (pp. 200–201). It helped toward that end that "the cost of a seat in Parliament rose rapidly in the late seventeenth and early eighteenth centuries as the Septennial Act [which required parliamentary elections only every seven years] made elections less frequent and thus increased the amount that wealthy families were prepared to spend on them." A further consequence was that "in the seven general elections between 1760 and the end of the century only a tenth of all the seats were disputed" in boroughs with small electorates (Mingay, *Landed Society*, p. 123; cf. 120). John Cannon reminds us that "it was really the landed interest as a whole which monopolized power," not merely the great lords, though they were the leading element in politics. But, because the ruling class of nobles and gentry was closely bound together not only by interest but also by ties of blood and marriage, the eighteenth-century House of Commons was "one of the most exclusive ruling elites in human history," and the opening of a Parliament was "a family reunion for many members." In 1754, he reckons, well over 70 per cent of the members "had or had had close relatives in the House" (pp. 114–115; cf. Mingay, *Landed Society*, p. 113).

"To a crucial extent," says Mingay, "the social supremacy of the landlords rested on their superior education and culture" (*Landed Society*, p. 131). The nobles and well-to-do gentry who were the ruling class received a classical education in the public schools, which were increasingly popular among them. Higher education, too, was steeped in a classicism that, in Cannon's words, "shaped the context of their lives intellectually and physically," prepared them "for that public life which was the destiny and duty of the upper classes," and "gave apparent validity to their rule" (pp. 34–35).

We need not pass judgment here on how valid their claim to rule was. Some twentieth-century scholars, however, have stated the case that can be made for it. Laslett, for example, says that "the great houses and the familial dynasties could not have ruled over English society by themselves. They acted as the agents, even as the representative of the bands of their supporters in the counties, as well as manipulators and controllers." Below the ranks of their supporters, who presumably were literate, there was the great majority of men, and even more of women, who could neither read nor write. One can understand "why the fully literate few could feel that they were thinking for the whole mass" (pp. 228, 233–234).

Namier asks: "Did then the eighteenth-century Parliament represent the men or the land of Great Britain? One might as well ask to whom the child owes its life, to the father or the mother? It represented both; or to put it more accurately, it represented British men rooted in the soil of Great Britain" (p. 28). Nor was the non-landed trading element of the population neglected. Even though the House of Commons was dominated by the great landed families, it was intensely interested in commercial questions, and did not judge a man qualified to be a statesman unless he had thoroughly studied the sources of British profits (ibid., pp. 34, 38–40). The commercial interest was at least "virtually" represented even where its urban centers did not elect Members of Parliament. When the agitation for parliamentary reform began in the last third of the eighteenth century, the great unrepresented towns, according to George Veitch, showed little enthusiasm for it (*The Genesis of Parliamentary Reform*, p. 100; cf. Mingay, *Landed Society*, pp. 262–263).

Laslett feels that the political system of pre-industrial England was "one of the most efficient, formidable and humane that the world has ever known" (p. 211). Mingay agrees that "the English gentry in general showed a strong sense of public duty and of social obligation towards their subordinates. Characteristically they wanted to be held in popular esteem, to be thought of as generous landlords, humane administrators, honest magistrates and trustworthy bulwarks against misfortune." The landed class, of which the gentry were the core, furnished the country "with leadership that in general was enlightened and progressive" (*The Gentry*, pp. 164, 187; cf. *Landed Society*, p. 115). Speaking of the aristocracy in the narrow sense as the nobility, Cannon concludes: "The aristocracy ran the country well, won its wars, fostered its trade, and extended its empire" (p. 175).

Of course, as he goes on to say, "there is a less attractive side . . . there was great deal of greed and pomposity" (ibid.), which is not unacknowledged by the writers most favorable to the aristocracy (see, e.g., Mingay, *Landed Society*, pp. 148–162). Bush, who leans to the left, is much more severe in his judgment on the ruling class: "Its paternalism was a selfish lust for power. Its charity consumed a minute proportion of its income and time, commendable only when measured against the resources of the recipient. When measured against the resources of the donor, aristocratic charity was meanness itself" (p. 76). Macpherson, following his thesis that by the seventeenth century England "approximated closely" to a "possessive market society" in which labor was a commodity, must regard eighteenth-century English society as exploitative. Hill insists that, in the spirit of capitalism, the treatment of the poor got worse in that century (pp. 212–213, 222–223).

Hobsbawm sees the development of agrarian capitalism as liquidating the social world that had cared for the poor: "The inhuman economics of commercial and 'advanced' farming strangled the human values of a social order." But, he says, the effects of this change did not reach catastrophic proportions that could not be ignored until the mid-1790s (pp. 99, 105). Even then, "there is indeed evidence that the eighteenth-century Poor Law, in spite of bourgeois theory, became more generous, and when poverty became catastrophic, . . . the country gentry went dead against the grain of economic theory in the 'Speenhamland system'." It was not until 1834, when the Industrial Revolution was well under way, that a "'New' Poor Law with these inhuman characteristics" of a laissez-faire free labor market was pushed through Parliament despite "the powerful prejudice of the agricultural community in favour of a stable social order, that is to say against the ruthless conversion of both men and land into mere commodities" (ibid., pp. 228–229; cf. Himmelfarb, pp. 40–41).

Until the French Revolution, English society apparently did not chafe under the rule of the aristocracy. Even then the aristocratic order continued to be very widely accepted, despite an emerging radical protest. It makes a good deal of difference, however, whether, in looking back at the eighteenth century, we see it as foreshadowing the age of industrial capitalism or as continuing and developing an aristocratic "world we have lost." It did both, of course, but for our understanding of Edmund Burke, much depends on which alternative we see emerging from what he himself said in his writings and speeches. That will determine our conclusion on what his conception of the role of property was in the world in which he lived.

2
The Soul That Animated

IN HIS ARTICLE "The Soul That Animated" (*Studies in Burke and His Time* 17: 27–41), George Fasel has thoroughly shown that property plays an important role in Edmund Burke's social and political thought. It is not the only or the primary role, however; nor does Fasel claim that it is. As he says, "The ideas of any person whose thought merits serious study are nearly always too complex to admit of explanation by means of a single concept," a caveat which "is especially applicable in the case of Edmund Burke" (p. 27). Yet, since Marxists and other simplifiers have taught us to reduce men's thoughts and actions to economic motives, we shall begin with some remarks on Burke's attitude toward the desire for material gain.

At the age of eighteen, while he was a student in Trinity College, Dublin, Burke began the publication of *The Reformer*. It was a thin little weekly sheet, which lasted only three months and "was managed, edited, and almost entirely written by Edmund Burke" (Samuels, *Early Life*, etc., p. 160). In No. 6 of this weekly, dated 3 March 1747–8, he says: "The Desire of Lucre is become almost the general Spring of Action, and it has never produced any but mean ones" (ibid., p. 313). In the following number he develops this theme. "The Riches of a Nation," he says, "are not to be estimated by the splendid Appearance or luxurious lives of its Gentry; it is the uniform Plenty diffused through a people, of which the meanest as well as greatest partake, that makes them happy, and the Nation powerful."

He then describes in grim detail the miserable poverty in which the mass of the people of Ireland live, "Poverty, as few Nations in *Europe* can equal." He sees nothing wrong in some people enjoying a higher standard of living than others, "but sure it is hard, that those who cultivate the Soil, should have so small a Part of its Fruits; and that among Creatures of the same Kind there should be such a Disproportion in their manner of living." We regard the wealth and power of kings, he says, as "by no means their Property, but a Depositum in their Hands, for the Use of the People." Similarly, "if we consider the natural Equality of Mankind, we shall believe the same of the Estates of Gentlemen, bestowed on them at the first distribution of Properties, for promoting the Public Good."

But the gentry of Ireland are far from taking this benevolent attitude toward their fellow-countrymen. Irish laborers "have an Acre of Land," but "at a very high Rent, to pay which they must work for their Master a great part of the Year," and in return get a bare subsistence even when times are good. "The poorer kind of Farmers . . . live nigh as miserably . . . , though they hold larger Quantities of Land, but at such a Rent as both hurts them and the Landlord." If the landlord takes his land into his own hands and tries to farm it on his own, he often finds that he cannot manage it and so rents it out for farming or grazing cattle to "rich Farmers or *Graziers*" who "hold vast Quantities of Land, and as they live like estated Men, equally contribute to the Poverty of the rest."

The reason Burke gives for this ruinous and heartless way of running the Irish agricultural economy is significant. "Gentlemen perceiving that in *England* Farmers pay heavy Rent, and yet live comfortably, without considering the Disproportion of Markets and every Thing else, raise their Rent high, and extort it heavily." What in England is a fair rent, in Ireland is a rack rent. Burke, however, does not advocate land reform and the redistribution of property. He accepts without question a country owned by a rentier class, but proposes intelligent and humane administration of estates as being in the interest of landlords and tenants alike. Lower rents on estates farmed by a large number of tenants, the improvement of the estates, and the encouragement of manufactures in the villages would "no doubt see this Nation in the most flourishing condition, notwithstanding all the Disadvantages we labour under" (ibid., pp. 314–317).

In later years Burke came to see great merit in the desire for lucre and became an unyielding defender of aristocracy and the existing distribution of property. But there was no radical break between the younger and the mature Burke. To the end of his days he continued to believe that the government of Ireland and the administration of its landed estates were an outrage on human nature; that property, like government, was a trust for the good of the community; and that where the social order was on the whole a good one, as in England he thought it was, it was founded on mutuality of interest among the several classes of society.

C. B. Macpherson has remarked that in Burke's *A Vindication of Natural Society*, published in 1756 before he began his political career, he "shows himself fully aware of the case that can be made against the political, legal, economic and moral order of eighteenth-century advanced societies" (*Burke*, p. 18). It is true that the *Vindication* is a satire, exaggerated for effect and designed to show that the Deists' case against revealed religion can be made with equal ease against civil society. But we must agree with Macpherson that Burke could not have written what he did without being aware of the faults, crimes, and sins of contemporary civil society, and in particular of the misery of the poor—and this not in Ireland alone (*Works* 1: 69–75). But for him, neither then nor later, were these defects a reason for radically restructuring the economic, social, or political order of society, but only for reforming it where it could be reformed and, where it could not be, for tolerating its unavoidable evils for the sake of the greater good of a civilized and prosperous order among men.

Valuable though property was as the material foundation of social order and necessary as the desire for material gain was as the incentive to the industry that created and improved property, Burke knew that acquisitiveness could become a vice. To cite a few examples: in *An Abridgment of English History*, which he began to write in 1758 but never finished, he remarks that the monks of seventh-century England "did not show that rapacious desire of riches, which long disgraced, and finally ruined, their successors" (*Works* 10: 269). Later in the same work he says that William the Conqueror "had vices in his composition, and great ones; but they were the vices of a great mind: ambition, the malady of every extensive genius; and avarice, the madness of the wise" (*Works* 10: 413). In 1779, in a letter to the Duke of Portland, he comments sarcastically on the way in which the recently deceased Lord Temple had bequeathed his property: "Lord Temples Will is perfectly like that of other Rich men, who living or dead abhor any thing that looks like distribution." That is to say, he left an enormous estate to his son, the present Lord Temple, and "not a shilling in Land or money" to his own three brothers and one sister (*Corr.* 4:

132). Finally, in 1789, in one of his speeches in the trial of Warren Hastings, the Governor-General of the East India Company's territories in India, Burke read to the House of Lords the following passage from a report that Lord Clive had sent back during his administration in India. He had discovered, said Clive, "'transactions, which seem to demonstrate, that every spring of this Government was smeared with corruption, that principles of rapacity and oppression universally prevailed, and that every spark of sentiment and publick spirit was lost and extinguished in the unbounded lust of unmerited wealth'" (*Works* 13: 425). Burke certainly admired wealth, but not the unbounded lust for it.

For Burke believed that human nature is a fallen nature, not totally depraved, but corrupt and corruptible. In *Letters on a Regicide Peace* he refers to "the nature of corrupted man" (*Works* 9: 95), and in another passage of the same document describes men as "a middle sort of beings, who, because they cannot be Angels, ought to thwart their ambition, and not endeavour to become infernal spirits" (*Works* 9: 42). What he says of ambition applies generally to all our desires: "Our physical well-being, our moral worth, our social happiness, our political tranquillity, all depend on that control of all our appetites and passions, which the ancients designed by the cardinal virtue of *temperance*" (*Works* 8: 376).

We must take men as they are, neither angels nor devils, and provide legitimate channels for their pursuit of wealth. Speaking of the East India Company's government in India, Burke said: "I should really think, that the Company deserved to be ill served, if they had not annexed such appointments to great trusts as might secure the persons entrusted from the temptations of unlawful emolument; and, what in all cases is the greatest security, given a lawful gratification to the natural passions of men" (*Works* 13: 434).

Speaking in still more general terms, Burke explains that political wisdom uses, rather than tries to crush, men's desire for wealth:

> There must be some impulse besides publick spirit, to put private interest into motion along with it. Monied men ought to be allowed to set a value on their money; if they did not, there could be no monied men. This desire of accumulation, is a principle without which the means of their service to the state could not exist. The love of lucre, though sometimes carried to a ridiculous, sometimes to a vicious excess, is the grand cause of prosperity to all states. In

this natural, this reasonable, this powerful, this prolifick principle, it is for the satyrist to expose the ridiculous; it is for the moralist to censure the vicious; it is for the sympathetick heart to reprobate the hard and cruel; it is for the judge to animadvert on the fraud, the extortion, and the oppression; but it is for the statesman to employ it as he finds it, with all its concomitant excellencies, with all its imperfections on its head. It is his part, in this case, as it is in all other cases, where he is to make use of the general energies of nature, to take them as he finds them [*Works* 8: 354].

Civil society will therefore protect property even though it thereby necessarily protects vice:

> It is impossible that any principle of law or government useful to the community should be established without an advantage to those, who have the greatest stake in the country. Even some vices arise from it. The same laws, which secure property, encourage avarice; and the fences made about honest acquisition are the strong bars, which secure the hoards of the miser. The dignities of magistracy are encouragements to ambition, with all the black train of villanies, which attend that wicked passion. But still we must have laws to secure property; and still we must have ranks and distinctions and magistracy in the State, notwithstanding their manifest tendency to encourage avarice and ambition [*Works* 10: 139–140].

Yet it does not follow that wealth is the highest goal of individual or social striving, or the object of a master passion to which all else should be subordinated. "If wealth is the obedient and laborious slave of virtue and of public honour," says Burke, "then wealth is in its place and has its use: but if this order is changed, and honour is to be sacrificed to the conservation of riches, riches which have neither eyes, nor hands, nor any thing truly vital in them, cannot long survive the being of their vivifying powers, their legitimate masters, and their potent protectors" (*Works* 8: 88; cf. 9: 83–84). In the same vein, he is reported as saying in a speech in the Commons:

> England was a commercial nation. . . . But if, by commercial nation, it was implied that commerce was her ultimate, her only end, he would deny it; her commerce was a subservient instrument to her greater interests, her security, her honour, and her religion. If the commercial spirit tended to break those, he insisted that it should be lowered [*Parl. Hist.* 30: 645; cf. *Corr.* 7: 85].

Society must allow men to seek wealth, first, because it cannot stifle a natural passion and, second, because society's prosperity and ability to pursue higher ends depend on the legitimate pursuit of private gain. Burke did not, however, subscribe to Bernard Mandeville's thesis in *The Fable of the Bees*, that private vices are public benefits (*Works* 13: 272; *W&S* 6: 396). Beneficial though the love of lucre is, it can become a vice and, consequently, a source of public corruption and damage to the community.

Property, therefore, must be kept in its proper place in the social scale of values. We can take Burke as being sincere in what he is reported as saying in the Commons on 11 April 1794: "If it were asked, did he prefer property to virtue? his answer would be no. To honour?—No. To arts and literature?—No. But he respected property inasmuch as it was the basis upon which they were all erected—the soul that animated, the genius that protected them" (*Parl. Hist.* 31: 381). Burke's thesis is that civilization and culture stand on and grow out of prosperity as their material base. But prosperity depends on private property, which stimulates industry, and industry depends on liberty, which in turn depends on order, outside of which it cannot perform its proper function.

He made the connection between property and industry a major theme of his *Tracts Relative to the Laws Against Popery in Ireland*, a fragmentary treatise that he wrote in 1761, while he was in Dublin serving as private secretary to William Gerard Hamilton. He never finished it, and it remained unpublished until after his death, though in the meantime it was passed around in manuscript form.

According to Burke, the chief, most extensive, and most certain operation of these penal laws against Catholics was upon property and, therefore, upon industry:

> Those civil Constitutions, which promote industry, are such as facilitate the acquisition, secure the holding, enable the fixing, and suffer the alienation of property. Every Law, which obstructs it in any part of this distribution, is, in proportion to the force and extent of the obstruction, a discouragement to industry. For a Law against property is a Law against industry, the latter having always the former, and nothing else, for its object.

The effect of these laws is most pronounced on "the acquisition of landed property, which is the foundation and support of all the other kinds." They have prevented "three fourths of the inhabitants of Ireland from acquiring any estate of inheritance for life or years, or any charge whatsoever, on which two thirds of the improved yearly value is not reserved for 30 years" (*Works* 9: 385; cf. 8: 400). Or, as Thomas H. D. Mahoney puts it in plainer language in his *Edmund Burke and Ireland*, "the penal laws made it impossible for Catholics to lease land for more than thirty-one years. Consequently, they lived in dread of the day when the lease would expire and they would be forced to begin all over again, if fortunate enough to secure another farm or bit of land" (p. 20).

"The desire of acquisition is always a passion of long views," said Burke. Give a man a tenure of only thirty years, and you give him no incentive "to build; to plant; to raise enclosures; to change the nature of the ground; to make any new experiment, which might improve agriculture; or to do any thing more than what may answer the immediate and momentary calls of rent to the landlord, and leave subsistence to the tenant and his family." Thus is stifled "that laudable avarice, which every wise State has cherished as one of the first principles of its greatness." Make it plain to a man that he may never have more than a temporary possession of property, and "you immediately and infallibly turn him to temporary enjoyments," which are "those of a thoughtless, loitering, and dissipated life" (*Works* 9: 387). As Burke said on another and much later occasion, "We know how little all Tenants, towards the expiration of their Lease, care how they havock the Estate; or rather with what industry they convert every thing to their temporary profit to the destruction of the Freehold Interest" (*Corr.* 8: 49).

The "avarice" that Burke praises is not "the unbounded lust of unmerited wealth." Rather, it is that desire for the means of self-support that enables a man to defer gratification in the hope of future gain, and rescues him from idleness and vice. We should also note that the access to property which Burke advocates does not question or deny the right of landlords to exact rents. What he advocates is the right of Catholics to rent, and even to buy, land.

Access to property also played an important part in a document entitled *Sketch of the Negro Code*, which Burke drew up in 1780, and years later sent to Henry Dundas, the Home Secretary and close associate of the Prime Minister, William Pitt the Younger, when Dundas requested it in 1792. A motion against the slave trade had been made for the first time in the House of Commons in 1776. It failed to pass, but the anti-slavery movement continued, and Burke wrote his document in support of it. His "sketch" is in fact a rather detailed set of proposals for ameliorating and eventually abolishing the slave trade, while at the same time preparing the slaves in the West Indies for emancipation. Among these proposals are the following.

First, the institution of the family must be fostered and protected among the slaves: "Whereas a state of matrimony, and the government of a family, is a principal means of forming men to a fitness for freedom, and to become good Citizens," all Negroes shall have the right, and the obligation, to marry. Conversely, slaveowners shall not have the right to sell slaves in such a way as to break up slave families. Married slaves who have resided on a plantation for twelve months may not be sold except along with the plantation. In other words, the slave becomes a serf (*Works* 9: 309, 311, 313).

Next, slaves shall have the right to acquire and hold property: "Whereas habits of industry and sobriety, and the means of acquiring and preserving property, are proper and reasonable preparatives to freedom, and will secure against an abuse of the same," married Negroes with children shall have all of Saturday and, after 37 years of age, all of Friday to work for themselves. Owners must respect the property acquired by their slaves and their right to pass it on to their heirs. The owners of field hands must allot them dwellings and plots of ground to be theirs for life (*Works* 9: 311–313). Some years later, when Philip Francis moved to bring in a bill to improve the condition of the slaves in the West Indies, Burke commented: "He had but one notion; that indeed perfectly agreed with mine—which was to give property to the Negroes" (*Corr.* 8: 451).

The *Sketch of the Negro Code* also provided that

> every Negro Slave, being thirty years of age, and who has had three children born to him in lawful matrimony, and who hath received a certificate from the Minister of his district, or any other Christian teacher, of his regularity in the duties of religion, and of his orderly and good behaviour, may purchase, at rates to be fixed by two Justices of Peace, the freedom of himself, or of his wife or children, or of any of them separately.

An official to be designated as "the Protector of Negroes" may also purchase "the freedom of any Negro, who shall appear to excel in any mechanical art, or other knowledge or practice deemed liberal" (*Works* 9: 314). The premise of these provisions is that a stable family, the acquisition of property, and freedom go together.

To return to the situation in Ireland: in 1778 the first of a series of Catholic Relief Acts was passed by the Irish Parliament. "By its terms," Thomas Mahoney explains, "Catholics were now enabled to lease land for a nine hundred and ninety-nine year period and their lands were made subject to the same conditions of sale and inheritance as those of Protestants" (p. 71; for fuller details, see the excerpts from the Act itself on pp. 332–334). That is to say, Catholics could now acquire freeholds, though in fact most of them were financially unable to do so. While the bill was pending in Parliament, Burke wrote to Edmund Sexton Pery, the Speaker of the Irish House of Commons, to commend him, and said that "the happy operation, which we expect from the benign and wise act you have in hand, is to create many small Estates—from the most minute, to perhaps three or four hundred [pounds] a year,—and that these will be the first, best, and most frequent results of encouraged and protected industry" (*Corr.* 3: 458). In Burke's mind, the great mass of landed property which belonged to the ruling class should correspond, not to a great mass of peons, but to a multitude of adequately well-off small farmers and freeholders.

After the Act was passed, he wrote to his Catholic cousin Garrett Nagle, of whose estate Burke was the legal leaseholder in order to protect it under the penal laws (Mahoney, p. 355, n. 45; cf. *Corr.* 3: 411–416, and notes), to congratulate him and all Irish Catholics on their new freedom. "Laws indeed cannot make men rich or happy," said Burke. "That they must do for themselves—but the Law now leaves their Natural faculties free. . . . Those who have nothing but the *means* of acquiring Substance, their Industry, Skill, and good oeconomy, have those *means* left free" (*Corr.* 4: 19).

In the same year Burke had had occasion to make the same point in regard to freeing Irish trade. He was at this time a Member of Parliament for Bristol, the second city of Great Britain and a major trading port. He incurred the wrath of Bristol's merchants (and partly for this reason, had to give up his seat in Parliament at the next election) by supporting a bill to relax a few of the restrictions that British law imposed on Ireland's trade with Britain and the colonies. In the spirit of mercantilism, Bristol could not see Ireland's gain as anything but Britain's loss. "It is hard to persuade us," Burke granted, "that every thing which is *got* by another is not *taken* from ourselves" (*Corr.* 3: 442). In one of a series of letters to his protesting constituents in Bristol, however, Burke replied that "England and Ireland may flourish together. The world is large enough for us both" (*Corr.* 3: 433).

More to the immediate point here, he insisted that by relaxing some of its restrictions on Irish trade, Britain was not giving Ireland a gift. "Do we in these resolutions *bestow* anything upon Ireland? Not a shilling. We only consent to *leave* to them, in two or three instances, the use of the natural faculties which God has given to them, and to all mankind" (*Corr.* 3: 433). To another constituent Burke declared: "When God has given any Men hands, and any other Men shall be found impious or mistaken enough, to say that they shall not work, my Voice shall not be with those Men" (*Corr.* 3: 438). To side with them would be against the law of God, as he wrote to a company of iron merchants in Bristol:

> God has given the earth to the Children of Man; and he has undoubtedly, in giving it to them, given them what is abundantly sufficient for all their Exigencies; not a scanty, but a most liberal provision for them all. The Author of our Nature has written it strongly in that Nature, and has promulgated the same Law in his written Word, that Man shall eat his Bread by his Labour; and I am persuaded, that no man, and no combination of Men, for their own Ideas of their particular profit, can, without great impiety, undertake to say, that he *shall not* do so; that they have no sort of right, either to prevent the Labour, or to withhold the Bread (*Corr.* 3: 442).

In answer to the complaint that the people of Ireland paid lower taxes than the British, and therefore should enjoy a smaller share of the benefits of the Empire, Burke replied that, to pay higher taxes, the Irish would first have to have the ability to pay them: "In the order of nature, the advantage must precede the charge. This disposition of things being the law of God, neither you nor I can alter it." But freeing Irish trade will increase Ireland's ability to pay taxes: "I believe it will be found, that if men are suffered freely to cultivate their natural advantages, a virtual equality of contribution will come in its own time" (*Corr.* 3: 433–434).

What government, under God, owes to its subjects is not their livelihood, but the freedom to earn it. Economic freedom, however, and the industry that depends on it, require a political and legal order that protects and fosters them. For example, there must be an imposition of taxes "the least likely to lean heavy on the active capital employed in the generation of that private wealth, from whence the publick fortune must be derived" (*Works* 5: 408). Again, speaking of the administration of Prime Minister Robert Walpole in the first half of the eighteenth century, Burke says: "The profound repose, the equal liberty, the firm protection of just laws during the long period of his power, were the principal causes of that prosperity which afterwards took such rapid strides towards perfection" (*Works* 6: 157).

Burke's early misgivings about the French Revolution concerned the lack of such an order. His first important judgment on the Revolution was expressed in a letter that he wrote Charles-Jean-François Depont. This was a young Frenchman who had visited England and been entertained by the Burke family in 1785. On 4 November 1789 he wrote a letter asking Burke to assure his young French friend and admirer that "the French are worthy of being free, that they will know how to distinguish liberty from licence and legitimate government from a despotic power," and that "the Revolution [now] begun will succeed" (*Corr.* 6: 31–32; my translation from the French). Burke's reply was considerably milder than what he wrote the following year in his *Reflections* (which were also ostensibly addressed to Depont), but it fell short of the assurance that Depont sought:

> When . . . I shall learn, that in France, the Citizen, by whatever description he is qualified, is in a perfect state of legal security, with regard to his life, to his property, to the uncontrolled disposal of his Person, to the free use of his Industry and his faculties;— When I hear that he is protected in the beneficial Enjoyment of the Estates, to which, by the course of settled Law, he was born, or is provided with a fair compensation for them;—that he is maintain'd in the full fruition of the advantages belonging to the state and condition of life, in which he had lawfully engaged himself, or is supplied with a substantial, equitable Equivalent;—When I am

assured, that a simple Citizen may decently express his sentiments upon Publick Affairs, without hazard to his life or safety, even tho' against a predominant and fashionable opinion; When I know all this of France, I shall be as well pleased as every one must be, who has not forgot the general communion of Mankind, nor lost his natural sympathy in local and accidental connexions [*Corr.* 6: 42–43].

Liberty and property were closely united in Burke's thought. R. B. McDowell explains his unrelenting opposition to the French Revolution on that premise:

> He fervently believed that the French revolutionary leaders in carrying through a ruthless reorganization of society were destroying liberty. By sweeping away old institutions and by displaying a contemptuous disregard of property rights they were destroying the guarantees of that individual independence which to Burke was an essential element in a civilized and just community [*Corr.* 9: xxi].

This consideration was also a main point in his condemnation of "Indianism," the system which he charged Warren Hastings (and others) with imposing on India, in his prosecution of Hastings before the House of Lords. Hastings, he told the Lords, was trying to pull the wool over their eyes by maintaining that "despotism was the only principle of government acknowledged in India" (*Works* 15: 62). He did this, said Burke,

> because your Lordships know, and because the world knows, that if you go into a country, where you suppose man to be in a servile state; where, the despot excepted, there is no one person who can lift up his head above another; where all are a set of vile, miserable slaves, prostrate and confounded in a common servitude, having no descendable lands, no inheritance, nothing that makes man feel proud of himself, or that gives him honour and distinction with others:—this abject degradation will take from you that kind of sympathy, which naturally attaches you to men feeling like yourselves, to men who have hereditary dignities to support and lands of inheritance to maintain, as you Peers have; you will, I say, no longer have that feeling which you ought to have for the sufferings of a people, whom you suppose to be habituated to their sufferings, and familiar with degradation [*Works* 15: 64–65].

Hastings's counsel had argued on this line before the Lords, said Burke, claiming that in India, before the English took over, "the people had no Liberty, no property, no Law—To be subject to arbitrary power was their sole privelege" (*Corr.* 7: 112). Whatever the merit of Burke's charge against Hastings may be, the premise on which he argued is clear: a people without securely protected property cannot be free, or even self-respecting.

English liberty, too, depended on property. The liberty for which Burke contended was not an abstract principle: "Abstract liberty, like other mere abstractions, is not to be found" (*Works* 3: 49). He had explained in his *Abridgment of English History* that the English people enjoyed certain liberties which could not be traced back to an "ancient constitution" and "Saxon laws" under which no one in the eighteenth century would care to live (*Works* 10: 555). The charter of English liberties given by Henry I in 1101 "was the first of the kind, and laid the foundation of those successive charters, which at last completed the freedom of the subject" (*Works* 10: 430–431). On a later page Burke says that the Great Charter and the Charter of the Forest, which King John signed at Runneymede in 1215, "disarmed the Crown of its unlimited prerogative, and laid the foundation of English liberty" (*Works* 10: 531–532). In 1790, in the *Reflections*, he says that English liberty is not claimed "on abstract principles 'as the rights of men'." Rather, it consists in concrete liberties, which were asserted in the Declaration of Rights in 1689, as "liberties, that had been long possessed, and had been lately endangered" (*Works* 5: 76–77).

In his *Speech on Conciliation with the Colonies* in 1775, having said that abstract liberty is not to be found, Burke continued: "Liberty inheres in some sensible object; and every nation has formed to itself some favourite point, which by way of eminence becomes the criterion of their happiness. It happened . . . that the great contests for freedom in this country were from the earliest times chiefly upon the question of taxing." Liberty was considered to rest on the principle "that, in all monarchies, the people must in effect themselves mediately or immediately possess the power of granting their own money [to the Crown], or no shadow of liberty could exist." This is the English conception of liberty, which the American colonists have inherited: "Their love of liberty, as with you, fixed and attached on this specifick point of taxing" (*Works* 3: 49–51). To put it in words other than Burke's: the line between absolute monarchy and limited monarchy is the line between the power of the king to tax without the consent of those whose property he taxes and their power to refuse to grant a tax (*Works* 3: 86; cf. 142; 9: 179). Their right to dispose of their property is the firm wall of liberty.

It is the bulwark of liberty because he who can take your property without your consent, having all property under his control, has all power. But those who have property that the government cannot take without their consent have power that limits the government. That property is power was an idea that Burke held until the French revolutionary state caused him, not to abandon it, but to modify it.

In his *Abridgment of English History* he refers to "that power, which always attends property" (*Works* 10: 391). He again alludes to the connection between property and power in his *Speech on Economical Reform*. He made this speech in the Commons in support of a bill, which he had written, designed to reduce the number of offices to which the king could appoint, in order thereby to diminish the king's power to influence the House of Commons by giving "places," i.e., jobs, to Members of Parliament. In this way the bill would safeguard the independence of the Commons from the Crown. In the course of this speech Burke said that, even if men were willing to serve without salaries in the great offices of state, "they ought not to be permitted to do so. . . . For as wealth is power, so all power will infallibly draw wealth to itself by some means or other; and when men are left no way of ascertaining their profits but by their means of obtaining them, those means will be increased to infinity" (*Works* 3: 316). Wealth and power go together, and if wealth does not bring power, power will bring wealth to itself. For this reason, property must control power.

That property, even if held in a moderate amount, should entail some share of political power led Burke to advocate giving Catholic freeholders in Ireland the right to vote for Members of Parliament. He wrote to Lord Kenmare, one of the small number of Catholic peers in Ireland:

> There are few Catholick Freeholders to take the Benefit of the privelege [of voting], if they were admitted to partake it: but the manner in which this very right in Freeholders at large is defended,

is not on the Idea, that they do really and truly represent the people, but that all people being capable of obtaining freeholds, all those, who by their industry and sobriety merit this privelege, have the means of arriving at Votes [*Corr.* 4: 410].

Because property is power, the road to property should lie open to all who are willing to work for it.

Burke repeated this proposal in a lengthy memorandum *On the State of Ireland*, which he wrote probably in 1792 and probably sent to Henry Dundas, the Home Secretary (see *Corr.* 1844, 4: 65, and Mahoney, p. 207). "I hold," he said, "that the measure of giving the Roman Catholics an interest in the landed property of the kingdom [the Catholic Relief Act of 1778] was not only the wisest policy, but the most fortunate event that ever took place in Ireland." The Irish Parliament should "now fill the measure by suffering property to give, in their hands, all that property can give," and "secure the right of election" (*Corr.* 1844, 4: 80–81).

As was mentioned above, the French Revolution shook Burke's conviction that property is power. Without going more deeply into a subject that will be treated in a later chapter, we may quote a treatise that he wrote in December 1791, under the title *Thoughts on French Affairs*. "That power goes with property," he now said, "is not universally true, and the idea that the operation of it is certain and invariable, may mislead us very fatally." In the National Assembly of France, "there are not quite fifty persons possessed of an income amounting to 100 £. sterling yearly." Whoever sees the significance of that fact "must discern clearly, *that the political and civil power of France is wholly separated from its property of every description*; and of course that neither the landed nor the monied interest possesses the smallest weight or consideration in the direction of any public concern" (*Works* 7: 51).

The French essay at democracy has created "a new species of interest merely political, and wholly unconnected with birth or property." This interest has produced and will increasingly produce a political class for which public office and the power and profit that go with it are an object of insatiable appetite. To such men "the glory of the state, the general wealth and prosperity of the nation, and the rise or fall of public credit, are as dreams; nor have arguments deduced from these topicks any sort of weight with them." If property does not check and direct power, political power will absorb property in the interest of politicians and their supporters, to the nation's harm (*Works* 7: 52–53).

Implicit in this proposition is Burke's belief that securely protected wealth, especially if it is old wealth joined to gentle birth and upbringing, disposes men to think in terms of the general welfare. He held that political power is a trust, derived from the people and held for the benefit of the people, not of the trustees (*Works* 2: 288; cf. *Corr.* 9: 169). Similarly, property is a trust, and property-owners, great landlords in particular, are more likely so to regard it. Subject though they are to all the weaknesses of human nature, they are better suited to fulfill the trust than are the poor whose natural guardians they are.

"The high ground of rank and dignity," said Burke in 1769, ". . . is trust implied" (*Works* 2: 9). In 1795 less than two years before he died, in *Thoughts and Details on Scarcity*, the most overtly laissez-faire piece he ever wrote, he argued that the rich "are the pensioners of the poor, and are maintained by their superfluity." The rich are also, he said,

> trustees for those who labour, and their hoards are the banking-houses of these latter. Whether they mean it or not, they do, in effect, execute their trust—some with more, some with less fidelity and judgment. But, on the whole, the duty is performed, and every thing returns, deducting some very trifling commission and discount, to the place from whence it arose. When the poor rise to destroy the rich, they act as wisely for their own purposes as when they burn mills, and throw corn into the river to make bread cheap [*Works* 7: 376–377; cf. *Parl. Hist.* 21: 191, and 30: 386].

Three distinct but related strands are interwoven in Burke's thought here. One is paternalism: the rich are trustees for the poor, and are obliged to care for them. Another is that there is a mutuality of interest between the rich and the poor which makes execution of the trust possible and probable. And, finally, whether the rich intend it or not, wealth circulates from the poor to the rich and back again. The wealth of the rich, however great it may be, is but a commission that they take and which is small in relation to the total wealth produced in the country, the greater part of which is consumed by the multitude of the poor. In all this, we must remember, Burke is thinking of a predominantly agricultural, pre-industrial society.

The idea of trusteeship as the office and function of wealth and power runs throughout Burke's writings, and here we need cite only a few instances of it. After the deaths of his son and his brother, both named Richard, in the same year, 1794, he wrote a typical eighteenth-century "character" of the two men. In it, he says: "Parents, in the order of Providence, are made for their Children, and not their Children for them; they are only their Trustees, at the most. They have no just title to any more than a distributory use of their goods even whilst they live." In the same document he expresses approval of the "settlement" or entailment of estates, because "the permanence of the commonwealth is greatly connected with the permanence of families. . . . The lead which Landed property ought to have in every well regulated State . . . demands also that everyone in the chain of succession should not have it in his power to destroy family property" (*Corr.* 7: 592, 594).

Government by the landed aristocracy is for the benefit, not of the aristocrats, but of the people at large, whose trustees the aristocrats are. In 1792, in a letter to a colleague in Parliament, Burke wrote that the former Rockingham Whigs, whose leader since the death of Lord Rockingham was Charles James Fox, have "thought proper to proscribe me on account of a book [*Reflections on the Revolution in France*]." But it was these Whig sympathizers with the French Revolution who had abandoned the Party's principles, not Burke. He thought himself "by the very constitution of the Party to be bound . . . to support those aristocratick principles, and the aristocratick Interests connected with them, as essential to the real Benefit of the Body of the people, to which all names of party, all Ranks and orders in the State, and even Government itself ought to be entirely subordinate" (*Corr.* 7: 52–53; cf. 9: 169).

Similarly, in his prosecution of Warren Hastings for plundering and otherwise misgoverning the East India Company's territories in India, Burke maintained: "When a British governour is sent abroad, he is sent to pursue the good of the people as much as possible in the spirit of the laws of this country [England], which in all respects intend their conservation, their happiness, and their prosperity." For "God forbid it should be bruited from Pekin to Paris, that the Laws of England are for the rich and the powerful; but to the poor, the miserable, and defenceless, they afford no resource at all." Moreover the East India Company and its officials were bound not only by laws of England, but by the charters through which they received powers from the Mogul Empire in India. By accepting those powers "they bound themselves (and bound inclusively all their servants) to perform all the duties belonging to that new office, and to be held by all the ties belonging to that new relation" (*Works* 13: 153, 18, 24).

The trust by which property and political power are held is much more likely to be executed, however, where there is a mutuality of interest between the governing rich and the governed poor. The burden of Burke's unending indictment of the government of Ireland under British rule was that such mutuality was lacking between a poor, Catholic, and subjugated Irish population and a rich, Protestant, and conquering class of British settlers who held Irish property and lived in fear that the natives would rise up in revolt and try to get it back again. This property-owning class left governing power in the hands of a political clique whose main interest, Burke said in 1792, was in getting and keeping well-paid government jobs:

> I am sure that it [the government of Ireland] is a job in its constitution; nor is it possible, a scheme of polity, which, in total exclusion of the body of the community, confines . . . to a certain set of favoured citizens the rights, which formerly belonged to the whole, should not, by the operation of the same selfish and narrow principles, teach the persons, who administer in that Government, to prefer their own particular, but well understood private interest to the false and ill calculated private interest of the monopolizing Company [i.e., class] they belong to [*Works* 9: 421–422].

In England, however, Burke thought that it was not so. To cite but one instance, he argued:

> In the case of the farmer and the labourer, their interests are always the same, and it is absolutely impossible that their free contracts can be onerous to either party. It is the interest of the farmer that his work should be done with effect and celerity: and that cannot be unless the labourer is well fed and otherwise found with such necessaries of animal life . . . as may keep the body in full force, and the mind gay and cheerful. . . . On the other hand, if the farmer cease to profit of the labourer, and that his capital is not continually manured and fructified, it is impossible that he should continue that abundant nutriment, and clothing, and lodging,

proper for the protection of the instruments he employs [*Works* 7: 383–384].

It would be all too easy, however, to persuade the poor, in England as well as in France, to believe French revolutionaries' propaganda and to regard the Revolution as a just revolt of the poor against kings, nobles, and the rich. "This doctrine," said Burke, "is highly dangerous, as it tends to make separate parties of the higher and lower orders, and to put their interests on a different bottom" (*Works* 7: 265). On the contrary, Burke thought, the interests of rich and poor are on the same bottom, because they are complementary. But the rich see that truth more easily when they are of the same blood and religion as the poor, and the poor accept it more readily when they are not blinded by ideological propaganda.

Property is not only an incentive to industry and the increase of a nation's wealth. It distributes itself throughout the population as landowners (and other rich men) spend their income. The owner of the land is a landed capitalist, and his capital performs the function not only of stimulating the production of wealth, but also of disbursing it; "the expenditure of a great landed property . . . is a dispersion of the surplus product of the soil" (*Works* 5: 292). The interest of the community is not to prevent capital formation, but to make sure that the capital redounds to the benefit of the community:

> In every prosperous community something more is produced than goes to the immediate support of the producer. This surplus forms the income of the landed capitalist. It will be spent by a proprietor who does not labour. But this idleness is itself the spring of labour; this repose the spur to industry. The only concern for the state is, that the capital taken in rent from the land, should be returned again to the industry from whence it came; and that its expenditure should be with the least possible detriment to the morals of those who expend it, and to those of the people to whom it is returned [*Works* 5: 290].

One way or another this surplus will be disbursed and make its way back to the original producers of the wealth. But it makes a great deal of difference by whom and for what purposes it is expended.

Burke discussed this question in his lengthy criticism of the French revolutionary government's confiscation of the property of the Church and specifically, at this point, of the monasteries. In answer to the objection that the latter "institutions savour of superstition in their very principle," he replies: "This I do not mean to dispute." But he asks whether it is wise to take the property from the monks and sell it to lay purchasers without some rational assurance that they

> will be in a considerable degree more laborious, more virtuous, more sober, less disposed to extort an unreasonable proportion of the gains of the labourer, or to consume on themselves a larger share than is fit for the measure of an individual, or that they should be qualified to dispense the surplus in a more steady and equal mode, so as to answer the purposes of a politick expenditure, than the old possessors" [*Works* 5: 288–291].

Burke's premise is clear: the landed capitalist is morally obliged to spend his capital in a moral way that will benefit the community.

Here the monks have the better of the argument. With all their faults, which Burke does not intend to dispute, the monks over the ages have spent their rental income on "the accumulation of vast libraries, . . . great collections of ancient records, medals, and coins, . . . paintings and statues, . . . grand monuments of the dead, . . . collections of the specimens of nature. . . ." These contributions to society and its culture may be compared favorably with the ways in which rich laymen have been known to spend their income:

> Does not the sweat of the mason and carpenter, who toil in order to partake the sweat of the peasant, flow as pleasantly and as salubriously, in the construction and repair of the majestick edifices of religion, as in the painted booths and sordid sties of vice and luxury; as honourably and as profitably in repairing those sacred works, which grow hoary with innumerable years, as on the momentary receptacles of transient voluptuousness; in opera houses, and brothels, and gaming-houses, and club-houses, and obelisks in the Champs de Mars? Is the surplus product of the olive and the vine worse employed in the frugal sustenance of persons, whom the fictions of a pious imagination raise to dignity by construing in the service of God, than in pampering the innumerable multitude of those who are degraded by being made useless domesticks, subser-

vient to the pride of man? Are the decorations of temples an expenditure less worthy a wise man than ribbons, and laces, and national cockades, and petit maisons, and petit soupers, and all the innumerable fopperies and follies in which opulence sports away the burthen of its superfluity [*Works* 5: 292–294]?

And yet, these fopperies and follies must be tolerated, "not from love of them, but for fear of worse. We tolerate them, because property and liberty, to a degree, require that toleration" (*Works* 5: 294). The economy depends on the circulation of wealth, and demands "the innumerable servile, degrading, unseemly, unmanly, and often most unwholesome and pestiferous occupations, to which by the social oeconomy so many wretches are inevitably doomed." Nonetheless, Burke accepts their sad lot as inevitable:

> If it were not generally pernicious to disturb the natural course of things, and to impede, in any degree, the great wheel of circulation which is turned by the strangely-directed labour of these unhappy people, I should be infinitely more inclined forcibly to rescue them from their miserable industry, than violently to disturb the tranquil repose of monastick quietude. . . . I am sure that no consideration, except the necessity of submitting to the yoke of luxury, and the despotism of fancy, who in their own imperious way will distribute the surplus product of the soil, can justify the toleration of such trades and employments in a well-regulated state [*Works* 5: 291–292].

We must bear in mind that in these pages of the *Reflections* Burke is attacking the confiscation of the monasteries in France, and is arguing that the lay purchasers of the confiscated lands will probably perform their duty of distributing the surplus product of the land less well than the monks. It is a polemical argument, in which Burke heightens for effect the contrast between the monks and the laity, and so appears to be inconsistent with his claim that on the whole the rich execute their trust. The latter claim, however, is Burke's more usual and genuine position. The rich, he believes, generally do perform their function, but they endanger their own ability to do so if they justify the confiscation of religious property on the ground that it is "superstitious."

Behind this argument lies Burke's awareness that any society that develops a high culture and civilization must generate capital in excess of what is needed for the sustenance of the population. Capital requires protection, not only by, but against, government. The French revolutionary government's confiscation of the monasteries was a crime not only against religion, but against property, and therefore against that security of capital on which the welfare of society, poor included, depends. Burke's defense of the monasteries is a defense of old, civilized, cultured (and, in this case, religious) property-owners against a tyrannical government and the newly enriched and greedy class who will benefit from the confiscation.

It remains, nonetheless, that he is willing to sacrifice a multitude of wretches to the great wheel of circulation. The reason he gives is that the income of landed capitalists must somehow be returned to the general population. The most common and obvious way is to give employment to the poor. Good and wholesome employments deserve to be commended. But "the innumerable servile, degrading, unseemly, unmanly, and often most unwholesome and pestiferous occupations" in which many people work from dawn to dark must be tolerated because they, too, "distribute the surplus product of the soil." Burke had satirically stated this as a politician's argument in *A Vindication of Natural Society* in 1756: "I am conscious, my Lord, that your politician will urge in his defence, that this unequal state is highly useful. That without dooming some part of mankind to extraordinary toil, the arts which cultivate life could not be exercised" (*Works* 1: 75). Here he restates the argument as his own.

That some evil must be tolerated to avoid greater evil was not a new thought in Christendom. But that not merely extraordinary toil, but "degrading, unseemly, unmanly" occupations must be tolerated for the sake of the great wheel of circulation was pushing that argument far indeed. It reflected a belief, of which Burke was not the originator, in "the natural course of things" which it is "generally pernicious to disturb," because left to itself, it will on the whole and in the long run produce greater benefits to society than intrusions by government, however well-intentioned, into the economy. Behind this was the Whig fear of government as a threat to, as well as a necessary protector of, society. It was better to leave society's welfare to society and the natural course of things, and to confine government to the defense of law and order.

Nonetheless, Burke was not a Manchester liberal or a social Darwinist. He always maintained that property was a trust held for the good of the whole community. Important though property undoubtedly was in his eyes, it was not the highest goal of human endeavor, and it deserved protection and esteem only because of the higher ends it served. Property, and the right to acquire it, was a stimulus to the industry that furnished a livelihood to all. It was a source of personal independence and self-respect, and a bulwark of liberty against the intrusive power of government. It generated a natural aristocratic governing class whose members were trustees for the whole community. Because of the independent power that their property gave them, they prevented the rise of a purely political ruling class whose source of wealth and power was their control of the government. Finally, property produced the capital which was the material wellspring of a high civilization and culture (see *Corr.* 7: 85). Property was therefore the ground on which all these good things stood and from which they sprang—"the soul that animated, the genius that protected them."

3
The Stability of Property

IN AN OFT-QUOTED PASSAGE in his *Reflections*, Burke accuses the French revolutionaries and their British partisans of being doctrinaire ideologues:

> They have "the rights of men." Against these there can be no prescription; against these no argument is binding: these admit no temperament, and no compromise: any thing withheld from their full demand is so much of fraud and injustice. Against these their rights of men let no government look for security in the length of its continuance, or in the justice and lenity of its administration. The objections of these speculatists, if its forms do not quadrate with their theories, are as valid against such an old and beneficent government as against the most violent tyranny, or the greenest usurpation [*Works* 5: 119–120].

A number of writers on Burke have therefore concluded that he rejected natural rights and natural law altogether (Peter J. Stanlis, *Edmund Burke and the Natural Law*, pp. 29–34, discusses several of them). But these writers miss Burke's point. He was, in the first instance, rejecting the ideological claim "that a representation in the legislature of a kingdom is not only the basis of all constitutional liberty, but of '*all legitimate government*: that without it a *government* is nothing but an *usurpation*.'" All men, that is to say, have by nature a right to vote for members of the legislature that makes the laws under which they live, and any government that denies it is ipso facto illegitimate. To this Burke answered, "as to the share of power, authority, and direction which each individual ought to have in the management of the state, that I must deny to be amongst the direct original rights of man in civil society" (*Works* 5: 115, 121).

On a deeper level Burke was denying that natural rights are those rights that belonged, in an abstract and unqualified form, to individual men in a pre-social and pre-political "state of nature." On the contrary, natural rights are derived from the natural, God-given goals of human nature and of the civil society that man must construct in order to achieve those goals. (For a fuller treatment of this topic, see Francis Canavan, *Edmund Burke: Prescription and Providence*, chap. 4.) As Burke explained:

> Far am I from denying in theory, full as far is my heart from withholding in practice (if I were of power to give or to withhold) the *real* rights of men. In denying their false claims of right, I do not mean to injure those which are real, and are such as their pretended rights would totally destroy. If civil society be made for the advantage of man, all the advantages for which it is made become his right [*Works* 5: 120].

Burke then proceeds to list, in summary fashion, those advantages. Among them is the right to property: "They have a right to the fruits of their industry; and to the means of making their industry fruitful. They have a right to the acquisitions of their parents . . ." (*Works* 5: 121). But property is one of the principal rights which the revolutionaries' "pretended rights" would totally destroy. For the right of every man in the state of nature to govern himself becomes, when he enters civil society, a natural and imprescriptible right to vote, and creates the possibility of a democratic tyranny. Burke, at any rate, feared that it would do so in a regime of untrameled majority rule. His fear was shared on the American side of the Atlantic by James Madison, who advocated ratification of the Constitution of 1787 as a safeguard against "a rage for paper money, for an abolition of debts, for an equal division of property, or for any other improper or wicked project," such as could sweep the people of a single state, but hardly the whole Union (*The Federalist*, no. 10, ad fin.).

Property, for Burke, is a natural right corresponding to a deep-seated impulse of human nature. He excuses the perhaps excessive attachment of the French nobility to their privileges in these words: "The strong struggle in every individual to preserve possession of what he has found to belong to him, and to distinguish him, is one of the securities against injustice and despotism implanted in our nature. It operates as an instinct to secure property, and to preserve communities in a settled state" (*Works* 5: 254; cf. *Corr.* 3: 456, where Burke refers to "the natural passions which Men have for fields and houses of their own").

Yet a natural right is not an absolute barrier to legal regulation. At the same time as he was writing the *Reflections*, Burke wrote to a friend concerning the claim of Protestant Dissenters (e.g., Presbyterians, Baptists, Congregationalists) to be exempted from the Test and Corporation Acts, which limited civil and military offices to Anglicans. The reason he gave for not supporting this claim would apply also to his attitude toward property as a natural right. The Dissenters, he said in 1790, will not get their exemption as long as they claim it as a *right*:

> Parliament will not hear of an *abstract principle*, which must render it impossible to annexe any qualification Whatsoever to the capacity of exercising a publick Trust; and I am myself much of the same Mind; though I would have these qualifications as few and as moderate as possible. This high claim of *Right*, leaves with Parliament no *discretionary* power whatsoever concerning almost any part of *Legislation*; which is almost all of it, conversant in qualifying, and limiting some *Right or other of mans original Nature* [*Corr.* 6: 102].

Burke considered the right to hold property more basic than the right to hold office. Twelve years earlier, while the Catholic Relief Act of 1778 was pending in Ireland, he expressed regret that the earlier English Catholic Relief Act had repealed only certain restrictions on Catholic property-holding and not certain penalties on religious practice. Yet the English act was wise,

> for it affirmed that *property* was to be encouraged in the acquisition, and quieted in the holding, whatever might become of religious toleration; and *disabilities* were to be removed though *penalties* might remain; as the latter however unjustifiable and opposite to Christian Charity and protestant principles, did not so directly sap the foundation of the national prosperity.

Besides, religious discrimination was less objectionable in regard to holding office than in regard to property rights: "We might give an exclusive preference to one religious Denomination with regard to publick Trust and official power, but that in point of property all Mankind ought to be upon a level" (*Corr.* 3: 455, 456).

Men's rights to their property should all stand on the same level, but it did not follow that those rights were absolute and immune from legal regulation. Burke explained in 1794:

> Now, although property itself is not, yet almost every thing concerning property, and all its modifications, is of artificial contrivance. The rules concerning it become more positive, as connected with positive institution. The legislator therefore always, the jurist frequently, may ordain certain methods, by which alone they will suffer such matters to be known and established, because, their very essence, for the greater part, depends on the arbitrary conventions of men [*Works* 14: 397–398].

"Property itself is not . . . of artificial contrivance." It is prior to, and therefore commands, positive law. In that sense, property is a natural right superior to "the arbitrary conventions of men." Yet, to have practical and effective existence in organized society, it must depend on rules of positive law which define how property will be recognized, acquired, protected, and transferred. There is nothing in the least surprising in this. It is true of almost everything of value in human life, indeed of life itself, which without the protection of positive laws on murder would be solitary, poor, nasty, brutish, and short.

The rights of property, therefore, though natural, are not independent of social definition and regulation. "Civil laws are not all of them merely positive," says Burke. Some of them are derived from principles of natural justice: "Those which are rather conclusions of legal reason, than matters of statutable provision, belong to universal equity, and are universally applicable." Such is the legal principle, found in the praetorian law of Rome, that a man is not so absolute a master of his own property that he may use it to the damage of his neighbors. On this point the law "has made many wise provisions, which, without destroying, regulate and restrain the right of *ownership*, by the right of *vicinage*. No *innovation* [in the owner's property] is permitted that may redound, even secondarily, to the prejudice of a neighbour" (*Works* 8: 185–186).

Property is subject to legal regulation, but not to arbitrary regulation, still less to outright confiscation. Burke thought that the revolutionary government's confiscation of the estates of the Church in France was outrageous, as he also thought that Henry VIII's plunder of "a part of the national church of his time and country" was (*Works* 8: 39). The National Assembly decreed the expropriation of Church lands in November 1789. Against this property a paper currency, called assignats, was issued. Its original purpose was to pay the creditors of the state, who could then use it to buy expropriated lands. (In this way the assignats would be retired; in fact, however, the state's need of ready money led to the continued issuance of assignats and an enormous inflation.) Burke's comment on these proceedings was: "We [the English] entertain a high opinion of the legislative authority; but we have never dreamt that parliaments had any right whatever to violate property, to over-rule prescription, or to force a currency of their own fiction [such as the assignats] in the place of that which is real, and recognized by the law of nations" (*Works* 5: 277).

Nor would he listen to the argument that the French Church had too much property:

> When once the commonwealth has established the estates of the church as property [as it has done in England], it can, consistently, hear nothing of the more or the less. Too much and too little are treason against property. What evil can arise from the quantity in any hand, whilst the supreme authority has the full, sovereign superintendance over this, as over any property, to prevent every species of abuse; and, whenever it notably deviates, to give to it a direction agreeable to the purposes of its institution [*Works* 5: 196; cf. 8: 32, 36]?

Although Burke does not explicitate it, there is at work in his thought on property a concept of nature and natural rights which is at odds with the dominant seventeenth- and eighteenth-century conception. In the latter, a natural right was a claim against all other men inherent in the nature of every individual antecedent to society and government. The function of government was to establish and protect a field of action on which every individual could exercise his rights in peace and security. The rights came first; society and government came after them and for them. Burke had a more teleological view of man's nature as oriented by God toward certain natural goals which could be attained only in and through society under government: "He who gave our nature to be perfected by our virtue, willed also the necessary means of its perfection—He willed therefore the state" (*Works* 5: 186).

The term "natural" for Burke, therefore, covered not only the constituent elements of human nature, but also that which nature needs to achieve its natural ends (as one might say, for example, that the body's digestive system is part of its natural constitution, but that food is also natural as the object of a natural and indispensable need; yet food may be as artificial as Twinkies or French-fried potatoes). So, too, a right can be natural as serving a natural need, yet exist in contingent, conventional, and changeable forms, rather than as an absolute claim prior to and independent of society. Subject to regulation and modification though it is, however, a right demands respect and protection because it flows from and serves the needs of man's nature.

Such a right was property, and because it was such, Burke could speak of it in terms which, to a nineteenth-century mind sounded like utilitarianism, but which in fact were compatible with the older tradition of natural law. So Burke was able to say: "In reality there are two, and only two foundations of Law, and they are both of them conditions, without which nothing can give it any force; I mean equity and utility." Of utility he says that it "must be understood, not of partial or limited, but of general and publick utility, connected in the same manner [as equity] with, and derived directly from, our rational nature" (*Works* 9: 351). Those rules and institutions are fundamentally natural which are derived from and serve man's natural needs. But since they exist in historically changing circumstances, their forms may be conditioned and regulated by convention, custom, and law.

The artificial and the natural are not necessarily opposed to each another. They can and should be complementary, because the artificial and the conventional are the means by which human nature realizes itself and achieves its natural ends:

> The state of civil society . . . is a state of nature, and much more truly so than a savage and incoherent mode of life. For man is by nature reasonable, and he is never perfectly in his natural state, but when he is placed where reason may be best cultivated, and most predominates. Art is man's nature [*Works* 6: 218].

Art is man's nature because by art and skill man constructs the civil society which, when properly constructed, is the environment in which his natural endowments can be fully developed. Burke can thus claim that civil society is in one sense natural, yet "commonwealths are not physical but moral essences. They are artificial combinations; and in their proximate efficient cause, the arbitrary productions of the human mind" (*Works* 8: 79). This is Burke's true position, as distinguished from his satirical attack on "artificial society" in his *Vindication of Natural Society*.

Property is a natural right because it is essential to the developed civil society which is the state that corresponds to man's developed human nature. Burke was not speaking as a mere utilitarian when he emphasized the importance to civilized society of stable and secure property. "I am sure," he said, "that everything which favours the stability of property is right, and does much for the peace, order, and civilisation of any Country" (*Corr.* 3: 404). It was not property as an end in itself, but its security and stability that was important to Burke. This concern showed itself throughout his career.

For instance, when Parliament first proposed to regulate the actions of the East India Company, the Rockingham Whigs, with Burke as their spokesman, were quick to defend the Company's chartered right to administer its own property. "We [Parliament] are to set ourselves up," Burke wrote to his friend Charles O'Hara, "as Judges upon a point of Law, to decide between the Subject and the Crown a matter of property of the greatest concern and magnitude without the least colour of right; at once Judge and party!" (*Corr.* 1: 303). When Parliament passed, among other acts regulating the Company, a bill rescinding a dividend of 12 per cent that the Company had declared, and limited it to 10 per cent, Rockingham and eighteen other peers submitted a protest to the House of Lords. Burke wrote this protest, which denounced Parliament's act as "an *ex post facto* law, rescinding a legal act of the Company in the exercise of its dominion over its own property, . . . without necessity or occasion, from any consideration of private justice or public utility" (*Parl. Hist.* 16: 353–354).

Burke's devotion to the Company's dividend no doubt was influenced by the fact that his cousin Will Burke had invested a large sum of money (supplied by his and Edmund's mutual friend, Lord Verney) in East India stock. Will held on to it too long, and when stock prices crashed in April 1773, "Will's paper fortune vanished" (Cone 1: 242). So did the Burke family's hope of financial independence. But Burke's and Rockingham's personal interests were not their only motives for protesting Parliament's action.

As the years went by, Burke was slowly but finally convinced that a company that administered an empire in India was not merely dealing in private property. It was itself an empire, with all the responsibilities of government toward the people it governed, and it was governing them very badly. Its "servants," i.e., officials, there were plundering the country, oppressing the natives, and lining their own pockets. It must therefore be controlled by Parliament (*Works* 4: 170; 11: 9).

The chief villain, in Burke's eyes, was Warren Hastings, the Governor-General of Bengal, whom he persuaded the House of Commons to impeach and try before the House of Lords. Few writers today think that Burke should have won his case against Hastings, and he didn't. He himself did not expect to win; as he wrote in December 1785 to Philip Francis, his principal associate in the prosecution: "Speaking for myself, my business is not to consider what will convict Mr. Hastings, (a thing we all know to be impracticable) but what will acquit and justify myself to those few persons, and to those distant times, which may take a concern in these affairs and the Actors in them" (*Corr.* 5: 243). But P. J. Marshall, who has made a thorough study of the case, credits Burke with a sincere idealism: "If Burke's judgement was disastrously at fault, if even Hastings' severest critics do not believe that he deserved his fate [an expensive trial that lasted from 1788 to 1794] . . . Burke's courage, his tenacity, and his devotion to what he believed were the interests of the Indian population are still not open to question" (*The Impeachment of Warren Hastings*, p. 191). What is of immediate interest here is that Burke's concern for the rights of property shifted from the chartered rights of the East India Company to the natural and legal rights of the people of India—but it was still a concern for property.

In his opening speech in the Hastings trial, Burke said: "There is a sacred veil to be drawn over the beginnings of all governments" (in *W&S* 6: 316–317, the "sacred veil" is a "secret veil," but this is the only notable difference from the text in *Works*). By that he meant, in context, that the ways in which the East India Company had acquired political dominion in Bengal would not bear close moral scrutiny. "But," he continued,

> whatever necessity might hide, or excuse, or palliate in the acquisition of power, a wise nation, when it has once made a revolution upon its own principles, and for its own ends, rests there. The first

step to empire is revolution, by which power is conferred, the next is good laws, good orders, good institutions, to give that power stability.

But the British in India had done the opposite, and took Bengal as a province to be exploited mercilessly (*Works* 13: 95–96).

Hastings, of course, was the chief offender:

> The first act of his Government in Bengal was the most bold and extraordinary, that I believe ever entered into the head of any man, I will say, of any tyrant. It was no more or less than a general (almost exceptless) confiscation, in time of profound peace, of all the landed property in Bengal upon most extraordinary pretences. Strange as this may appear, he did so confiscate it; he put it up to a pretended publick, in reality to a private corrupt, auction; and such favoured landholders, as came to it, were obliged to consider themselves as not any longer proprietors of the estates, but to recognise themselves as farmers under Government [*Works* 13: 230–231].

The crimes of Hastings, according to Burke, were many, but crimes against property ranked high among them. Convicting him would safeguard the property of many proprietors in India against lesser criminals, who might profit by the example of Hastings's punishment. "You will punish Mr. Hastings," Burke urged the Lords, "and no man will hereafter dare to rob widows, to give to the vilest of mankind, their own base instruments for their own nefarious purposes, the lands of others without right, title, or purchase" (*Works* 13: 380–381).

Burke also emphasized the importance of stable property in a passage of his *Speech on the Economical Reform* in 1780. His purpose was to abolish a number of royal offices, but, speaking of certain very profitable sinecure offices, he said that they could not be taken from their present holders, and that reform of these offices must await their deaths and the appointment of new officeholders who would get the offices on new terms. The reason he gave for this necessary delay was:

> These places, and others of the same kind which are held for life, have been considered as property. They have been given as a provision for children; they have been the subject of family settlements; they have been the security of creditors. What the law respects shall be sacred to me. If the barriers of the law should be broken

down, upon ideas of convenience, even of public convenience, we shall have no longer any thing certain among us. If the discretion of power is once let loose upon property, we can be at no loss to determine whose power, and what discretion it is that will prevail at last [*Works* 3: 308].

Burke did not mean, however, that property rights should be regarded as absolute. He went on to say: "There are occasions, I admit, of public necessity, so vast, so clear, so evident, that they supersede all laws. Law being only made for the benefit for the community, cannot in any one of its parts resist a demand which may comprehend the total of the publick interest." But such was not the case here. The reform of these offices could therefore wait (*Works* 3: 308–309).

In his *Reflections* Burke noted another instance in which exceptional measures might be justified in exceptional circumstances. "Had your nobility and gentry," he told his French correspondent, ". . . resembled those of Germany, at the period when the Hanse-towns were necessitated to confederate against the nobles in defence of their property . . . too critical an inquiry might not be advisable into the means of freeing the world from such a nuisance." This would have been "the dreadful exigence in which morality submits to the suspension of its own rules in favour of its own principles." But such was not the case in France when the property and the persons of the nobility, as of the clergy, were attacked (*Works* 5: 247–248).

In more general terms, massive confiscations of property are no way to reform a state: "In all mutations (if mutations must be) the circumstance which will serve most to blunt the edge of their mischief, and to promote what good may be in them, is, that they should find us with our minds tenacious of justice, and tender of property" (*Works* 5: 283). If the people, deluded by democratic theories, should ever become convinced that they are "the entire masters" of the state and have the right to do with it what they will, the result would be disastrous:

> No certain laws, establishing invariable grounds of hope and fear, would keep the actions of men in a certain course, or direct them to a certain end. Nothing stable in the modes of holding property, or exercising function, could form a solid ground on which any parent could speculate in the education of his offspring, or in a

choice for their future establishment in the world [*Works* 5: 181–182].

Not only a democratic but a monarchical state could become a menace to society by the monarch's disregard of property rights, as Burke explained in relation to an incident that took place during the American War of Independence. After the Dutch entered the war on the American side, a British fleet under Admiral George Brydges Rodney captured the island of St. Eustatius, a Dutch entrepôt in the Antilles, in February 1781. Rodney confiscated private property "with a complete disregard for law" (Editor's note, *Corr.* 4: 343). Burke commented sarcastically on this seizure of Dutch and other, including even British, property: "The plunder of that people or of people connected with them or indeed the plunder of any people whatsoever, friends or foes, is at present, a thing extremely pleasing to the generality of the Nation. In this they sympathize with their Rulers" (*Corr.* 4: 350).

Burke also argued in the Commons that Rodney's actions violated the principle of the law of nations that the conqueror must treat the conquered who have freely surrendered as he would his own subjects. As for what a monarch owes to his own subjects, Burke is reported as explaining it in these terms:

> It was ridiculous to suppose, for a moment, that the subject could lose his effects, and all the benefit of regal protection, and yet be bound by the duty of allegiance; or that a monarch could retain that character when the whole property of the state was vested in himself: he might then be called lord of the soil, or sole processor of it, but he could not arrogate the title of king. This is a principle inspired by the Divine Author of all good; it is felt in the heart; it is recognized by reason; it is established by consent [*Parl. Hist.* 22: 230].

This is to say that natural law makes the protection of private property an obligation of government.

Speaking of the problems that the French state faced in collecting an adequate revenue, Burke remarked: "Too many of the financiers by profession are apt to see nothing in revenue but banks, and circulations, and annuities on lives, and tontines, and perpetual rents, and all the small wares of the shop." These things have their uses in "a settled order of the state." They are not its true wealth, however.

> When men think that these beggarly contrivances may supply a resource for the evils which result from breaking up the foundations of publick order, and from causing or suffering the principles of property to be subverted, they will, in the ruin of their country, leave a melancholy and lasting monument of the effect of preposterous politicks, and presumptuous, short-sighted, narrow-minded wisdom [*Works* 5: 432–433].

The stability and security of property is the indispensable condition for people's acquisition of property, therefore for increasing the wealth of the community and its ability to support the state through taxation. Prosperity demands respect for property and for the order on which property depends:

> Good order is the foundation of all good things. To be enabled to acquire, the people without being servile, must be tractable and obedient. The magistrate must have his reverence, the laws their authority. The body of the people must not find the principles of natural subordination by art rooted out of their minds. They must respect that property of which they cannot partake. They must labour to obtain what by labour can be obtained; and when they find, as they commonly do, the success disproportioned to the endeavour, they must be taught their consolation in the final proportions of eternal justice. Of this consolation whoever deprives them, deadens their industry, and strikes at the root of all acquisition as of all conservation. He that does this is the cruel oppressor, the merciless enemy of the poor and wretched; at the same time that by his wicked speculations he exposes the fruits of successful industry, and the accumulations of fortune, to the plunder of the negligent, the disappointed, and the unprosperous [*Works* 5: 432].

How much consolation the poor found in this advice, coming from a member of the lesser gentry, is questionable. But, without exculpating Burke, it is worth mentioning that he himself commonly found the success disproportioned to the endeavor. Neither he nor the members of his close-knit family circle ever got rich. Carl Cone reports that both Burke's brother and his son "died intestate and poor. Will Burke was a financial burden and a legal liability, living under the threat of imprisonment for debt." Burke himself "had no regular income except £500 a year from his land; his debts amounted to twenty-five or thirty thousand pounds," and in 1795 he seriously considered leaving the country because of them (*Corr.* 8: 280, n. 4). Prime Minister William Pitt was able to arrange pensions and grants for him, however, which enabled him "to satisfy his most clamant creditors, and . . . have £2,500 a year for the rest of his life" (Cone 2: 446–448).

Nor was he more successful in his political career. Indeed, by his decision in 1766 to hitch his wagon to Lord Rockingham's political star, he effectively renounced the hope of a career. In the two brief periods in the 1780s in which his party was in power, Burke was appointed Paymaster of the Forces. It was a post that was understood to be a legitimate means of getting rich quickly. But instead of taking this opportunity, Burke reformed the office and limited its emoluments to a fixed salary (ibid., pp. 29–32; cf. *Corr.* 8: 116–117). He was never seriously considered for a cabinet post, and he failed to get the peerage he would have loved to pass on to his son.

Not only did he not pursue the *cursus honorum* that such of his contemporaries as Alexander Wedderburn followed, but he was generally unsuccessful in the political causes to which he dedicated himself. He did not deter the British government from the policies that lost the American colonies. He failed to win a conviction of Warren Hastings, and it is doubtful that "the impeachment had a salutary influence upon future Indian administrations" (Cone 2: 256); on the contrary, it has been judged "largely irrelevant to the future of British rule in India" (P. J. Marshall, p. 191). He certainly contributed to relieving the lot of Irish Catholics, but he died warning the government of the rebellion it was provoking by the bigoted policies it persisted in following, a rebellion which in fact broke out in the year after he died. He also died in near-despair over what he saw as the half-heartedness of the British government in opposing the French Revolution.

Finally, he spent his last years in a political wilderness. Having dedicated his public life to the Rockingham Whigs, he ended in exile from its successor party, the Foxite Whigs, after his break with them over the attitude to be taken toward the French Revolution. Yet he was never really received by William Pitt and his Tories. L. G. Mitchell comments: "The fact that Pitt and his friends were as reluctant as Fox to give credibility to Burke's views meant that, in abandoning Foxite Whiggery, Burke would not find an alternative political home in Pitt's entourage. There followed the terrible isolation in politics that was Burke's lot after 1791" (*W&S* 8: 20; cf. *Corr.* 7: 460, 8: 335). It does not follow that Burke was therefore wrong in the stand he took against the French Revolution. But, politically, he was largely a failure, so that he, too, was forced to find his consolation in the final proportions of eternal justice (see Canavan, *Prescription and Providence*, pp. 73–77, 174–179).

To return to the main theme of this chapter: Burke maintained that the stability and security of property depended on prescription as a title to it. Long-continued possession of property in good faith established a right to it that overrode all earlier claims to own it. For Burke, prescription was not a mere principle established by custom or statute law, but a principle of the law of nature, which positive law ought to recognize and incorporate into itself.

On this point Burke was in flat disagreement with William Warburton, an eighteenth-century bishop of Gloucester. Burke would have largely agreed, however, with Warburton's definition of prescription: "*Prescription* is, when a Man, by enjoying for a certain Course of Time without Opposition, the Property of another, but possessed by him *bona fide* and by a lawful title acquires in that others Property, a full Right, in such sort, that the true Proprietor has no longer any claim to it, or Civil Action for the recovery of it." Warburton holds, however, that prescription is against natural law:

> Now this by the generality of Writers is agreed to have its sole foundation in the *Civil Law*. The incomparable *Cujas* says expressly—*That the Law of Prescription directly contradicts the Law of Nature and of Nations, because the true Proprietor is dispossessed of his own, without his Consent.* And indeed nothing can be more evident. For what I once had the right to, I must ever have, till I resign, transfer or forfeit it by a direct Act of the Will.

Yet Warburton goes on to say that states rightly deviate from the law of nature for the sake of "public Good, the Peace of Civil Society, and stifling the Seeds of Chicane and Process. It is of the highest Concernment to the State that its Citizens be assured of their Possession without Contest" (*The Alliance Between Church and State*, 1766 ed., p. 127).

Paul Lucas, writing in the twentieth century, confirms Warburton on the reasons for which the old natural-law writers asserted prescription as a title to property. It was

> not on grounds of divine, eternal, and immutable truths, or even of equity, but for considerations of public utility . . . [and] upon the need to restrain litigiousness, to secure existing rights to property in order to encourage its improvement for the benefit of all men, and to maintain prosperity, order, tranquillity, and stability in society [*Historical Journal* 11: 39].

But, as we shall see, those were the reasons that Burke offered for insisting that prescription, as he said in his *Reflections*, "is a part of the law of nature" (*Works* 5: 276). Although he often called prescription a principle of natural equity, he ultimately justified it in terms of its utility in serving the needs of human nature.

Nor was this a position to which he came late in life, in reaction to the French Revolution and its massive confiscations of property. He had held it all along, as is shown by his argument for two nullum tempus bills early in his political career. The occasion for the first of them arose when, in 1768, a Sir James Lowther asserted a flaw in the title to certain lands belonging to his political rival (and one of Burke's political leaders), the Duke of Portland. The Duke had inherited these lands from ancestors who had originally received them as royal grants. Sir James alleged that there were defects in the grants, and "*nullum tempus occurrit regi*"—no length of time runs against [the rights of] the king. If there was a flaw in the original grant, then the king still owned the lands, and the Crown could now lease them to Sir James.

The Rockingham Whigs replied to this threat with Sir George Savile's Nullum Tempus bill, which defined a period of time after which the title of the Crown lapsed and a prescriptive title to former Crown lands would be recognized in the present possessor. The bill failed, but by only twenty votes, and was passed by Parliament the following year because the ministry chose not to oppose it.

In the meantime Burke had two letters published in the press under the pen name Mnemon. In one of them he called *nullum tempus occurrit regi* a "practical Menace to all Landed Property," and said that "the Principle of this Grant [to Lowther] has given

A SHOCK TO THE WHOLE LANDED PROPERTY OF ENGLAND." In a later letter he admitted that *nullum tempus occurrit regi* is a principle of English law, but to its disgrace: "The best Judges have always cast an Odium upon it, as being fundamentally contrary to natural Equity, and all the Maxims of a free Government." It is unjust because the Surveyor-General "is only bound to prove, that the Lands in Question have been in some former Age in the hands of the Crown. This is not difficult: All the Lands of the Kingdom have been so."

It is a menace to liberty as well as property because the Ministers of the Crown thus have a weapon for "breaking the Fortunes and depressing the Spirit of the Nobility, for drawing the common People from their reliance on the natural interests of the Country, to an immediate Dependance on the C---n, and principally for enabling Ministers . . . to domineer and give the Law in all future Elections" (*W&S* 2: 78, 80–81, 82). Nearly three decades later, Burke still took pride in having had "a very full share" in bringing prescription "to its perfection" in "Sir George Savile's Act called the *Nullum Tempus* Act" (*Works* 8: 48).

In 1772, Burke supported a similar Nullum Tempus bill against dormant claims of the Church. This bill, he argued, would "render the principle of prescription a principle of the Law of this Land, and incorporate it with the whole of your jurisprudence" (*Works* 10: 143). Lucas remarks that Burke thereby admitted that "prescription was a gift of parliamentary statute, not an ancient right of Englishmen" (p. 55). Yet Burke had not said that it was an ancient right of Englishmen, but that it was a principle of the law of nature which parliamentary statute should recognize and make enforceable by the courts. In so doing, Parliament would do justice: "If the principle of prescription be not a constitution of positive law, but a principle of natural equity, then to hold it out against any man is not doing him injustice" (*Works* 10: 144). On the contrary, men deserved to be protected against the revival of old and forgotten claims, and were entitled to prescription, "the end of which is to secure the natural well-meaning ignorance of men, and to secure property by the best of all principles, continuance" (*Works* 10: 146).

Burke thought that parliamentary enactment of a law of prescription was necessary because he did not want judges recurring directly to natural law. That was the function of legislators, as he explained in his *Letter to the Sheriffs of Bristol* in 1777:

> Legislators ought to do what lawyers cannot; for they have no other rules to bind them, but the great principles of reason and equity, and the general sense of mankind. These they are bound to obey and follow; and rather to enlarge and enlighten law by the liberality of legislative reason, than to fetter and bind their higher capacity by the narrow constructions of subordinate artificial justice [*Works* 3: 144; cf. 10: 66].

But as Burke said in a speech on a subject other than prescription:

> A Judge, a person exercising a judicial capacity—is neither to apply to original justice, nor to a discretionary application of it. He goes to justice and discretion, only at second hand, and through the medium of some superiours. He is to work neither upon his opinion of the one nor of the other, but upon a fixed Rule, of which he has not the making, but singly and solely the *application* to the case [*Works* 10: 66–67].

On the same premise, if prescription were to be enforceable, it would have to be enacted by parliamentary statute, not left to judges enforcing their own opinions of natural justice.

For Burke, a prescriptive title to property assumed that the present proprietor held the property in good faith: "Prescription can only attach on a supposed *bona fide* possession" (*Works* 10: 144). Burke himself asserted in 1777 that he would never have accepted legal ownership of the estate of his Catholic cousins, the Nagles, "if . . . I had reason to think there had been any original wrong in the obtaining it though not by my act or consent" (*Corr.* 3: 413). Prescription was not at issue in this instance, since the conveyance of the estate to Burke's brother Garrett, from whom Edmund inherited it, had taken place in the relatively recent past, far short of the period of time which prescription required. But for precisely that reason, Edmund said that he could not and would not have accepted a suspect title to the property: prescription had not yet had time to obliterate whatever defect may have been in the title and thus confirm him in good faith possession.

On the other hand, where prescription has had time to operate, there is no need to examine the original validity of the title. In his *Letter to the Sheriffs of Bristol* Burke explained that, although he urged Parliament to abandon the effort to tax the American colonies because of its imprudence and unwisdom, he did not question Parliament's right to tax them:

> When I first came into a publick trust, I found your parliament in possession of an unlimited legislative power over the colonies. I could not open the statute book, without seeing the actual exercise of it, more or less, in all cases whatsoever. This possession passed with me for a title. It does so in all human affairs. No man examines into the defects of his title to his paternal estate, or to his established government [*Works* 3: 177].

Although political revolutions are sometimes justified because they are unavoidably necessary, we must otherwise accept the long-established constitution of government on which so much depends. Under the British Constitution that "I actually enjoy," said Burke, ". . . I know that no power on earth, acting as I ought to do, can touch my life, my liberty, or my property" (*Works* 10: 104). One does not lightly question the legitimacy of such an old and beneficent constitution.

The case for respect for property is even stronger, as Burke explained to Captain Thomas Mercer. After Burke had attacked the principles of the French Revolution in his *Speech on the Army Estimates* in February 1790, Mercer wrote him a letter objecting to his criticism of the French for subverting their ancient government and their church. Mercer, a North of Ireland Protestant, thought that both those institutions deserved what had been done to them. Burke replied with an extended defense of prescription.

As a Member of Parliament, he said, "I am in *trust* religiously to maintain the rights and properties of all descriptions of people in the *possession* which legally they hold; and in the *rule* by which alone they can be secure in any possession." The rule is "that grand title, which supersedes all other title, and which all my studies of general jurisprudence have taught me to consider as one principal cause of the formation of states; I mean the ascertaining and securing *prescription*." It is not enough to call churchmen, as Mercer had done, "pampered and luxurious prelates," or their use of expensive liturgical vessels "pageantry and hypocrisy," or their estates "accumulations of ignorance and superstition" derived from donations made in "ages of ignorance and superstition." Suppose they were that: "It proves that these donations were made long ago; and this is *prescription*; and this gives right and title" (*Corr.* 6: 93–95).

Knowing, and knowing that Mercer knew, that most of the land in Ulster had been confiscated from the native Irish after their several unsuccessful uprisings against the English, Burke went on: "It is possible that many estates about you were originally obtained by arms, that is, by violence, a thing almost as bad as superstition, and not much short of ignorance: but it is *old violence*; and that which might be wrong in the beginning, is consecrated by time, and becomes lawful." Call this superstition and ignorance, if you will, "but I had rather remain in ignorance and superstition than be enlightened and purified out of the first principles of law and natural justice." Why the consecration of property by time is such a principle, Burke did not explain clearly here but said emphatically that an expropriating government is a tyrannical one, and an expropriating democracy is the worst, because the most unchecked, tyranny of all (*Corr.* 6: 95–96).

His son, Richard, Jr., gave a reason (which he surely had learned from his father) in a letter he wrote to Henry Dundas on 18 April 1792. He enclosed a Declaration of the Catholics of Ireland, which had been adopted by the Catholic Committee, whose agent he was, to be transmitted to King George III. Among other things, the Catholics declared: "We do hereby solemnly disclaim and for ever renounce all interest in, and title to, all forfeited lands resulting from any rights of our ancestors, or any claim, title or interest therein: nor do we admit any title as a foundation of right which is not established and acknowledged by the laws of the realm as they now stand." Richard's comment is that this renunciation is "wholly superfluous" because the titles that the Catholics renounce have long since been superseded by the period of prescription which English law fixed, "upon a presumption (Founded in natural justice and recognised in its principles, by the laws of all countries) that no claim of right, can, after vicissitudes of so many years, be ascertain'd with any sort of probability" (*Corr.* 7: 126–128). Natural justice requires that property be secure. After some period of time, therefore, property titles must be safeguarded against the revival of claims from so far in the past that their validity cannot be determined "with any sort of probability." It is for positive law, however, to fix that period of time.

Later in the same year Burke wrote a lengthy letter to his son (but which he never completed or sent), in which he makes much the same point in more emphatic terms. The Protestant holders of forfeited Irish estates are fearful that if they make any concessions to Irish Catholics, the latter will lay claim to their ancestral lands. The present proprietors should stop insisting that the Protestants who originally got those estates received them with legal and valid titles. What difference does that make? Burke asked:

> Might one not ask these gentlemen, whether it would not be more natural, instead of wantonly mooting these questions concerning their property, as if it were an exercise in Law, to found it on the solid rock of prescription; the soundest, the most general, and the most recognized title between man and man, that is known in municipal or in publick jurisprudence? a title, in which not arbitrary institutions, but the eternal order of things gives judgment; a title, which is not the creature, but the master of positive Law; a title, which, though not fixed in its term, is rooted in its principle, in the law of nature itself, and is indeed the original ground of all known property; for all property in soil will always be traced back to that source, and will rest there [*Works* 9: 449].

Prescription is the master, not the creature, of positive law, because it is *rooted in its principle* in the law of nature. Burke was surely aware of Locke's argument that the original ground of property was occupancy of and labor on the soil. But Burke's proposition is that prescription is the original ground of all *known* property. We have no way of knowing which human beings in the impenetrable mists of the remote past first occupied any piece of soil. But we can know whether the present occupant has held it in good faith for long enough that justice requires us to protect his title as a matter of right. For if we do not—and this is the ultimate argument—no title will be secure.

Besides, Burke points out, the native Irish are not questioning the title of the present proprietors:

> The miserable Natives of Ireland, who ninety-nine in an hundred are tormented with quite other cares, and are bowed down to labour for the bread of the hour, are not, as gentlemen pretend, plodding [plotting?] with antiquaries for titles of centuries ago to the estates

of the great Lords and Squires, for whom they labour. But if they
were thinking of the titles, which gentlemen labour to beat into
their heads, where can they bottom their own claims but in a presumption and a proof, that these lands had at some time been
possessed by their ancestors? These gentlemen, for they have Lawyers amongst them, know as well as I, that in England we have had
always a prescription or limitation, as all nations have, against each
other. . . . All titles terminate in prescription; in which (differently
from Time in the fabulous instances) the son devours the father,
and the last prescription eats up all the former [*Works* 9: 449–450].

Burke knew that the argument, which he said the Irish peas-
antry did not use, was used by French peasants during the
Revolution:

They know, that almost the whole system of landed property in its
origin is feudal; that it is the distribution of the possessions of the
original proprietors, made by a barbarous conqueror to his barbarous
instruments; and that the most grievous effects of the conquest are
the land rents of every kind, as without question they are. The
peasants, in all probability, are the descendants of these ancient
proprietors, Romans or Gauls [*Works* 5: 395].

They will not listen to the argument that the passage of time has
obliterated their right to the lands that barbarians seized from their
remote ancestors. Still, since it would be difficult to prove, after
so many centuries, which peasant today is descended from the
proprietor of a particular piece of land in the Roman Empire, they
have found another argument to fall back on:

If they fail, in any degree, in the titles which they make on the
principles of antiquaries and lawyers, they retreat into the citadel
of the rights of men. There they find that men are equal; and the
earth, the kind and equal mother of all, ought not to be monopolized to foster the pride and luxury of any men, who by nature are
no better than themselves, and who, if they do not labour for their
bread, are worse. They find, that by the laws of nature, the occupant and subduer of the soil is the true proprietor; that there is no
prescription against nature; and that the agreements (where any
there are) which have been made with the landlords, during the
time of slavery, are only the effect of duresse and force; and that
when the people re-entered into the rights of men, those agreements were made as void, as every thing else which had been

settled under the prevalence of the old feudal and aristocratick tyranny [*Works* 5: 395–396].

Against this argument, Burke is convinced, no property is safe, and the National Assembly of France made a grievous mistake when it reprobated the doctrine of prescription:

> If prescription be once shaken, no species of property is secure, when it once becomes an object large enough to tempt the cupidity of indigent power. I see a practice perfectly correspondent to their contempt of this great fundamental part of natural law. I see the confiscators begin with bishops, and chapters, and monasteries, but I do not see them end there [*Works* 5: 276].

For, as Burke explained in 1796, in his *Letter to a Noble Lord*, "the principles and the examples which lead to ecclesiastical pillage," lead also "to a contempt of *all* prescriptive titles, thence to the pillage of *all* property, and thence to universal desolation" (*Works* 8: 40).

To Burke's mind, when prescription goes, everything goes, and this was the essence of his indictment of the French democracy:

> A People who thirst for blood and confiscation in the bosom of Peace, who could endure even to hear of a maxim that the goods of any one Citizen possessed by a long acknowledged legal title belong to the State, and that those who assume the exercise of sovereign Authority are free to take it from him and to make such a distribution of it as they please, such a People are not fit to sit in a seat of Judgment, or for any other function, because they despise the very foundation of social Union [*Corr.* 6: 108].

We may see here an answer to the puzzle of how Burke could call prescription a principle that makes injustice just, or in his own words, "that principle of natural and legal limitation by which wrong enures into right" (*Corr.* 1844, 4: 81). A possession may have originated in an unjust conquest or confiscation, but prescription turns it into just ownership when a sufficiently long period of time has passed since the initial injustice. Burke calls this a principle of natural equity, but it seems rather to be rooted in that other source of law, namely, that utility which is "derived directly from our rational nature" (*Works* 9: 351). While Burke does not fully spell out this argument, it runs as follows. Man's nature as created by God, and therefore as part of the moral order of the universe, is social. Organized civil society is man's true state of nature, because it is the best environment for the development of his nature toward the perfection that God intends for it. In this human social development, property plays an essential role, and is therefore a natural right. But property cannot perform its role in society unless it is adequately protected from depredation and confiscation.

Even that property must be protected which originated in such confiscations as Henry VIII's expropriation of monastery lands, once it has passed into the general mass of private property and been inherited by successive generations or sold to purchasers who bought it in good faith. So much depends on the security of property that prescription satisfies a basic need of man's nature, and therefore must be recognized as a principle of natural law. That the acquisition of a piece of property was originally unjust may be admitted, but for the good of man and his society, that claim must at some time lapse and die.

4
Property and Government

IN Burke's political theory, the protection of property ranked high among the goals of civil society. Sometimes he spoke of it as the only, or at least the primary, goal. At other times, however, it was but one in a broad range of goals, to which he referred in very general terms. He therefore gives the impression of being vague, perhaps inconsistent, in his views on the purposes for which civil society exists.

We need not be surprised at this, since what he said on the subject was never spelled out in a formal treatise. His remarks always occurred in writings on particular political issues, to which his statements on the ends of society and government were relevant without being fully elaborated. How he related property to the other ends of social and political life is not a matter that he made entirely clear. Any effort to clarify it, consequently, is an attempt to put discrete statements and remarks together to form a mosaic, and the result may be the imposition of a pattern on Burke's thought rather than the discovery of an underlying unity in it. But, unless we are to take Burke as a political hack who spoke only as the occasion and his immediate purpose demanded, we must run that risk.

Furthermore, Burke could, and sometimes did, speak a language that sounds as if he borrowed it from John Locke, even though he does not acknowledge Locke as its source. For example, in his early and never completed *Tracts Relative to the Laws Against Popery in Ireland*, he says: "Every body is satisfied that a conservation and secure enjoyment of our natural rights is the great and ultimate purpose of civil society; and that therefore all forms whatsoever of Government are only good as they are subservient to that purpose, to which they are entirely subordinate" (*Works* 9: 364). He had already stated earlier in the same tracts that "a Law, which shuts out from all secure and valuable property the bulk of the people" is unjust, because it is "repugnant to the essence of Law, which requires that it be made as much as possible for the benefit of the whole" (*Works* 9: 352).

In a speech that he made in Parliament in 1772, Burke identified life, liberty, and property as the goals of society: "To take away from men their lives, their liberty or their property, those things for the protection of which society was introduced, is great hardship and intolerable tyranny" (*Works* 10: 16). For their sake, he had said a year earlier, the laws must also protect men's reputations against libels: "Undoubtedly the good fame of every man ought to be under the protection of the Laws, as well as his life, and liberty and property. Good fame is an out-work, that defends them all, and renders them all valuable" (*Works* 10: 115–116). In other writings and speeches, Burke mentions property as if it were the sole or principal purpose of government. "Prescription," he said in 1782, "is the most solid of all titles, not only to property, but, which is to secure that property, to government" (*Works* 10: 96). Speaking in 1785 of the abuses of British power in India, Burke declared that when "the supreme authority . . . secures publick robbery by all the careful jealousy and attention with which it ought to protect property from such violence, the commonwealth then is totally perverted from its purposes" (*Works* 4: 317). In 1793 he complimented a member of the Irish Parliament on having "well shewn [that] property is the first origin, the continued Bond, and the ultimate End" of civil society (*Corr.* 7: 359). In 1791, he had written to a member of the National Assembly of France: "As you had a constitution formed upon principles similar to ours, my idea was, that you might have improved them as we have done, conforming them to the state and exigencies of the time, and the condition of property in your country, having the conservation of that property, and the substantial basis of your monarchy, as principal objects in all your reforms" (*Works* 6: 58). Two years later he wrote to an émigré French nobleman, "It is the contempt of Property, and the setting up against its principle, certain pretended advantages of the State, (which by the way exists only for its conservation) that has led to all the other Evils which have ruined France, and brought all Europe into the most imminent danger" (*Corr.* 7: 389). Finally, in one of his concluding speeches in the trial of Warren Hastings, he told the House of Lords:

> It will not be improper for me to remind your Lordships of the legitimate ends to which all controlling and superintending power ought to be directed. . . . The first is to take care of the vital principle of every State, its Revenue. The next is to preserve the magistracy and legal authorities, in honour, respect, and force. And the third to preserve the property moveable and immoveable, of all the people committed to his [the governor's] charge [*Works* 15: 340].

It would be consistent with many of Burke's other statements to conclude that, of these three ends, it is the last, property, that is the highest, for the sake of which the revenue and the magistracy exist.

Nonetheless, another line of passages in Burke's writings reveals that he often spoke of the ends of civil society in much broader terms. In his *Tracts on the Popery Laws* he did not make a nation's wealth consist in real estate and other material goods alone: "The stock of materials, by which any nation is rendered flourishing and prosperous, are its industry; its knowledge, or skill; its morals; its execution of justice; its courage; and the national union in directing these powers to one point, and making them all centre in the publick benefit" (*Works* 9: 385). These were elements of the common good, for which the community exists and which it is the purpose of society to preserve and develop.

All government is a trust to be exercised for the good of the governed, according to Burke. If he were the Lord-Lieutenant of Ireland, he wrote to Father Thomas Hussey (who later became the Catholic Bishop of Waterford), "I should feel myself turned out of my Situation, the moment I was deprived of the power of being just, and of protecting the people under my Care, from the tumults of the Multitude, and the insolence of the Rich and powerful; For, in the name of God, for what else are Governours and Governments made?" (*Corr.* 8: 139). In his speech on Charles James Fox's East India Bill in 1783, he said that he regarded protection of the people's natural rights as an object of the trust which the people had conferred on government (*Works* 4: 11). Defending the bill against the charge that it violated "the chartered rights of men," i.e., the rights conferred on the East India Company by its charter, he replied: "The rights of *men*, that is to say, the natural rights of mankind, are indeed sacred things, and if any publick measure is proved mischievously to affect them, the objection ought to be fatal to that measure, even if no charter at all could be set up against it." But this charter confers rights on the Company which do not deserve to be regarded as natural rights: "The East-India charter is a charter to establish monopoly, and to create power. Political power and commercial monopoly are *not* the rights of men; and the rights of them derived from charters it is fallacious and sophistical to call 'the chartered rights of men'" (*Works* 4: 8–9). Incidentally, that statement alone is enough to cast doubt on the notion that Burke did not believe in natural rights, but only in historically evolved ones.

Burke used the same argument in his *Reflections* against the revolutionary "rights of men." Men do have basic natural rights, he said, but a share in government is not among them: "As to the share of power, authority, and direction which each individual ought to have in the management of the state, that I must deny to be among the direct original rights of man in civil society; for I have in my contemplation the civil social man, and no other," i.e., *not* man in a pre-civil state of nature (*Works* 5: 121). In this passage in the *Reflections*, however, "the direct original rights of man in civil society" turn out to be all the benefits that men can gain by living in society under law and government:

> If civil society be made for the advantage of man, all the advantages for which it is made become his right. It is an institution of beneficence; and law itself is only beneficence acting by a rule. Men have a right to live by that rule; they have a right to do justice, as between their fellows, whether their fellows are in politick function or in ordinary occupation. They have a right to the fruits of their industry; and to the means of making their industry fruitful. They have a right to the acquisitions of their parents; to the nourishment and improvement of their offspring; to instruction in life, and consolation in death. Whatever each man can separately do, without trespassing on others, he has a right to do for himself; and he has a right to a fair portion of all which society, with all its combinations of skill and force, can do in his favour [*Works* 5: 120–121].

Burke took a similarly expansive view of the goals of civil society in other writings as well. In his *Speech on the Reform of the Representation* in 1782, he speaks of "temporal prosperity and eternal happiness, the ends for which society was formed" (*Works* 10: 102). In 1793 he said that Britain and her allies in the war against the revolutionary government in France must persuade the French people "that we come to maintain their legitimate monarchy in a truly paternal French government, to protect their privileges, their laws, their religion, and their property" (*Works* 7: 143). In his *Fourth Letter on a Regicide Peace* (1796) he contrasted anarchy with "Government pursuing the peace, order, morals, and prosperity of the People." Later in the same piece, he says of "our humanity, our manners, our morals, our religion" that "the constitution is made by those things, and for those things: without them it cannot exist, and without them it is no matter whether it exists or not" (*Works* 9: 70, 106).

The goals of civil society thus become coterminous with the ends of human life, both here and hereafter. In May 1792, when a group of Unitarians petitioned Parliament for the repeal of certain statutes that limited their freedom to express their religious opinions, Burke spoke against them. He had generally been in favor of religious toleration, but now he saw the Unitarians as sympathizers with French republican principles, enemies of the Established Church, and a danger to the State. In explaining his position he made the care of religion one of the principal purposes of the State:

> In a Christian Commonwealth the Church and the State are one and the same thing, being different integral parts of the same whole.... Religion is so far, in my opinion, from being out of the province or the duty of a Christian Magistrate, that it is, and it ought to be, not only his care, but the principal thing in his care; because it is one of the great bonds of human society; and its object the supreme good, the ultimate end and object of man himself [*Works* 10: 44].

One sees the difficulty of reconciling that view with the proposition that "property is the first origin, the continued Bond, and the ultimate End" of civil society. Or, for that matter, with what Burke wrote to the Speaker of the Irish House of Commons concerning the then-pending Catholic Relief Bill of 1778: the governing power must be "thoroughly convinced, that it is the Sole Business of his Office to make his people happy and prosperous, and not to convert them to any System of Theology—That he is to be their ruler and not their Apostle." A Protestant government ought not to try to force Catholics into Protestantism. Similarly, "in India we have got a Pagan and a Mohammedan Country to govern; and as a Mohammedan and pagan Country we ought to make the most of it, for the Benefit of the people and our own" (*Corr.* 3: 457–458; cf. *Works* 8: 315).

Perhaps these and others of Burke's statements cannot be fully reconciled, and one should not try too hard to harmonize all the remarks that he made in different contexts and on different occasions. But it will go some way toward synthesizing them to advert to a distinction that Burke made in the same year as his statement on the duty of a Christian magistrate: "In the word *State*, I conceive there is much ambiguity. The state is sometimes used to signify *the whole commonwealth*, comprehending all its orders, with the several privileges belonging to each. Sometimes it signifies only *the higher and ruling part* of the commonwealth, which we commonly call *the Government*." Burke made this distinction in order to say that excluding a whole class of people from the state in the first sense— he is speaking of the Catholics in Ireland—is reducing them to slavery, but to exclude them from the "*Supreme Government . . .* cannot be considered as *absolute slavery*" (*Works* 6: 306–307). If it is permissible to go beyond Burke's immediate point, we may say that his broad conception of the goals of civil society fits the first sense of the term "state" as signifying the whole commonwealth and all that it can and should do for its members. The ends of the state in the second sense, as the government, may be much narrower and, to Burke's Whig mind, they were.

Less than two years before he died, Burke expressed what we may take as his last thought on the role of government in society, and therefore on what should be left to the other institutions of society. It is perhaps a somewhat exaggerated statement of his thought, since it occurs in his *Thoughts and Details on Scarcity*, which he wrote in November 1795 as a protest against a scheme for governmental subsidy of the wages of farm laborers in a period of economic distress. It will be discussed more fully in a later chapter, but these words are relevant here:

> It is one of the finest problems in legislation, and what has often engaged my thoughts whilst I followed that profession, "What the state ought to take upon itself to direct by the publick wisdom, and what it ought to leave, with as little interference as possible, to individual discretion." Nothing, certainly, can be laid down on the

subject that will not admit of exceptions, many permanent, some occasional. But the clearest line of distinction which I could draw, whilst I had my chalk to draw any line, was this; that the state ought to confine itself to what regards the state, or the creatures of the state, namely the exterior establishment of its religion; its magistracy; its revenue; its military force by sea and land; the corporations that owe their existence to its fiat; in a word, to every thing that is *truly and properly* publick, to the public peace, to the publick safety, to the publick order, to the publick prosperity. . . . Statesman who know themselves will, with the dignity which belongs to wisdom, proceed only in this the superiour orb and first mover of their duty steadily, vigilantly, severely, courageously: whatever remains will, in a manner, provide for itself. But as they descend from the state to a province, from a province to a parish, and from a parish to a private house, they go on accelerated to their fall. They *cannot* do the lower duty; and, in proportion as they try it, they will certainly fail in the higher. They ought to know the different departments of things; what belongs to laws, and what manners alone can regulate. To these, great politicians may give a leaning, but they cannot give a law [*Works* 7: 416–417; cf. 8: 367].

Burke's immediate purpose in writing the above was to argue that it was simply not the function of government to relieve the sufferings of the poor in hard times, but he was enunciating a broader principle, which he had already stated in an earlier writing in 1791. A king of France, he said, and by implication any king, must possess "every degree of power necessary to the state, and not destructive to the rational and moral freedom of individuals, to that personal liberty, and personal security, which contribute so much to the vigour, the prosperity, the happiness, and the dignity of a nation" (*Works* 6: 61). The energies of society spring from below, and do not descend from above. The state as commonwealth will prosper, grow, and develop if private individuals and institutions are left free to deploy their energies within an order of law which the state as government creates and maintains. But government will only harm them and the commonwealth if it tries to take their place and do what it should leave them free to do. How far one should carry that argument is, of course, a major issue in politics to this day. In *Thoughts and Details* Burke carried it as far as he ever did, but the principle was not then a new one with him (see, e.g., *Works* 3: 323–324, 4: 39).

As far back as 1761 he had written: "The coercive authority of the State is limited to what is necessary for its existence. . . . It considers as crimes (that is, the object of punishment) trespasses against those rules, for which society was instituted" (*Works* 9: 371). Among these rules are those which define, protect, and foster property, which can therefore be called, in a narrow sense, the end, or a principal end, of the state. Although property is, as Burke admitted, inferior in worth to virtue, honor, morals, arts and literature, the latter were ends of society as the commonwealth. Government would make its contribution to these higher ends of society by securing property as "the basis upon which they were all erected—the soul that animated, the genius that protected them." In this sense, then, Burke was able to say in the same passage that "for the protection of property, all governments were instituted" (*Parl. Hist.* 31: 380–381; cf. 30: 645).

In order to keep government's grasping hands off property, and to confine government to its proper and limited ends, the property of the nation must govern it. The property-owning class best fitted for this task was the landed aristocracy of nobles and gentry, from whom came the natural leaders of the country. Burke did not limit participation in politics to the landed aristocracy or consider the mere possession of large property as a sufficient qualification for governing. Rather, he believed that old, landed wealth tended to breed a class of men with the qualities that prepared them to govern wisely and well.

He left room, of course, for the ascent of "new men" into the governing class; after all, he was one of them. Lucy S. Sutherland says that "he was in no sense a social climber. He expressed his views freely to his aristocratic colleagues, but he made no claim to social equality with them." He rarely visited them in their country houses, and when he did, it was usually on business (*Corr.* 2: xiv–xv). Yet he was aware of his own worth.

In 1770, he wrote to his schooldays friend Richard Shackleton, "Whatever advantages I have had, have been from friends on my own Level; As to those that are called great, I never paid them any Court; perhaps since I must say it, they have had as much benefit from my Connection, as I have had" (*Corr.* 2: 131). His cousin Will Burke reports a speech that Burke made in the Commons around the same time, in which he defended himself as a *novus homo*:

> He expatiated upon the Impropriety and danger of discouraging new Men: This rising merit stamp'd with Virtue would indeed seek to rise, but under the wings of establish'd Greatness, and if their industry and their Virtue was greater than &c. &c. &c. they must be equal, nay the superior to the lazy something that came by inheritance. . . . All wise governments have encouraged rising merit, as useful and necessary; we know not in what mountain of Scotland, what bog of Ireland, or what wild in America that Genius may be now rising who shall save this country [*Corr* 2: 128–129].

The Burke family had a coat of arms (*Corr.* 6: 209, n. 3), which indicated gentry status or at least pretensions thereunto. Burke himself became a member of the landed gentry of England in 1768, when he bought an estate of 600 acres near Beaconsfield in Buckinghamshire (and went into debt for the rest of his life in order to do it). In 1780 he described himself to the chairman of the county meeting of Buckinghamshire as "an inhabitant and freeholder of this county (one indeed among the most inconsiderable)" (*Corr.* 4: 228; cf. 5: 144). Other persons certainly took him as such. Not long after he bought the estate, Thomas Bradshaw, Secretary to the Treasury, described an earlier county meeting, which Burke had attended, as consisting principally of boys "and of *new Men* who have just acquired (God knows how) a small property in the County, and not in the least of Men of Great Estates or of old Buckinghamshire families" (*Corr.* 2: 80, note). Burke remained forever, as he wrote to the Duke of Portland during the French Revolution, a man "who had, comparatively with men of your description, a very small Interest in opposing the modern System of morality and policy" (*Corr.* 7: 438).

In 1794, when Burke was planning to retire from the House of Commons, he hoped to get a peerage which his son would inherit. The Prime Minister, William Pitt, thought for a short while of getting it for him, but changed his mind (*Corr.* 7: 550–552). William Windham, Burke's political pupil, who was joining Pitt's government at that time, complained to Pitt that Burke's "poverty, the consequence of his virtues, is made a reason for witholding [sic] honours from him . . . the want of fortune, and of the port, and consequence, which that gives, is really at the bottom of all the obstacles, that now remain" (*Corr.* 7: 550, note).

A man treated in this way might entertain anti-aristocratic feelings, and there are writers who think he did. Yet this writer is convinced that Burke was completely sincere when he told Lord Fitzwilliam (Rockingham's nephew and heir), "I am an Aristocrate in Principle; In situation, God knows nothing less" (*Corr.* 8: 185). He could be contemptuous of individual aristocrats, as he was in *A Letter to a Noble Lord* (1796), where he caustically put down the young, very rich, and bumptious Duke of Bedford, who had criticized the government for giving Burke a pension; or even of the whole House of Lords for acquitting Warren Hastings (*Corr.* 8: 206, 217; cf. 110). But the evidence of his public writings and private correspondence throughout his career leaves no doubt about the honesty and intensity of his belief in aristocracy as a social and political institution.

He was not, however, an apologist for aristocratic domination. As he said in a speech in the Commons in 1781:

> I am accused, I am told abroad, of being a man of aristocratick principles. If by aristocracy they mean the Peers, I have no vulgar admiration, nor any vulgar antipathy, towards them; I hold their order in cold and decent respect. I hold them to be of an absolute necessity in the Constitution; but I think they are only good when kept within their bounds.

Burke believed that no part of the constitution was good except within its bounds; furthermore, he was very much a House of Commons man.

He went on, however, to say that if by aristocracy "they mean an adherence to the rich and powerful against the poor and weak," he did not subscribe to that kind of aristocracy; "and if it should come to the last extremity, and to a contest of blood, God forbid! God forbid!—my part is taken; I would take my fate with the poor, and low, and feeble" (*Works* 10: 138–139). We need not take this declaration too seriously. Burke did believe that society existed for the benefit of all its members—a Christian statesman must "first provide for the *multitude* because it is the *multitude*; and is therefore, as such, the first object . . . in all institutions" (*Works* 5:

192)—but he also believed that only a society governed by the rich and the good would benefit all its members.

He was convinced from the beginning of his career that, as he said in *An Abridgement of English History*, a strong and stable society needed to be structured by "those orders and connected classes of men, that are necessary to a regular commonwealth" (*Works* 10: 237). When the Roman Empire collapsed and the legions withdrew from Britain, "there was among the Britains no royal family, no respected order in the state, none of those titles to government confirmed by opinion and long use, more efficacious than the wisest schemes for the settlement of the nation" (*Works* 10: 248). The Britons were therefore helpless before the invading barbarians from across the North Sea.

At the end of his life he pointed out that the various nations that made up the commonwealth of Christendom prior to the French Revolution were all "countries of states [or "estates," as in "Estates-General"]; that is, of classes, orders, and distinctions" (*Works* 8: 183). This structure of society, he had explained in *Reflections*, was the result of the habits of life in civil society, which are a "second nature" that modifies our first and common human nature. From the operation of this second nature "arose many diversities amongst men, according to their birth, their education, their professions, the periods of their lives, their residence in towns or in the country, their several ways of acquiring and of fixing property, all which rendered them as it were so many different species of animals." Ancient legislators were wise enough to take this into account and to divide their citizens into classes, which they combined into one commonwealth. But the legislators of the French Revolution "have attempted to confound all sorts of citizens . . . into one homogeneous mass," and have ignored the utility of a division into classes as "a strong barrier against the excesses of despotism" (*Works* 5: 331–333). Class-division is also, he said in 1791, a check on the "envy of men" toward "the mercantile or any other class," and a barrier against newly acquired commercial wealth's gaining too much power too soon:

> It is the natural operation of things where there exists a crown, a court, splendid orders of knighthood, and an hereditary nobility;— where there exists a fixed, permanent landed gentry, continued in

greatness and opulence by the law of primogeniture [cf. *Works* 6: 189] and by a protection given to family settlements;—where there exists a standing army and navy;—where there exists a church establishment, which bestows on learning and parts an interest combined with that of religion and the state;—in a country where such things exist, wealth, new in its acquisition, and precarious in its duration, can never rank first, or even near the first; though wealth has its natural weight, further, than as it is balanced and even preponderated amongst us as amongst other nations, by artificial institutions and opinions growing out of them [*Works* 7: 23–24].

On other hand, Burke felt that the French nobility before the Revolution had made a serious mistake in being too exclusive of rising wealth: "Those of the commons, who approached to or exceeded many of the nobility in point of wealth, were not fully admitted to the rank and estimation which wealth, in reason and good policy, ought to bestow in every country" (*Works* 5: 253; but cf. 7: 22).

He was keenly aware that, as he told the merchant-class electorate of Bristol in 1774, Great Britain's "prosperity and dignity arose principally, if not solely, from two sources; our constitution and commerce" (*Works* 3: 7). He had some years earlier praised Lord Rockingham's brief administration from July 1765 to July 1766 as "the first which proposed and encouraged publick meetings and free consultations of merchants from all parts of the kingdom; by which means the truest lights have been received; great benefits have been already derived to manufacturers and commerce; and the most extensive prospects are opened for further improvements" (*Works* 2: 4). In a later defense of the Rockingham Whigs, Burke declared: "The universal alarm of the whole trading body of England will never be laughed at by them as an ill-grounded or a pretended panick. The universal desire of that body will always have great weight with them in every consideration connected with commerce" (*Works* 2: 161).

From this conviction of the importance of commerce and its harmony with the landed interest within the aristocratic order, Burke never departed. The advent of the French Revolution only caused him to emphasize more and more strongly the primacy of the aristocratic order over all other political considerations. As he put it in the *Reflections*, "Even commerce, and trade, and manufacture, the gods of our oeconomical politicians, are themselves perhaps but creatures; are themselves but effects, which, as first causes, we choose to worship." They have developed and flourished in a civilization which has "depended for ages upon two principles; . . . I mean the spirit of a gentleman, and the spirit of religion" (*Works* 5: 154–155). These latter are the base, Burke suggests, of which the economy is the superstructure; hence, the primary importance of preserving the aristocratic and Christian order of Europe. In nations so conceived, the landed proprietors were the most important part, and ought to play the leading role. Having reckoned their number in pre-revolutionary France as not "less than seventy thousand," Burke remarked, "I am sure, that if half that number of the same description were taken out of this country, it would leave hardly any thing that I should call the people of England" (*Works* 7: 140–141). The successful outcome in English history of the people's struggles for liberty, he said, has been due, under God, to this, "that while the landed interest, instead of forming a separate body, as in other countries, has at all times, been in close connection and union with the other great interests of the country, it has been spontaneously allowed to lead and direct, and moderate all the rest" (*Works* 8: 400–401).

Leadership, therefore, as Burke wrote to Lord Rockingham in 1770, belonged to "the sober, large-acred part of the Nation" (*Corr.* 2: 175; cf. 7: 310, 8: 80). He did not, however, advocate plutocracy, that is, government by the rich, merely as rich. It was landed wealth that sustained and carried on the families which provided the nation with a strong and stable tradition, and with men who would govern by its traditional principles. Burke was not merely flattering a great lord (whom in fact he regarded as something of an eccentric) when he wrote to the Duke of Richmond in 1772:

> You people of great families and hereditary Trusts and fortunes . . . if you are what you ought to be are the great Oaks that shade a Country and perpetuate your benefits from Generation to Generation. In my eye—The immediate power of a D[uke] of Richmond or a Marquis of R[ockingha]m is not so much of moment but if their conduct and example hands down their principles to their successors; then their houses become the public repositories and offices of Record for the constitution, . . . in full vigour and acting

with vital Energy and power in the Characters of the leading men and natural interests of the Country [*Corr.* 2: 377].

This was the role of the great noble families and, more broadly, of the gentry, which was composed to a significant extent of their younger sons and other relatives (see *Works* 13: 67). They led the country rather than monopolized high offices of state in order to govern it. The British constitution, Burke wrote in a draft for a speech in 1774, "nourishes and is nourished by Virtue only—an English gentleman [in contrast with] a Nobleman of the Continent—has no rank above his fellow Citizens—but what his Manners, his affability, his Knowledge, his justice, the popular use of his fortune give him" (*W&S* 2: 230).

Ten years later, when the head of the powerful Grenville family, Lord Temple, died, his nephew succeeded to his title and vast wealth. Now being a noble, the nephew had to surrender his seat in the House of Commons as a member for Buckinghamshire. He then put forward his brother as a candidate for that seat. Burke felt it necessary to explain to the Duke of Portland, a leading member of the Rockingham Whigs, who was supporting the brother, why he, Burke, opposed him. It was because he agreed with those who objected to the arrogance of the Grenvilles and "did not like to let the County become an heirloom in a family, which is known to be as tenacious of power as lofty and rigorous in the use of it" (*Corr.* 4: 130). The Duke replied that "surely there was nothing unnatural or unreasonable in Lord Temple's wishing to be succeeded by His Brother. His Rank His Fortune His Property in the County all concur in forming his title to it" (*Corr.* 4: 137). Burke answered that a seat in the Commons was a gift, not an entitlement:

> I certainly never meant to exclude the younger Branches of illustrious families, which your Grace well knows I always considered as the permanent substantial parts, the Bones and sinews of every free commonwealth, from popular Trusts and favour . . . but these things are only to be solicited under circumstances of prepossession, and not claimed, as it were, as matter of right; and with circumstances of haughtiness. . . . They ought to be begged not demanded, let the . . . worth of ancestry be what it may [*Corr.* 4: 152].

In Burke's mind, wealth, social class, and character went together as qualification for the exercise of public trust, and this not accidentally, but by natural conjunction. Such was the case in the Roman Republic in its best days (*Corr.* 2: 377). He developed this theme at length in his *Reflections*. Speaking of legislative bodies, he said: "Nothing can secure a steady and moderate conduct in such assemblies, but that the body of them should be respectably composed, in point of condition in life, of permanent property, of education, and of such habits as enlarge and liberalise the understanding" (*Works* 5: 91–92). Such is the British House of Commons which (in contrast to the Third Estate in France), "without shutting its doors to any merit in any class, is, by the sure operation of adequate causes, filled with everything illustrious in rank, in descent, in hereditary and acquired opulence, in cultivated talents, in military, civil, naval, and politick distinction, that the country can afford" (*Works* 5: 96).

Burke was careful to make clear that he did not "wish to confine power, authority, and distinction to blood, and names, and titles." As a "new man," how could he? On the contrary: "There is no qualification for government but virtue, actual or presumptive." Wherever it is found, it should open the doors "to human place and honour." But, since such merit is rare, "the road to eminence and power from obscure condition, ought not to be made too easy, nor a thing too much of course" (*Works* 5: 106–107).

For ability, necessary though it was to the state, was dangerous when the talents of ambitious men were disjoined from property, and in particular, from large property:

> Nothing is a due and adequate representation of a state, that does not represent its ability, as well as its property. But as ability is a vigorous and active principle, and as property is sluggish, inert and timid, it never can be safe from the invasions of ability, unless it be, out of all proportion, predominant in the representation. It must be represented too in great masses of accumulation, or it is not rightly represented. The characteristick essence of property, formed out of the combined principles of its acquisition and conservation, is to be *unequal*. The great masses therefore which excite envy, and tempt rapacity, must be put out of the possibility of danger. Then they form a natural rampart about the lesser properties in all their gradations [*Works* 5: 107–108].

Burke's thesis is that the protection of large property is a bulwark to lesser properties which would otherwise lack sufficient force to defend themselves against the envy of the unpropertied and the ambition of demagogues. We recognize here his picture of the British Parliament, which serves the good of the commonwealth by representing property, that material source of its welfare and stability. Parliament does this all the more effectively when the property it represents is hereditary: "The power of perpetuating our property in our families is one of the most valuable and interesting circumstances belonging to it, and that which tends the most to the perpetuation of society itself." The House of Lords is composed entirely of hereditary property, and the House of Commons "is always so composed in far the greater part." Be these large hereditary proprietors what they will (and they may be among the best of men), "they are at the very worst, the ballast in the vessel of the commonwealth." Burke therefore concludes: "Some decent regulated pre-eminence, some preferences (not exclusive appropriation) given to birth, is neither unnatural, nor unjust, nor impolitick" (*Works* 5: 108–109; cf. 6: 188, 15: 370).

Burke further explained the union of wealth and rank with civil wisdom and virtue in the sequel to *Reflections*, *An Appeal from the New to the Old Whigs*:

> To enable men to act with the weight and character of a people, and to answer the ends for which they are incorporated into that capacity, we must suppose them (by means immediate or consequential) to be in that state of habitual social discipline, in which the wiser, the more expert, and the more opulent conduct, and by conducting, enlighten and protect the weaker, the less knowing, and the less provided with the goods of fortune. When the multitude are not under this discipline, they can scarcely be said to be in civil society [*Works* 6: 216].

Civil society necessarily generates an elite, as we would say today, or a natural aristocracy in Burke's (and Thomas Jefferson's) words, that closely resembles the aristocracy of nobility and gentry that governed Burke's England. He explained the composition of this natural aristocracy in a lengthy passage, which we may summarize by saying that it is made up of those who have been raised in upper-class households; have held military or naval commands; are members of the clergy, especially of the higher clergy; have administered law and justice; have taught in universities; or are "amongst rich traders." All of these pursuits sharpen men's minds and broaden their views. "These are the circumstances," says Burke, "of men, that form what I should call a *natural* aristocracy, without which there is no nation." Society united under their governance is "this beautiful order, this array of truth and nature, as well as of habitual prejudice," which is "the natural order of life" (*Works* 6: 217–219).

In this order, the nobility plays an essential role. In his *Letter to a Noble Lord*, in which Burke ridiculed the hapless young Duke of Bedford, he stated in terms of warm approval the views of the late Lord Keppel, who "valued ancient nobility":

> He considered it as a sort of cure for selfishness and a narrow mind; conceiving that a man born in an elevated place, in himself was nothing, but every thing in what went before, and what was to come after him . . . he felt, that no great commonwealth could by any possibility long subsist without a body of some kind or other of nobility, decorated with honour, and fortified by privilege. This nobility forms the chain that connects the ages of a nation. . . . He felt that no political fabrick could be well made without some such order of things as might, through a series of time, afford a rational hope of securing unity, coherence, consistency, and stability to the state. He felt that nothing else can protect it against the levity of courts, and the greater levity of the multitude [*Works* 8: 66–67; cf. 7: 67–68; *Corr.* 7: 143–144, 160].

Burke wrote the above words at a time when he knew that he would never be made a peer and when, his son having died, he no longer cared. He was not arguing *pro domo sua*—for he now had no house to argue for—but for an aristocracy which, however little it heeded his exhortations to defend itself against the spread of the Revolution, he still regarded as the indispensable bulwark of civilization. "Kings," he had said in his *Speech on Economical Reform* in 1780, "are naturally lovers of low company" and "are rather apt to hate than to love their nobility, on account of the occasional resistance to their will, which will be made by their virtue, their petulence, or their pride." He had to admit that "many of the nobility are as perfectly willing to act the part of flatterers, tale-bearers, parasites, pimps, and buffoons, as any of the lowest and vilest of mankind can possibly be" (*Works* 3: 318;

cf. 7: 64–66). In *A Letter to a Noble Lord* he said that he had defended "those, who hold large portions of wealth without any apparent merit of their own" and that he had "strained every nerve to keep the duke of Bedford in that situation, which alone makes him my superior." He did this, not for the sake of individuals, but "to defend an order of things, which, like the sun of heaven, shines alike on the useful and the worthless" (*Works* 8: 32, 48). Burke thought the aristocratic order was valuable and necessary, but he was not bedazzled by aristocrats merely because of their wealth and rank.

Nonetheless, aristocrats were the natural leaders of the country. The qualifications for the exercise of public trust were not possessed by men who, "from their want of rank, fortune, character, ability, or knowledge, are likely to betray or to fall short of their trust" (*Works* 4: 121). It was "madness" in "the common people," Burke said in 1780, to "dream that they could be any thing without the Aid of better fortunes and better heads than their own" (*Corr.* 4: 295). He had said this before (*Corr.* 3: 218, 280; 4: 240), and would say it again, in stronger language, during the French Revolution (*Works* 6: 5, 12–13, 17–18, 38). Toward the end of his life he said that there was "a British publick," of about 400,000 in England and Scotland, consisting of persons of sufficient education, leisure, and means of information that they could "in any political view . . . be called the people" (*Works* 8: 140). They were capable of forming and expressing a public opinion that leaders could appeal to for support in the war against revolutionary France. But, as he said on another occasion, poor workingmen are "utterly incapable of comprehending" the ground of such a war, "and, indeed, it is not every man in the highest classes who is altogether equal to it" (*Works* 7: 262–263).

If this was capitalism, it was capitalism with a difference. It was not the "creative destruction" of an economic system geared to the production of more and more material goods and the constant replacement of old with new goods. As Burke conceived of it, it was not primarily an economic but a political system which, indeed, protected property and fostered prosperity. But property's primary purpose was to generate and sustain a ruling class that would govern the nation for its general welfare, of which material prosperity was not the only or the highest part.

For that reason, the leading role in the state was best left in the hands of the possessors of old, landed property rather than of busily acquisitive entrepreneurs. More than on material goods, the welfare of the commonwealth depended on a civil wisdom rooted in a realistic understanding of human nature and in the "second nature" of a sound cultural, moral, and religious tradition. The tradition maintained and transmitted the manners of civility and the virtues of moderation, restraint, and devotion to the common good of society. Hereditary landed property made possible the continuity and stability of the families that were the chief guardians of the tradition. They thereby guaranteed the safe combination of liberty with order.

Burke's faith in this aristocratic order rested on the assumption that the several peoples of Great Britain—Anglo-Saxons, Cornish, Welsh, and Scots—had a basic commonality of economic, cultural, and religious interests. The aristocracy, supported by "the British publick," could therefore represent and act for them all. In that sense, the whole people of Great Britain had a stake in the British constitution.

Such, however, was not the case in Ireland, but quite the opposite. To understand Burke's belief in aristocracy properly, and to see that it was not a blind faith in government by property, we must next consider his savage denunciation of the government of Ireland under British rule.

In Burke's lifetime, Great Britain and Ireland were separate kingdoms with separate parliaments but under the same Crown. Politically, however, the kingdom of Ireland was an English and Anglican colony in Ireland and under British control. The native Irish Catholics and, to a large extent, the Dissenting and largely Scottish colonists in the North were excluded from any share in power. In his *History of Ireland*, Edmund Curtis, a twentieth-century professor of history in the same Trinity College that Burke attended, described the situation in Ireland as it was at the time when Burke began to write his *Tracts on the Popery Laws*:

> The Protestant ascendancy in Church, government, law, parliament, local government, industry, was complete. It was a replica on a small scale of that of England, but at least in England the Anglican aristocracy for all its faults ruled in the Church of a majority and had the support of a nation. It was otherwise in Ireland,

where both the ruling aristocracy and Church represented an alien minority.... It was in effect a despotism worked from Dublin but controlled from Westminister in a double interest, that of the Protestant ascendancy at home [in Ireland] and that of England in its relations to a subject kingdom [pp. 292–293].

The government of Ireland was headed by a Lord-Lieutenant who was always, with but one exception, a titled Englishman appointed by the British government. He came over from England for only a few weeks at the beginning of each biennial session of Parliament, until 1767, after which date he was required to live in Dublin. In his absence, the country was governed by a handful of Lords Justices who "managed" it through what Burke called "jobbing": the distribution of government jobs, bribes, and pensions, many of them sinecures, and some of them very lucrative. After 1767 the Lord-Lieutenant took over this patronage power, but administered it through such powerful Irish officials as John Beresford, John Fitzgibbon, and the rest of what Burke called "the Junto." Burke was convinced that they were the real power governing Ireland, and that England's sin was letting them do it.

The Irish Parliament consisted of a House of Lords composed of the great territorial lords and some bishops of the Established Church of Ireland, and a House of Commons even more unrepresentative than the one in England. "The members," says Thomas Mahoney, "were largely notorious jobbers and placemen" (p. 13). This Parliament won an apparently significant degree of legislative independence from Great Britain in 1782, but the change did not lessen the power of the Ascendancy and only increased the Lord-Lieutenant's need to exercise his patronage power. "This policy," Curtis remarks, "was not difficult in a parliament where out of 300 members the only unbought men were those from the thirty-two counties [numbering 64], elected by the forty-shilling freeholders, and a few of the great towns" (p. 323).

Burke's judgment on the government of his native country was simple, clear, and severe. It was, he wrote to Henry Dundas in 1792, "the curse, scourge, and bane of the Irish nation," and its chief occupation was "the great staple trade, never carried to its full perfection but in Ireland—the whole art and mystery of jobbing" (*Corr.* 1844, 4: 66). The government of Ireland, he said on another occasion, was "a job in its constitution" (*Works* 9: 421), an accusation he repeated on many other occasions (*Corr.* 7: 31, 287, 289–290, 301; 8: 175, 192, 231, 263, 286; 9: 330, 338, 368). In 1794, he described the Irish government to his friend and disciple William Windham as "*Non regnum sed magnum latrocinium* [not a kingdom but a large band of robbers]—the Motto that ought to be put under the Harp" (*Corr.* 8: 41). Historians generally speak of the Ascendancy in more measured terms, but they might agree with Windham when he wrote to a mutual friend of his and Burke's, "Mr. B. is wrong by excess and exaggeration, I dare say; but whether he is so in the main, I should much doubt" (*Corr.* 9: 339, n. 2).

The "Protestant Ascendancy," Burke's son wrote in 1792, was "a new name which the enemies of the Catholics have adopted" (*Corr.* 7: 241–242). His father's comment was:

> New ascendency is old mastership. It is neither more nor less than the resolution of one set of people in Ireland to consider themselves as the sole citizens of the commonwealth; and to keep a dominion over the rest by reducing them to absolute slavery under a military power; and thus fortified, to divide the publick estate, which is the result of general contribution, as a military booty solely amongst themselves [*Works* 9: 425–426; cf. *Corr.* 9: 254–255].

We remarked earlier that the laws against "Popery" in Ireland discouraged industry among Catholics by denying them the right to acquire permanent or long-term property in land. These laws were in fact much more detailed and oppressive, but it will be enough here to quote Burke's summary judgment of them in a long letter (obviously designed to function as a pamphlet), which he wrote to Sir Hercules Langrishe, an Irish M.P., who was proposing a new Catholic Relief bill in 1792:

> Their declared object was to reduce the catholicks of Ireland to a miserable populace, without property, without estimation, without education. The professed object was to deprive the few men who, in spite of those laws might hold or obtain any property amongst them, of all sort of influence or authority over the rest. They divided the nation into two distinct bodies, without common interest, sympathy or connexion. One of these bodies was to possess *all* the franchises, *all* the property, *all* the education; the other was to be composed of drawers of water and cutters of turf for them [*Works* 6: 303–304].

Later in the same letter he gives the Popery Laws their due as a legal system perfect in its kind:

> For I must do it justice: it was a complete system, full of coherence and consistency; well digested and well composed in all its parts. It was a machine of wise and elaborate contrivance; and as well fitted for the oppression, impoverishment, and degradation of a people, and the debasement, in them, of human nature itself, as ever proceeded from the perverted ingenuity of man [*Works* 6: 375].

A common Protestant objection to relaxing the legal restrictions on Catholics was that they were an ignorant, superstitious, undisciplined people, and prone to violence. But, Burke asked, "Are we to be astonished when, by the efforts of so much violence in conquest, and so much policy in regulation, continued without intermission for near an hundred years, we had reduced them to a mob; that whenever they came to act at all, many of them would act exactly like a mob, without temper, measure, or foresight?" The wise response to this situation would be, not more repression, but the creation of a propertied Catholic aristocracy:

> You ought to raise an aristocratick interest; that is, an interest of property and education amongst them; and to strengthen by every prudent means, the authority and influence of men of that description. It will deserve your best thoughts, to examine whether this can be done without giving such persons the means of demonstrating to the rest, that something more is to be got by their temperate conduct, than can be expected from the wild and senseless projects, of those, who do not belong to their body, who have no interest in their well being, and only wish to make them the dupes of their turbulent ambition [*Works* 6: 304].

Burke referred in those last words to Deists and Dissenters whom he judged suspect of republicanism and "French principles" (see also *Corr.* 8: 248). They must be offset by allowing respected leaders to emerge from among the Catholics: "Men of consideration from their age, their profession, or their character, men of proprietary landed estates, substantial renters, opulent merchants, physicians, and titular bishops," who could hardly by suspected of fomenting or taking part in "the disorder of an oppressed or a licentious populace" (*Works* 6: 313). The lesson that the governing Protestants must learn is this: "Lawful enjoyment is the surest method to prevent unlawful gratification. Where there is property there will be less theft; where there is marriage, there will always be less fornication" (*Works* 6: 315–316). Property will be the unifying bond of a whole people if access to it is widely available.

At this date, 1792, the Catholic Relief Act of 1782 had allowed Catholics to "purchase, hold, and bequeath freehold land and leases on the same terms as Protestants" (Curtis, p. 313). Apart from a large number of humiliating restrictions on the public practice of their religion, the Catholics' chief remaining grievance was their lack of the right to vote for Members of Parliament. This right, Burke argued, was necessary to give them a stake in their country's constitution, and would benefit Protestants by securing Catholics' loyalty to that constitution.

Two hundred years of efforts to make the bulk of the Irish people Protestant have failed, Burke wrote. "The result is—you cannot make the people Protestant—and they cannot shake off a Protestant Government." This being the case, and it was the case in 1792, the question is, "are we to make the best of the situation, which we cannot alter?" (*Works* 9: 439). The question answers itself.

To begin with, the existing distribution of property must be accepted as confirmed by prescription. Protestants on their part must stop taking that distribution of property as a reason for regarding Catholics as permanent internal enemies:

> The operation of the Popery laws, through the medium of infinite private calamity, and much public detriment, has put the Protestants in possession of three-quarters of the landed property of the kingdom; and, [since they are] possessed of all that is beneficial and honourable in Church and State, can any thing be more absurd than for *them* perpetually to remind those whom they have deprived of all these things, that there is a perpetual irreconcilable opposition between their interests? Would it not be a much more natural and wiser policy, in the sect of the *rich reigning few*, to persuade that of *the humble and the many*, that their interests were not at all incompatible . . . [*Corr.* 1844, 4:73]?

In order to bring about this harmony of interests, it will be necessary to admit Catholics to the franchise, on the basis of property, of course, but not exclusively of large property. Burke had little use for the remnants of the old Catholic gentry and nobility who still remained in Ireland, because they despised their poor co-religionists, hated those of them who had got rich in trade, and sought only to join the ruling upper class without having to renounce their religion (*Corr.* 7: 9–10; cf. 9: 172). But, as Burke's son wrote to Henry Dundas, "the country gentlemen and men of landed property, *if* they had them, are not the strength of the R[oman] C[atholics]" (*Corr.* 7: 25). When members of the Catholic Committee, now controlled by rich merchants who had replaced Lord Kenmare and his friends, began to talk of seeking the franchise on the basis of a freehold valued at £100 a year, Burke objected strongly:

> The hundred pound qualification is not a thing to be even whisperd, because it would tend to make the world believe . . . that . . . the Committee are like Lord Kenmare and his friends, who look only to the accommodation of a few Gentlemen, and leave the common people who are the heart and strength of the Cause of the Catholicks, and are the great Objects in all popular representation, completely in the Lurch [*Corr.* 7: 83].

What Burke had in mind was not mass democracy—far from it—but a right to vote attached to the possession of a relatively modest freehold. As he told his son, "there are not probably two hundred people [among the Catholics] who can take advantage of that Franchise." Protestants therefore need not have nightmares about the Catholics taking the country away from them. But Irish Catholics (and, obviously, more than a mere two hundred of them) need the vote for two reasons: (1) "That alone can give their interests fair play, by bringing them into a connexion of mutual obligation with the great and powerful [who will have to solicit their votes in elections]. That alone can raise to anything like equality, a people habitually injured, because habitually despised" (*Corr.* 1844, 4: 77). (2) They need it to protect their property and their right to earn a living:

> It is a known fact . . . that the Roman Catholics have been, and are every day, turned out of very beneficial farms, deprived of the maintenance of themselves and their families, lost their honest occupations, and the exercise . . . of their industry and capitals, because they could not vote at an election, and to make room for

those that could. *A fortiori*, they have, in multitudes of instances, failed to obtain leases, nor can they ever obtain them on equal terms [*Corr.* 1844, 4: 67].

Worsening relations between Britain and revolutionary France, and fear of an Irish revolt accompanied by a French invasion of Ireland, led the British government to force the Irish Parliament to pass a new Catholic Relief Act in 1793. It granted Catholics the right to hold property and to vote for Members of Parliament on the same terms as Protestants (but not to be elected to Parliament). It also repealed the laws incapacitating Catholics from holding military and naval commissions and most civil offices. "But," Burke wrote to Lord Fitzwilliam in the following year, "such has been the operation of the immense Code of penal Statutes striking at their property, that they have not been in effect restored to any degree of proportionable importance" (*Corr.* 8: 22). In 1796, when another of his friends and admirers, Dr. French Laurence, wrote to ask for a copy of *Tracts on the Popery Laws*, Burke replied, "You know that the far greater and the most oppressive part of those Laws has been repealed." But, he continued, this has not greatly improved the lot of the Catholics of Ireland: "The ill will of the governing Powers is their great Grievance who do not suffer them to have the Benefit of those capacities to which they are restored, nominally, by the Law" (*Corr.* 9: 124–125; cf. 8: 132).

The Ascendancy's stubborn refusal to accept Catholics into the commonwealth, Burke feared, was driving Irish Catholics into "Jacobinism" and reliance on French arms to free them from the Protestant and British yoke. He wrote to his friend, the Rev. Thomas Hussey: "You state, what has long been but too obvious, that it seems the unfortunate policy of the Hour, to put to the far largest portion of the King's Subjects in Ireland, the desperate alternative, between a thankless acquiescence under grievous Oppression, or a refuge in Jacobinism with all its horrors and all its crimes." But if the Irish are driven to the latter, it will not be "that Jacobinism, which is Speculative in its Origin . . . but the Jacobinism which arises from Penury and irritation, from scorned loyalty, and rejected Allegiance" (*Corr.* 9: 162; cf. 120, 171, 256–257, 283, 345).

In the same year, 1796, Burke wrote to Lord Fitzwilliam that Ireland was headed for disaster, largely because of the obstinacy of the Irish government:

> It is plainly in Ireland little less than a war declared between property and no property—between the high and the Low, the rich and the poor, brought on, partly by the Circumstances of the Country; but, I may say, much more by the fault of Government, which has fomented the Evil, and widend the Breach between the parties. The nature of this War now being made between Wealth and want, renders it almost above human Wisdom, to tell what Course ought to be taken. As long as Government Stands, and sides with that property (which it must do or it will not long be Government) it must be victorious; being possessed of all the Revenues and all the forces of the State. The other party can do nothing at all but aggravate the Tyranny by provoking it, unless by the aid of a foreign Jacobin force and in that Case their Victory would be the utter subversion of human Society itself, of all religion, all Law, all order, all humanity, as well as of all property [*Corr.* 9: 188–189; cf. 8: 272].

Burke, incidentally, was a good prophet in this instance. There were armed uprisings in the year after his death, but they were ruthlessly put down, and the French aid, when it came, was too little and too late. But the rebels did succeed in founding the Irish republican tradition, which triumphed in most of Ireland in the twentieth century.

Burke himself never wanted Irish independence any more than he had wanted American or Indian independence. He was always a staunch believer in the British Empire, but in an empire that should be a benefit to all its constituent parts. "My poor opinion is," he said, "that the closest connexion between Great Britain and Ireland, is essential to the well being, I had almost said, to the very being of the two Kingdoms" (*Corr.* 9: 257; cf. 8: 247, 9: 113). That it was not a benefit to Ireland was the fault of the local Ascendancy rather than of the British government. Catholics are wrong, he told his son in 1792, in casting the blame on Britain's government:

> They think that Ministers here [in England] instruct the Castle [the seat of the Lord-Lieutenant's government] and that the Castle sets the jobbing ascendency in motion; whereas it is now, wholly, and has, ever since I remember, been for the greater part, the direct

contrary. The Junto in Ireland entirely governs the Castle; the Castle, by its representations of the Country governs the Ministers here [*Corr.* 7: 283].

As time went on, however, while he continued to deny the charge that "'all the Evils of Ireland have originated from this Country'" (*Corr.* 9: 189), Burke was less inclined to excuse the government in England as being merely ignorant or misinformed about Ireland, and blamed it more for keeping the Junto in power for its own political ends (*Corr.* 9: 113, 121, 134, 158, 357). In any case, his solution to the misgovernment of Ireland was to break the power of the Ascendancy, get rid of the Junto (see, e.g., *Corr.* 8: 189–190), and give Irish Catholics the "real Benefit of a *sympathetic* Representation" within an aristocratic constitution (*Corr.* 9: 256).

How practicable a solution that was is open to question, and was so even in Burke's mind: "If that junto was thrown out tomorrow, . . . Government has proceeded in such a manner, and committed so many in violent declarations on this subject [Catholic emancipation] that a compleat emancipation would no longer pass with its former facility" (*Corr.* 9: 336). But it is clear that Burke wanted a government by the rich and the good who would govern for the benefit of the whole Irish people. He did not defend government by the rich merely as rich, or by property for the sake of property alone. Rightly or wrongly, he sincerely believed that government by a good aristocracy was best for the country fortunate enough to have one. What a good aristocracy might be appears in his idealized portrait of the Rockingham Whigs.

5
True Whigs and True Whiggism

BURKE WAS AND ALWAYS REMAINED a Whig, even after what he called his "expulsion from the [Whig] party" (*Corr.* 8: 401; cf. *Works* 7: 352). His principles, he said, continued to be "exactly such as the sober, honourable, and intelligent in that party, have always professed." But, if those who expelled him insist that his principles are contrary to those of "their Whig party," so be it: "I shall always wish to be thought a Tory" (*Corr.* 9: 446). In the last year of his life he wrote that the old parties of Whig and Tory were "nearly extinct," and had been replaced by those of Jacobins and anti-Jacobins (*Works* 8: 317–318). Nonetheless, Burke never abandoned Whiggism as he understood it.

It was, he maintained, the old and traditional English political creed, on which English liberty was founded. When the French Revolution was hailed in certain quarters in England as the belated French counterpart of England's Glorious Revolution of 1688, Burke denied that it was any such thing. The French Revolution was a total revolt, not merely against an absolute monarchy, but against the whole social, cultural, and religious order of Christendom. Not so what the English had done a century earlier:

> What we did was in truth and substance, and in a constitutional light, a revolution, not made, but prevented. . . . In the stable fundamental parts of our constitution we made no revolution; no, nor any revolution at all. We did not impair the monarchy. . . .
>
> The nation kept the same ranks, the same orders the same privileges, the same franchises, the same rules for property, the same subordinations, the same order in the law, in the revenues, and in the magistracy; the same lords, the same commons, the same corporations, the same electors.
>
> The church was not impaired. . . . The church and the state were the same after the revolution that they were before, but better secured in every part [*Works* 5: 20].

The original Whig argument for the Revolution of 1688, as Burke recounted it and fully agreed with it, was this: "That it was justified *only* upon the *necessity* of the case; as the *only* means left for the recovery of that *antient* constitution, formed by the original contract of the British state; as well as for the future preservation of the *same* government" (*Works* 6: 148; cf. *Corr.* 7: 168). Few scholars, if any, today agree with Burke on that point. As Carl Cone says, "The eighteenth-century constitution that Burke revered was not the ancient constitution, or that under which the seventeenth century had lived; the sovereignty of parliament after 1688 was a reality, no longer merely an aspiration" (Cone 2: 361–362). Nonetheless, as Peter Stanlis says in his *Edmund Burke: The Enlightenment and Revolution*, "Burke's argument is in essence the standard conservative Whig interpretation of the Revolution of 1688" (p. 224).

In Burke's eyes, Whiggism stood for the power of property in the hands of a landholding Whig aristocracy as the necessary check both on efforts to expand the power of the Crown and on proposals to increase the power of the people though parliamentary reform and extension of the franchise. He never denied that all three elements—king, aristocracy, and people—were legitimate and necessary parts of the British constitution. But prior to the French Revolution, Whiggism principally meant resistance to attempts at arbitrary power by the Crown, and after it, resistance to the threat of a democratic revolution that would end in the arbitrary power of the state.

After Burke's death, his friend and disciple Walker King, as co-editor of the original set of Burke's *Works*, accurately described his master's understanding of Whiggism:

> The assumption of arbitrary power, in whatever shape it appeared, whether under the veil of legitimacy, or skulking in the disguise of state necessity, or presenting the shameless front of usurpation; whether the prescriptive claim of ascendancy, or the brief career of official authority, or the newly-acquired dominion of a mob, was the sure object of his detestation and hostility [*Works* 13: viii].

That Burke may have seen attempts at arbitrary power where they did not exist, and that he may have exaggerated the necessity of a landed aristocratic elite to check them, may well be true. But resistance to arbitrary power was what he thought was the essence of Whiggism. It was therefore the ultimate meaning of the role of property in the state.

The menace of royal power that alarmed Whigs, and especially those of them who followed the Marquis of Rockingham, showed itself in the ambitions of the young king, George III, after his accession to the throne in 1760. He took into his own hands the patronage that the earlier Georges had allowed Whig leaders to exercise for the control of Parliament, and he insisted on his right to choose his own ministers independently of any "faction" or "party" in Parliament.

His most offensive choice was to make his personal confidant, the Scottish peer Lord Bute, a minister in 1761 and Prime Minister in 1762, passing over the leading politicians of the day. No one denied his legal right to do so but, as Richard Pares said in his *King George III and the Politicians*, "it was a choice which meant that court favour alone was enough to make a minister" (p. 100). Bute resigned a little less than a year later and, says Pares, "Having given up the idea of governing through a friend, George III had now to govern through politicians. . . . Ministries of politicians could not be formed without some negotiation" (p. 109).

Although Bute was now out of office, the king continued for some time to correspond with him, and the belief that he was an *éminence grise* hung on. According to Thomas Copeland, "In August 1766 the King and Bute broke off all correspondence, yet the Rockingham group continued to believe that Bute was the power behind the Throne. Only after he retired to the Continent in 1769 did these suspicions die" (*Corr.* 1: 169, n. 3). But even without Bute, Burke was still talking about "secret advisers of the Crown" in 1784 (*Works* 4: 138, 152, 178).

In opposition to the king's wish to choose his ministers from whatever group, faction, or party he wanted, the Rockinghams claimed that he should choose a Prime Minister who would present him with a list of ministers committed to a party program. Burke brilliantly propounded the theory of party government in *Thoughts on the Cause of the Present Discontents* (1770), which he published as, in his own words, "the political Creed of our Party" (*Corr.* 2: 136; cf. xiv; *W&S* 2: 242). "Party," he said there, "is a body of men united, for promoting by their joint endeavours the national interest, upon some particular principle in which they are all agreed"

(*Works* 2: 335; cf. *Corr.* 8: 39). The result of accepting this definition as the basis of ministries would be to make a ministry responsible to Parliament as well as, and even more than, to the king. It would thus preserve the nation from the danger of arbitrary power in the Crown. It would in fact be a significant transfer of executive power from the king to his ministers and their supporters in Parliament, but, in British constitutional terms, that is what saving the constitution from executive tyranny meant: limited, constitutional monarchy. The Whigs were sincere monarchists, not crypto-republicans. When Burke said in 1774, "We are members in a great and ancient *monarchy*; and we must preserve religiously, the true legal rights of the sovereign, which form the key-stone that binds together the noble and well-constructed arch of our empire and our constitution" (*Works* 3: 21–22), he was speaking to the constituents in Bristol who had just elected him to Parliament, and was expressing an appropriately royalist sentiment. But there is no reason to doubt his sincerity.

On the other hand, there can be no doubt that he, like the Rockingham party generally, saw the innate tendency of the Crown to expand its power as the great standing threat to constitutional liberty. Rockingham wrote to Burke in 1769 that "the great and continual increase of the power and influence of the Crown in the course of this century (if the Crown should be unfortunately led by weak—wicked and arbitrary ministers and surrounded by evil counsellors) would operate most dangerously to the Constitution" (*Corr.* 2: 38; cf. 3: 205, 4: 219, 5: 154–155). It was therefore urgent to keep the king from being advised by ministers who would lead him into dangerous paths, and to prevent the formation of what Burke in 1784 called "a prerogative party in the nation . . . in derogation from the authority of the commons of Great Britain in parliament assembled" (*Works* 4: 151).

In the *Present Discontents* it was Burke's thesis that there was in the royal government a *"double cabinet."* The "exteriour" administration was composed of the ministers of state, but they were manipulated and controlled by an "interiour" administration, which was a "court cabal," a "faction," or "junto" composed of men "distributed with art and judgment through all the secondary, but efficient, departments of office, and through the households of all the branches of the royal family." These men were the real but hidden government of the kingdom. They controlled the exterior administration by keeping it from being staffed by any single party with one leader and set of policies. In this way, said Burke, "the discretionary power of the crown in the formation of ministry, abused by bad or weak men, has given rise to a system, which, without directly violating the letter of any law, operates against the spirit of the whole constitution" (*Works* 2: 247–260).

Carl Cone has described Burke's talk of a "double cabinet" and an "interiour administration" as "sheer nonsense," to be taken as hyperbolic political rhetoric, but used out of a real fear for "the safety of traditional usages" (Cone 1: 202; but cf. *W&S* 2: 249–250). Burke himself, however, seems to have believed his own rhetoric, a fault not unknown among politicians before and since his time. In the same year in which he published the *Present Discontents*, for example, he remarked in a personal letter to a friend, "I do not know whether the apparent ministers triumph or not. They may last some time for the interiour managers have nothing to fear from them" (*Corr.* 2: 148).

In the *Present Discontents* he argued that the power of the "secret government" depended on making Parliament indifferent to "the persons, rank, influence, abilities, connexions, and character of the ministers of the crown," so that Parliament would support the king's choice of ministers (*Works* 2: 233). The "lovers of absolute monarchy" could only view "in a very invidious light" the method George III's Hanovarian predecessors had used, "of governing, by men of great natural interest or great acquired consideration" (*Works* 2: 231; cf. 238). Such men were the surest check on the overweening ambitions of the court party, because their exalted rank, great property, and earned consideration made them independent of court cabals. They were, that is to say, the noble, the rich, and the good:

> It is true, that the peers have a great influence in the kingdom, and in every part of the publick concerns. While they are men of property, it is impossible to prevent it, except by such means as must prevent all property from its natural operation: an event not easily to be compassed, while property is power; nor by any means to be wished, while the least notion exists of the method by which the spirit of liberty acts, and of the means by which it is preserved [*Works* 2: 245].

So far the noble and the rich, not all of whom are good. Some of them are men of virtue, however, and it is they who have earned the people's trust and the privilege of serving them in the high offices of state:

> If any particular peers, by their uniform, upright, constitutional conduct, by their publick and private virtues, have acquired an influence in the country; the people, on whose favour that influence depends, and from whom it arose, will never be duped into an opinion, that such greatness in a peer is the despotism of an aristocracy, when they know and feel it to be the effect and pledge of their own importance [*Works* 2: 245–246].

These peers were, of course, the Rockingham Whigs.

The peers, however, are not the only bulwark against the abuse of executive power. The House of Commons is peculiarly the people's watchdog: "It was not instituted to be a controul *upon* the people. . . . It was designed as a controul *for* the people." Its function is to keep "a vigilant and jealous eye over executory and judicial magistracy; an anxious care of publick money, an openness, approaching towards facility, to publick complaints" (*Works* 2: 288–289). Yet in saying this Burke by no means wished to increase the power of the people in choosing members of Parliament or to reform the existing system of representation. The system as it was gave the people a fully adequate representation of their interests, as he argued in his *Speech on the Reform of the Representation* in 1782. Seeking to improve it by enlarging the electorate would only disturb its time-tested balance and harm the country (*Works* 10: 100–108). Though Burke did not say so, it would also diminish aristocratic influence in the House of Commons.

From the Whig point of view, the threat to the constitution was not aristocratic influence but, first and foremost, the influence of the Crown on Parliament. The way to combat it was to resist any increase in the Crown's patronage and, if possible, to reduce it. When the government began to move to assert control over the East India Company's government of India, Lord Rockingham wrote to Burke: "All thinking men must already acknowledge that the influence of the Crown and the means of corruption are become very dangerous to the Constitution and yet the enormous addition of power, which Government are aiming at, by subjecting the E. India Company to their controul, does not strike and alarm so much as it ought" (*Corr.* 2: 344). At the same time Burke was writing to William Dowdeswell, the Rockingham party's leader in the Commons, that a "leading object in the Politicks of the Court is, to seize upon the East India Patronage of Offices" (*Corr.* 2: 351; cf. 399, 407). Burke and the Rockingham Whigs later changed their minds and argued for the need to bring the Company under political control, but they did not abandon their opposition to the patronage power of the Crown.

The power of the Crown is the king's power, Burke wrote to Rockingham in 1779, and the existing system of weak and divided ministries is his system:

> The whole depends on the King. As long as the King thinks proper to keep them [Lord North's administration], though they will quarrel [among themselves], they will remain: And as to the King himself, though the Interest of his Kingdom would have led him to a change long enough ago, yet the Interest of his System, which is far nearer and dearer to him, will, I am much afraid, make him defer a change, until it is so evident that a change can do no good, that the System may remain, from the apprehensions which will deter every sober man from meddling in the management of affairs so completely ruined [*Corr.* 4: 156; cf. 161, 163].

In the *Present Discontents* Burke had described how Parliament's failure to control the expenditure of the money voted for the king's civil list had allowed that money to become a slush fund for influencing elections to the House of Commons (*Works* 2: 308–324). Now, toward the end of 1779, he announced that he would introduce legislation to reduce the Crown's power. The first object of this plan for "economical reform" was to supervise and diminish the expenditure of civil list funds. In January 1780, he explained to one of his political supporters in Bristol, what the issue was:

> The Court has spoken out very distinctly. You are to consider Whether you are to speak your Sentiments or not—I mean supposing, that you do think that the public money ought to be well accounted for, and that it ought not to be employed for corrupt influence, but for national Service. This at present is the Question, and the whole question [*Corr.* 4: 200].

The other main object of economical reform was to reduce the size of the royal household in order to eliminate sinecure offices held by Members of Parliament, who were known as "placemen."

Burke succeeded in achieving neither of these objectives to any great extent in 1780, when the House of Commons voted down the most important parts of his plan (*Corr.* 4: 215, 219-220, 240). In 1782, with the Rockingham party finally in office, Burke was able to get a more extensive part of his economical reform through Parliament, but even then he did not achieve all that he had proposed in 1780 (*Corr.* 4: 433-434). To break the grip of the Crown on the electoral system, however, was as far as Burke and the leading Rockingham Whigs (the Duke of Richmond being an exception) were willing to go in parliamentary reform. Widening the franchise would destroy the aristocratic constitution which, said Burke, had produced "the happy experience of this Country of a growing liberty and a growing prosperity for five hundred years" (*Works* 10: 100; cf. 8: 13-14, 19).

Yet, although an aristocratic constitution was one in which large private property, represented and overrepresented in Parliament, kept the Crown within due bounds, not all great wealth performed that role. The wrong kind of wealth could corrupt politics. In his *Speech on the Nabob of Arcot's Debts* in 1785, Burke accused William Pitt's government of having won its smashing victory over the Whigs in 1784 with the aid of Paul Benfield and others whom Burke charged with having enriched themselves by criminal means in India (*Works* 4: 308, 312-316, 319). Later, in the trial of Warren Hastings, he told the House of Lords: "It is well known, that enormous wealth has poured into this country from India through a thousand channels, public and concealed; and it is no particular derogation from our honour to suppose a possibility of being corrupted by that, by which other empires have been corrupted, and assemblies, almost as respectable and venerable as your Lordships, have been directly or indirectly vitiated" (*Works* 13: 17; cf. 15: 8; *Corr.* 5: 314).

The kind of aristocracy that Burke admired and would trust with power was exemplified by "the great Whig connexions" that had governed Great Britain earlier in the eighteenth century. It was their power, more than the personal power of William Pitt the

Elder, that the "new court faction" surrounding the young George III set out to destroy:

> For, with a good deal less of popularity [than Pitt], they possessed a far more natural and fixed influence. Long possession of government; vast property; obligations of favours given and received; connexion of office; ties of blood, of alliance, of friendship (things at that time supposed of some force); the name of Whig, dear to the majority of the people; the zeal early begun and steadily continued to the royal family: all these together formed a body of power in the nation [*Works* 2: 238].

The most worthy heirs of those traditional Whigs, said Burke in 1769, but without naming them, are the Rockingham Whigs, "many of them of the first families, and weightiest properties in the kingdom; but infinitely more distinguished for their untainted honour publick and private, and their zealous but sober attachment to the constitution of their country, than they can be by any birth, or any station" (*Works* 2: 195; cf. *Corr.* 4: 143, 8: 80; *Works* 9: 232). Rockingham himself referred to his followers as "men of high rank and fortune, of known principles and of undoubted abilities" (*Corr.* 3: 215). The Rockingham party were obviously not lacking in self-esteem, but they based it chiefly on their conviction that they were devoted to principles rather than to attaining political office.

Burke named the leading Rockingham Whigs in his *Letter to the Sheriffs of Bristol*, written while he sat in the Commons for that city:

> If [as some people charge] I have wandered out of the paths of rectitude into those of interested faction, it was in company with the Saviles, the Dowdeswells, the Wentworths, the Bentincks, with the Lenoxes, the Manchesters, the Keppels, the Saunders's; with the temperate, permanent, hereditary virtue of the whole house of Cavendish; names among which, some have extended your fame and empire in arms, and all have fought the battle of your liberties in fields not less glorious [*Works* 3: 197].

He did not need to explain to his readers that among those names were those of several noble families of the highest rank in the kingdom.

These landed lords and country gentlemen were rather reluctant statesmen and not overly eager politicians. Burke, who was a kind of party manager for them, was often frustrated by the difficulty he found in getting them to come to London a few days before the opening of a session of Parliament to discuss policy and tactics. They were the natural governing class, but were not obsessed with governing. Thus, he wrote to the Duke of Richmond in 1772:

> You are in general somewhat Languid, scrupulous and unsystematick. But men of high Birth and great property are rarely as enterprising as others and for reasons that are very natural. . . . However with all these faults it is better you should be rich and honest and numerous than needy, and profligate and composed of a few desperate politicians though they have advantages in their own way which you must always want [*Corr.* 2: 373–374; but cf. 3: 40).

In 1776, the Marquis of Rockingham wrote to Burke from Wentworth Woodhouse, his mini–Versailles in the fields of Yorkshire: "I leave this place *as usual* with infinite regret—I confess I lend an unwilling ear to the calls of duty, and I begin to think, that it is mere vanity to imagine that this country can or will be served by anything like honest, integrity—or policy" (*Corr.* 3: 297). A few months later Burke wrote to Rockingham, urging the advisability of his party's ostentatiously staying away from Parliament, with a statement of their reasons for doing so, as a means of calling attention to their protest against the government's American policy. But he admitted that the friends he talked to seemed to be "willing to fall in with this design, because it promised to emancipate them from the servitude of irksome Business, and to afford them an opportunity of retiring to ease and Tranquility" (*Corr.* 3: 311).

Perhaps it was just as well that a party whose chief aim was to prevent government from governing too much should not be too active in politics. Burke wrote to Charles James Fox, the party's rising star, in 1777:

> I have ever wished a settled plan of our own, founded in the very essence of the American Business, wholly unconnected with the Events of the war, and framed in such a manner as to keep up our Credit and maintain our System at home, in spite of any thing which may happen abroad. I am now convinced by a long and somewhat vexatious experience that such a plan is absolutely impracticable. I think with you, that some faults in the constitution of those whom we most love and trust are among the causes of this impracticability. They are faults too, that one can hardly wish them perfectly cured of, as I am afraid they are intimately connected

with honest disinterested intentions, plentiful fortunes, assured rank, and quiet homes. A great deal of activity and enterprize can scarcely ever be expected from such men, unless some horrible calamity is just over their heads; or unless they suffer some gross personal insults from power, the resentment of which may be as unquiet and stimulating a principle in their minds, as ambition is in those of a different complexion [*Corr.* 3: 381].

Finally, many years later, during the French Revolution, Burke complained of the imperturbability of Earl Fitzwilliam, Rockingham's nephew and heir, and the Duke of Portland:

There are two men high in the Party, who would certainly be affected by these things [the slave revolt in Hispaniola] if they ever attended to them, or combined them with each other, or followed them up to their principle—But one of them does not even read the Newspaper—and the Business is not suffered to occupy their reflexions. It is still a foreign concern, and they do not like much to reflect upon what they will never permit themselves to act [*Corr.* 6: 439].

Burke, we see, was well aware of the faults of his natural aristocrats. But he regarded them as faults that only exaggerated the virtues that made them fit to govern the country with safety to its constitution. They were already rich, very rich, and presumably beyond the consuming avarice that corrupts politics. Their wealth was chiefly in land, the least fluid and most stable kind of property; it therefore fostered a desire to preserve and only gradually to expand property rather than to make a killing in trade or finance. Moreover, while the Rockingham party was open to and glad to get "new men" like Burke, its leaders had been born to old, landed wealth and high rank. They were thus presumably beyond the consuming ambition that sees in politics the avenue to personal power and wealth through the possession and expansion of governmental power. Whig aristocrats like Rockingham and his associates, who really were exempt from driving greed and lust for power, were therefore the natural bulwark of constitutional liberty. If they preferred the enjoyment of life on their country estates to the hurly-burly of political strife, it might be more a benefit than a loss to the nation.

Constitutional liberty was what the Rockingham Whigs stood for above all: "A constitution of things in which the liberty of no one man, and no body of men, and no number of men, can find means to trespass on the liberty of any person, or any description of persons, in the society. This kind of liberty is, indeed, but another name for justice; ascertained by wise laws, and secured by well-constructed institutions" (*Corr.* 6: 42). Burke wrote those words in 1789, in his first extended comment on the French Revolution. Five years earlier, after the defeat of the Whigs by the younger William Pitt and his Tories in the elections of 1784, he had explained the Whig ideal of government:

> An independent house of Commons; an house of Commons like the last, equally an Enemy to indefinite prerogative, and to wild unprincipled Liberty; an house of Commons fitted and disposed to support, the only plan of Government that deserves to be supported, or indeed that at all deserves the name of Government; a scheme of method and reason, and not of fancy and Caprice [*Corr.* 5: 143].

In 1792, after he had broken with Fox and what had been the Rockingham Whigs over the French Revolution, Burke looked back on his former party and its virtues:

> The party with which I acted had, by the malevolent and unthinking, been reproached, and by the wise and good always esteemed and confided in, as an aristocratick party. Such I always understood it to be, in the true sense of the word. I understood it to be a party, in its composition, and in its principles, connected with the solid, permanent, long-possessed property of the country; a party which, by a temper derived from that species of property, and affording a security to it, was attached to the ancient tried usages of the kingdom; a party, therefore, essentially constructed upon a ground-plot of stability and independence; a party, therefore, equally removed from servile court compliances, and from popular levity, presumption, and precipitation [*Corr.* 7: 52–53; cf. 6: 161, 450].

But the party was not a class party, dedicated to the interests of one part of the community against the others. Even new men such as himself, Burke continued,

> I conceived, without any formal engagement, by the very constitution of the Party to be bound, with all the activity and energy of Minds animated and awakened by great hopes and Views, to support those aristocratick principles, and the aristocratick Interests

connected with them, as essential to the real Benefit of the Body of the people, to which all names of party, all Ranks and orders in the State, and even Government itself ought to be entirely subordinate [*Corr.* 7: 53].

Burke's conception of Whiggism explains why he did not consider himself inconsistent in his differing attitudes toward the American and French Revolutions (*Works* 6: 120–127; *Corr.* 9: 241), or in his change from severe critic of the British Crown to defender of all crowns against republicanism. Many of his contemporaries were astonished at his attack on the French Revolution, which they thought wildly inconsistent with his previous beliefs and practices. The opening words of the English edition of Thomas Paine's *The Rights of Man, Part I,* are well known: "From the part Mr. Burke took in the American Revolution, it was natural that I should consider him a friend to mankind," and therefore a friend to the French Revolution. Another man who found Burke's attitude toward the French Revolution incomprehensible was that strange character, a Prussian who became a French revolutionary and called himself Anacharsis Cloots, the Orator of the Human Race. He had visited Beaconsfield in 1784, and got the impression that Burke and his friends were hostile to the British constitution, when in fact they were only Whig politicians "at the height of their indignation against George III and the House of Lords, for having rejected Fox's India Bill and dismissed the Fox–North Coalition" (*Corr.* 6: 110, n. 2). In May 1790, having heard of Burke's first attacks on the French Revolution, Cloots wrote to him to remind him of the views he had expressed in 1784:

> Our conversations, often prolonged far into the night, had for their object the greatest interests of humanity. You were very discontented with your Upper Chamber and the frightening advances of the royal authority. The dark picture you painted for me of your Constitution, reconciled me a bit to *my Bastille and my Lenoir* [a lieutenant in the Paris police]. Your friends Fox, Sheridan, Powis, Lord Inchiquin, Duke St. John, etc., used the same language with me. On this ground, I expected to find in Mr. Burke one of the most ardent apologists for the admirable revolution which sets France above all the nations in the world [*Corr.* 6: 110; my translation from the French].

Fox and Sheridan in particular admired the French Revolution from the beginning and continued to defend it against the criticism of Burke and others. In November 1792, Burke wrote to Lord Fitzwilliam and mentioned what he had learned in conversation from William Windham:

> He had, not long since, seen Fox. He found him in no way altered. His opinion was, that the danger to this Country chiefly consisted in the growth of Tory principles, and that what happened in France was likely to be useful to us in keeping alive and invigorating the Spirit of Liberty. He was disposed to lower and palliate whatever seemed shocking in their procedure [*Corr.* 7: 315].

Fox, that is to say, still thought as he and Burke had thought in 1784, and saw in the French Revolution only a revolt against absolute monarchy which, despite excesses, would lead the French to the liberty the English had sealed in 1688. Burke had not switched sides; he remained a Whig, with a Whig's mistrust of political power. But he saw in the French Revolution the rise of a state power which, justifying itself on the principles of democratic sovereignty, would pose a threat to liberty greater than anything George III had ever ambitioned. As he wrote to Captain Mercer in 1790:

> The tyranny of a multitude is a multiplied tyranny. If, as society is constituted in these large countries of France and England, full of unequal property, I must make my choice (which God avert!) between the despotism of a single person, or of the many, my election is made. As much injustice and tyranny has been practised in a few months by a French democracy, as in all the arbitrary monarchies in Europe in the forty years of my observation [*Corr.* 6: 96].

Burke saw no such threat in the newly independent American republic. Nor was he entirely displeased with American independence, because it was preferable to the enormous access to the power of the Crown that would have resulted from a military conquest of America: "We lost our colonies; but we kept our constitution" (*Works* 8: 13). Once America left the British Empire, he largely lost interest in it, because it was now outside his sphere of action, and therefore said little about it.

But we do find some passing comments on the United States, none of them unfriendly. In September 1788, when enough States had ratified the U.S. Constitution to make it operative, he remarked in a letter to a friend, "America looks as if she were taking something like a form" (*Corr.* 5: 415). In the following year, in a letter introducing a young American to Lord Charlemont, he said: "America and we are not under the same Crown, but if we are united by mutual goodwill and reciprocal good Offices, perhaps it may do almost as well" (*Corr.* 5: 452; cf. *Works* 8: 315). Later in 1789, when he was aware of what was going on in France, he wrote to William Windham:

> What has happened puts all speculation to the blush; but still I should doubt, whether in the End France is susceptible of the Democracy that is the Spirit, and in good measure too, the form, of the constitution they have in hand: It is except the Idea of the Crowns being hereditary much more truly democratical than that of North America [*Corr.* 6: 25].

Finally, he is reported as saying in the Commons in May 1791: "The people of America had, he believed, formed a constitution as well adapted to their circumstances as they could." It was a republican constitution, because it had to be one: "They had not the materials of monarchy or aristocracy among them. They did not, however, set up the absurdity that the nation should govern the nation; that prince prettyman should govern prince prettyman: but formed their government, as nearly as they could according to the model of the British constitution" (*Parl. Hist.* 29: 365–366).

To Burke's mind, his disagreement with Fox and the bulk of what had been the Rockingham Whigs was not a mere difference of opinion over the attitude to be taken toward a revolution in a foreign country. It concerned the attitude of Englishmen toward the British constitution and, indeed, toward the whole idea of limited constitutional government, as opposed to radical majoritarian democracy. "I have the misfortune," he told Lord Fitzwilliam in June 1791, "totally and fundamentally to differ with that party in constitutional and publick points of such moment, that all those, on which I have hitherto ever differed from other men and other Parties, are, in comparison, mere toys and Triffles" (*Corr.* 6: 275).

Two months later, Burke published his *An Appeal from the New to the Old Whigs*, the New Whigs being Fox and his apostate followers, and the Old Whigs the Fathers of true Whiggism. Having quoted several of the more radically revolutionary and treasonable pages of *The Rights of Man*, without naming Thomas Paine as their author, Burke concluded: "These are the notions which, under the idea of whig principles, several persons, and among them persons of no mean mark, have associated themselves to propagate" (*Works* 6: 187–200). Earlier in the same book he had spelled out the doctrines he was attributing to Fox and company in these words:

> These new whigs hold, that the sovereignty, whether exercised by one or many, did not only originate *from* the people (a position not denied [and which Burke himself had affirmed in 1770, *Works* 2: 288], nor worth denying or assenting to) but that, in the people the same sovereignty constantly and unalienably resides; that the people may lawfully depose kings, not only for misconduct, but without any misconduct at all; that they may set up any new fashion of government for themselves, or continue without any government at their pleasure; that the people are essentially their own rule, and their will the measure of their conduct.

"These doctrines concerning the *people*," said Burke," . . . tend, in my opinion, to the utter subversion, not only of all government, in all modes, and of all stable securities to rational freedom, but of all the rules and principles of morality itself" (*Works* 6: 147–148).

Burke himself, in 1793, described the Foxite Whigs as "a confederacy of about fifty persons of eminence; men, for the far greater part, of very ample fortunes either in possession or in expectancy" (*Works* 7: 279). It is unlikely that these rich aristocrats held democratic views as radical as the ones Burke ascribed to them, and, at least at first, he did not believe they did. Shortly after the publication of *An Appeal*, he wrote to his son that no more than a handful of men in both houses of Parliament "think with the French Revolution." He then said, "It may be asked, why I represent the whole party as tolerating, and by a toleration countenancing, those proceedings. It is to get the better of their inactivity, and to stimulate them to a publick declaration of, what every one of their acquaintance privately knows, to be as much their Sentiments as they are yours and mine" (*Corr.* 6: 316–317). Three months later he told his son that "the deviation" of the New Whigs was "not *from* Principle, but the pushing an allowed principle of our own to a mischeivous *extreme*," and this was why Fitzwilliam and the Duke of Portland found it so hard to repudiate their old friends among the New Whigs (*Corr.* 6: 441; cf. 418).

The desire to disabuse them may also explain why, in his letters to Fitzwilliam and Portland, Burke judged the New Whigs so severely (and as time went by, more and more really meant what he said). After their break with him over the French Revolution, he told Fitzwilliam, "The Leaders [of the New Whigs] have ever since gone on, and are with all their might going on, to propagate the principles of French Levelling," whose "great Object is not, (as they pretend to delude worthy people to their Ruin) the destruction of all absolute Monarchies, but totally to root out that thing called an *Aristocrate* or Nobleman and Gentleman" (*Corr.* 6: 451; cf. 273, 416, 7: 60, *Works* 7: 270–271). The leading New Whigs, he insisted, know what they are doing. Other aristocrats, he told Portland, may be merely deceived by them:

> It is truly alarming to see so large a part of the Aristocratick Interest engaged in the Cause of the new species of democracy, which is openly attacking or secretly undermining the System of property, by which mankind has hitherto been governed: But we are not to delude ourselves. No man, who is connected with a party, which professes publickly to admire, or may be justly suspected of secretly abetting, this French revolution, who must not be drawn into its vortex, and become the instrument of its designs [*Corr.* 7: 437].

The issue as Burke saw it was clear and profoundly important. He thought it foolish to regard it as a matter of being for or against absolute monarchy. What was at stake was the maintenance of "that Aristocratick principle, without which every Dominion must become a mere despotism of the Prince, or the brutal Tyranny of a ferocious and atheistick populace [such as the Parisian mob]; The latter infinitely a greater Evil; and infinitely more shocking to every Liberal and well instructed mind, than even despotism itself" (*Corr.* 7: 160). The Revolution was an effort to destroy aristocracy, its system of property, and the whole body of laws, morals, and religion that held its world together (*Corr.* 7: 232). Those Englishmen were inexcusable who refused to see that if it triumphed in France, it would surely triumph in other countries, including Great Britain (*Corr.* 6: 419; cf. 416, 453; 7: 177–178, 218–219; 8: 300–301, 335, 343; *Works* 6: 20; 7: 235; 8: 215).

Equally inexcusable were enlightened despots like Marie Antoinette's brother, Emperor Leopold II of Austria, of whom Burke said:

> The Truth is, I am afraid, that the Emperor and some of his Ministers though he does not approve; (as he cannot approve) of the destruction of the monarchy [in France], is infinitely pleased with the Robbery of the Church property and the humiliation of the Gentry; and that in the lust of philosophick spoliation, and equalization, he forgets that he cuts down the supports of Monarchy, and indeed destroys those principles of property, or order and regularity for which alone any rational man can wish Monarchy to exist [*Corr.* 6: 413; cf. 7: 263; *Works* 7: 67–72, 100].

"*Je suis Royaliste, mais Royaliste raisonné,*" Burke wrote to a French émigré. He was no fanatic for kings, he continued, but valued them for their functions: to protect the peoples against the encroachments of the great, and the great against the invasions of the people; to keep everything in its place and habitual order, to consolidate the whole, to contain everything within the bounds of a sound situation, to even everything out under the equality of justice, and not of the foolish and insolent chimeras that they preach and practice in France (*Corr.* 7: 263).

In *An Appeal from the New to the Old Whigs* he answered the charge that by his defense of monarchy in the *Reflections* he had been inconsistent with the Whiggism he had previously professed. Writing of himself in the third person, he said:

> Mr. Burke thought, with a majority of the house of commons, that the influence of the crown at one time was too great; but . . . his majesty had by a gracious message, and several subsequent acts of parliament, reduced it to a standard which satisfied Mr. Fox himself, and, apparently at least, contented whoever wished to go farthest in that reduction [*Works* 6: 127].

Burke may have been disingenuous in this self-exculpation; if the French Revolution had not happened, he might have spent the rest of his life resisting real or imagined extensions of the influence of the Crown. He came nearer to his real point two pages later, when he stated the issue in these terms: "If, say his accusers, the dread of too great influence in the crown of Great Britain could justify the degree of reform which he adopted, the dread of a return under the despotism of a monarchy might justify the people of France in going much further, and reducing monarchy to its present nothing" (this in 1791, when revolutionary France had not yet deposed the king and proclaimed itself a republic). Burke comes to a very different conclusion: "That a monarchy is a thing perfectly susceptible of reform; perfectly susceptible of a balance of power; and that, when reformed and balanced, for a great country, it is the best of all governments" (*Works* 6: 129).

A year earlier, in his *Reflections*, he had asked concerning the French revolutionaries, "Have they never heard of a monarchy directed by laws, controlled and balanced by the great hereditary wealth and hereditary dignity of a nation; and both again controlled by a judicious check from the reason and feeling of the people at large acting by a suitable and permanent organ?" (*Works* 5: 229). That was the Whig idea as Burke had always understood it (the reader will recognize the "suitable and permanent organ" as the House of Commons controlled by the property-owners of the country). He restated this ideal as existing fact in *A Letter to a Noble Lord* in 1796, where he said that "the British monarchy" is "not more limited than fenced by the orders of the state," and as long as it stands together with "the lords and commons of this realm,— the triple cord, which no man can break," as "the firm guarantees of each others being, and each others rights; the joint and several securities, each in its place and order, for every kind and every quality of property and of dignity," so long shall we be "all safe together—the high from the blights of envy and spoliations of rapacity; the low from the iron hand of oppression and the insolent spurn of contempt" (*Works* 8: 49–50; cf. 7: 368). Or, as he had said on an earlier occasion, "without monarchy in England, most certainly we never can enjoy either peace or liberty" (*Works* 6: 46).

The Whig ideal was liberal in that it guaranteed English liberties, but conservative in its dependence on and protection of a society structured by unequal levels of property and rank. To that ideal Burke remained devoted to the end. As John Morley put it in his *Burke*, "He changed his front, but he never changed his ground" (p. 167).

6
Burke's Economics

BURKE WAS NOT a professional economist, but in *A Letter to a Noble Lord* (his *apologia pro vita sua*), he claimed to have steeped himself in his country's economic affairs from the beginning of his parliamentary career: "The first session I sat in parliament, I found it necessary to analyze the whole commercial, financial, constitutional and foreign interests of Great Britain and its empire" (*Works* 8: 26; cf. *W&S* 2: 3). Observers gave him credit for this; Charles Lee, for example, who wrote: "'An Irishman, one Mr. Burke, is sprung up in the House of Commons, who has astonished every body with the power of his eloquence, his comprehensive knowledge in all our exterior and internal politics and commercial interests.'" In a revealing comment on the aristocratic world that Burke was entering, Lee added: "'He wants nothing but the sort of dignity annexed to rank, and property in England, to make him the most considerable man in the Lower House'" (quoted in Cone 1: 162).

Burke also claimed to have brought to Parliament a study of "political oeconomy . . . from my very early youth . . . even before . . . it had employed the thoughts of speculative men in other parts of Europe," and at a time when it "was still in its infancy in England." Then, in a remark which may be the source of what Carl Cone has called "a dubious tradition" (ibid., p. 326), Burke went on to say: "Great and learned men thought my studies were not wholly thrown away, and deigned to communicate with me now and then on some particulars of their immortal works" (*Works* 8: 27).

The dubious tradition is that Adam Smith consulted Burke in writing *The Wealth of Nations*. Another tradition, accepted by a number of scholars (on whom see Stanlis, *Burke: Enlightenment and Revolution*, p. 57, n. 63), is that Smith once said that Burke was "the only man I ever knew who thinks on economic subjects exactly as I do without any previous communication having passed between us." But this tradition seems to be derived from Robert Bisset's

Life of Edmund Burke, published in 1800 (2: 429); at least he is the source given by Dixon Wecter (*Notes and Queries* 174: 311). Since Bisset never documents his own sources, we do not know how reliable the tradition is.

It is certain the Burke knew and admired Smith, and maintained cordial if distant (necessarily so, given the distance between London and Scotland) relations with him (see ibid., pp. 310–311). But, as Carl Cone says, the "supposed agreement of ideas" between them "would be better substantiated if one could prove Burke's authorship of the favorable review [of *The Wealth of Nations*] published in the *Annual Register* for 1776, or if one could find Burke attacking the protectionist system of the Empire as vigorously as Smith" (Cone 1: 326). Nonetheless, Burke often sounded like Smith in his advocacy of economic freedom and the free market economy. In one of his earliest published political writings, he remarked that the very attempt to confine trade and manufacturing would certainly destroy them. But left to themselves, "they "frequently change their place; and thereby, far from being lost, are often highly improved. Thus some manufactures have decayed in the west and south, which have made new and more vigorous shoots when transported into the north" (*Works* 2: 63; cf. 64).

In his *Speech on American Taxation* in 1774, he criticized George Grenville, whose administration introduced the policy of taxing the American colonies, at the same time more rigorously enforcing the navigation acts that restricted their trade:

> Mr. Grenville thought better of the wisdom and power of human legislation than in truth it deserves. He conceived, and many conceived along with him, that the flourishing trade of this country was greatly owing to law and institution, and not quite so much to liberty; for but too many are apt to believe regulation to be commerce, and taxes to be revenue [*Works* 2: 390].

On the contrary, said Burke in his *Speech on Economical Reform* in 1780, "Commerce . . . flourishes most when it is left to itself. Interest, the great guide of commerce, is not a blind one. It is very well able to find its own way; and its necessities are its best laws" (*Works* 3: 323).

Commercial enterprises must be free to run on certain elementary principles. For example, "the active, awakened, and enlightened principle of self-interest," which inspires "the regulations by mercantile men for their mercantile purposes," provides "a better system for the guard of that interest than the cold, drowsy wisdom" of state regulation "ever contrived for the publick" (*Works* 13: 52). Or again: "The principle of buying cheap and selling dear is the first, the great foundation of mercantile dealing" (*Works* 4: 95). There is therefore a natural and general freedom of trade. Without suggesting that it was beyond the power of government to grant monopolies, Burke said that "the monopoly of the East India Company was a derogation from the general freedom of trade belonging to his majesty's people" (*Works* 4: 165–166). In an undated note for a speech, he laid it down that "'Monopoly' is contrary to 'Natural Right.'" He then defined it: "Monopoly is the power, in one man, of exclusive dealing in a commodity or commodities, which others might supply if not prevented by that power." A monopoly, therefore, cannot become a prescriptive right, because it is "contrary to common right. Its only lawful origin is in the convention of parties, which gets the better of law." The state, however, "may grant a monopoly," because "representing all its individuals," it "may contract for them." But it ought to do so only for purposes that contribute to "the good of the whole" (*Corr.* 1844, 4: 459–460). Burke favored the mobility, not only of capital, but of labor as well. In 1774, he denounced the Settlement Act of 1662, under which magistrates had the power to return poor people to their parish of origin, lest they become a charge on the parish they had moved to: "The laws of settlement and removals are the essence of slavery . . .—if you will not let me live where I please, which necessarily implies, where I can best maintain and support myself, I am a slave—I am tied to my native spot, and cannot leave it without the consent of another" (*W&S* 2: 402).

All this fits into a general approval of the internal development of Great Britain by private capital. Burke seldom spoke of the enclosure movement, which was an important part of that development, but he was in favor of it if carried out in a fair and legal way, as he explained in an unpublished letter to the press in 1768:

> I readily grant that the Nation would receive a great and solid Benefit from a general enclosure of all Waste Lands, whether they belong to the Subject [or the] Crown. But this must be taken with several

Qualifications. The scheme of an enclosure in order to be a Benefit must be carried on openly in the face of day, with a quiet and deliberate procedure. . . . It must be pursued with due Notice to and full consent of all Parties; carried into execution by impartial, reputable and intelligent commissioners, and not the lowest Slaves and Tools of single Interest only. . . . Above all a sacred regard ought to be paid to property of what nature so ever, or in whatever hands it may be found.

Nor should the rights of the poor be neglected: "Multitudes of the poor not less perhaps than some hundreds of thousands owe almost their whole being to their use of Common, for which they are acquainted with no other Title, than antient undisturbed possession of their forefathers and the absolute necessity of the continuance of that possession for their own subsistence" (*W&S* 2: 84–85).

In his *Speech on Economical Reform* in 1780, Burke advocated selling the smaller landed estates of the Crown to private owners, because such estates were more suitable for private than public management. In selling off the Crown's forest lands, Burke would not allow bidders to run up the price, lest "the expence of that purchase may weaken the capital to be employed in their cultivation." Instead, he thought, some "rule of fair preference" might be established to prevent favoritism. "The principal revenue which I propose to draw from these uncultivated wastes," he explained, "is to spring from the improvement and population of the kingdom; which never can happen, without producing an improvement more advantageous to the revenues of the crown, than the rents of the best landed estate which it can hold" (*Works* 3: 271–274).

Burke's final remark on this subject, near the end of his life, was: "To what ultimate extent, it may be wise or practicable, to push inclosures of common and waste lands, may be a question of doubt, in some points of view: but no person thinks them already carried to excess" (*Works* 8: 396–397; cf. 398).

For all his conviction about the benefits of commercial freedom, however, Burke was not an absolute free-trader. He was an enlightened imperialist, who thought that the British Empire could and should be a blessing to all its parts (*Works* 3: 126). His imperialism included imperial protectionism, certainly against countries outside it, and even within it. This emerges clearly in his writings on America, Ireland, and India.

During the American crisis, he insisted that the Empire was a single economic whole. To regard the balance of trade between Britain and its colonies as the indicator of their value to Britain was therefore foolish:

> The whole import from Ireland and America, and from the West Indies, is set against us in the ordinary way of striking a balance of imports and exports, whereas the import and export are both our own. This is just as ridiculous, as to put against the general balance of the nation, how much more goods Cheshire receives from London, than London from Cheshire. The whole revolves and circulates through this kingdom, and is, so far as regards our profit, in the nature of home trade, as much as if the several countries of America and Ireland were all pieced to Cornwall [*Works* 2: 72; cf. 73-75].

Yet Burke knew that the American colonies "were evidently founded in subservience to the commerce of Great Britain," and that "the whole system of our laws concerning them became a system of restriction." Under the navigation acts the colonies were allowed to import only from Great Britain and to export only to Great Britain, so far as what they exported "can serve any purpose here." Furthermore, "it was contrived that they should send all their products to us raw, and in their first state; and that they should take every thing from us in the last stage of manufacture" (*Works* 2: 162; cf. 163; *Corr.* 3: 15). Burke therefore granted that the commercial system imposed on the Americans by the navigation acts would be "a condition of as rigorous servitude as men can be subject to," if it did not also benefit them (*Works* 2: 383).

But there was a real benefit: "The Americans trade, navigate, cultivate, with English capitals; to their own advantage, to be sure; for without these capitals; their ploughs would be stopped, and their ships wind-bound" (*Works* 2: 164; cf. 384). Nonetheless, it was folly to try to tax colonies that were subject to the mother country's monopoly of their trade, when that monopoly was the real source of her profit from them (*Works* 2: 162-164). Nor had it been British policy to tax them prior to 1764 (*Works* 2: 380-386).

In his great *Speech on Conciliation with the Colonies* in 1775, Burke explained his idea of an empire: "An empire is an aggregate of many states, under one common head; whether this head be a monarch, or a presiding republick." There must be a "supreme common authority," and in the British Empire, that must be Parliament: "We are indeed, in all disputes with the colonies, by the necessity of things, the judge" (*Works* 3: 69–71). But our supreme authority, Burke told the electors of Bristol in 1774, was "consistent with all the liberties a sober and spirited American ought to desire" (*Works* 3: 7).

When the Rockingham administration in 1766 repealed the first law taxing the colonies, it joined to the repeal a Declaratory Act which asserted that the British Parliament had authority to legislate for the colonies "in all cases whatsoever." Burke firmly believed in the principle of the Declaratory Act, but maintained that if Parliament used its authority wisely and prudently, it would refrain from trying to tax the colonies. It could then keep the imperial commercial system and the trade laws that defined it. This he urged Parliament to do: "For without idolizing them, I am sure [these laws] are still in many ways, of great use to us," and, he believed, they are not "the true ground of the quarrel" that the colonies have with Britain (*Works* 3: 78–79). It is doubtful if the colonies were in fact willing to settle the quarrel on those terms in 1775. By 1777, Burke himself was ready to renounce, even in principle, Parliament's authority to tax them (*Works* 3: 193–194; 9: 203, 213–214). But this renunciation was a concession to necessity, not a loss of faith in the imperial commercial system or in the Empire's need of a central authority to hold it together.

Ireland was a somewhat different case, since it was legally a distinct kingdom from Great Britain, with the same king, but with its own legislative and taxing power, and it voted its own money to the Crown. But, as Burke remarked in *Conciliation with the Colonies*, "Ireland has ever had from the beginning a separate, but not an independent legislature" (*Works* 3: 113). Until 1782, Irish legislation had to be sent to England for acceptance or amendment by the British government. Even after that date, the British kept the Irish government under control by "management."

In practice, Britain treated Ireland as a colony whose trade must be restricted to keep it from competing with British manufacturers and merchants. Burke wanted Irish independence even less than he wanted American independence, but he argued for easing the restrictions on Irish trade for the sake not only of justice, but also of the mutual benefit of the two countries.

In 1778, when Lord North's administration brought forward proposals for removing certain restriction on Irish trade, Burke vigorously supported them. But the proposals aroused an angry response from the manufacturing and trading cities of England, not least from Burke's own constituency of Bristol, which let him know that he was in danger of losing his seat in Parliament (as in fact he did in 1780).

One of the critics who wrote to Burke was Samuel Span, Master of the Merchants Society of Bristol. In his reply, Burke pointed out that trade is not a zero-sum game. The more trade, the better for all parties to it. "Ireland, being a Country of the same Nature with this can never be beneficial to this Kingdom, but by pursuing several, if not all, of the Objects of Commerce and manufacture which are cultivated here." But we should not fear this. "The world, I apprehend, is large enough for all; and we are not to conclude, that what is gained to one part of it, is lost, of Course, to the other." The opposite is true: "The prosperity, arising from an enlarged and Liberal System, improves all its objects and the *participation* of a Trade with flourishing Countries is much better than the *monopoly* of want and penury" (*Corr.* 3: 426). Poor people are of necessity poor customers, and so "it is the interest of the commercial world that wealth should be found everywhere" (*Corr.* 3: 436). "Believe me," Burke assured some other Bristol merchants, "if Ireland is beneficial to you, it is so, not from the parts in which it is restrained; but from those in which it is left free, though not unrivalled. The greater its freedom, the greater must be your advantage" (*Corr.* 3: 444).

The North administration collapsed in the face of the opposition of the British manufacturers and merchants, and reduced its concessions to Ireland to insignificance (*Works* 9: 243–244; cf. 3: 368). Now Ireland was aroused. An illegal army of Irish Volunteers sprang up, ostensibly to defend the country against possible French and Spanish invasions during the American war, but in fact threatening England. Burke described this situation in dramatic terms to the electors of Bristol in 1780:

> The people of Ireland demand a freedom of trade with arms in their hands. They [here meaning their Parliament] interdict all commerce

between the two nations. They deny all new supply [to the Crown] in the house of commons, although in time of war. They stint the trust of the old revenue, given for two years to all the king's predecessors, to six months [*Works* 3: 369].

Although Burke disliked and feared illegal armies, he praised the Irish Parliament for what it had done (*Works* 9: 248).

The North administration gave in again, this time to Ireland, and a frightened British Parliament, said Burke, "made an universal surrender of all that had been thought the peculiar, reserved, uncommunicable rights of England;—the exclusive commerce of America, of Africa, of the West Indies—all the manufactures— iron, glass, even . . . the sacred fleece [wool] itself, all went together" (*Works* 3: 369–370). In a letter to a Bristol manufacturer, he added that not only did Parliament make "an unlimited and untimely surrender . . . of every one of the objects of former restraints, but virtually of the whole legislative power itself, which had made them." It was not the freeing of Irish trade that alarmed Burke, but the British Parliament's surrender of the power to regulate the commerce of the Empire unless it got the consent of the Irish Parliament where Irish trade was concerned (*Corr.* 4: 224).

As he wrote to a member of the Irish Parliament, he would have preferred to start with small commercial concessions to Ireland, in the hope that one concession would lead to another, as the people of England discovered by experience that the dire consequences they had feared did not in fact follow. "But that, to which I attached myself the most particularly, was to fix *the principle* of a free trade in all the ports of these Islands, as founded in justice, and beneficial to the whole; but principally to this, the seat of the supreme power" (*Works* 9: 235–236). Freedom of trade indeed, but within the imperial commercial system and under the control of the imperial Parliament.

Ireland, however, had not got a full "free trade in all the ports of these Islands." (For a brief account of what she did get, see Mahoney, pp. 141–142.) In 1785, William Pitt the Younger, who was by then the Prime Minister, proposed a plan that would give Ireland commercial equality with Great Britain in return for an Irish monetary contribution to imperial defense. British commercial and manufacturing interests were once again galvanized against the plan. This time they were strongly supported by the Fox-

North coalition which Pitt had defeated in the elections of 1784. Parliament eventually passed Pitt's proposals, but in so amended a form that the Irish Parliament would not accept them.

"Burke's attitude to Pitt's Irish Propositions remains obscure," says Holden Furber, one of the editors of Burke's *Correspondence*. "He took little part in the debates. Although the few speeches he made were not frontal attacks on the Propositions themselves, he voted with his party against the Propositions." Why he did so is not entirely clear, but "contemporaries . . . felt that Burke was being inconsistent with his previous attitude towards Irish trade, and in general regarded the attack on the Propositions as factious" (*Corr.* 5: 221, n. 1). Thomas Mahoney, having reviewed the explanations offered by several writers for Burke's conduct, concludes that "Burke was guilty here of factiousness and as such cannot avoid the charge of inconsistency" (pp. 149–150).

Whatever the explanation, it is clear that devotion to free trade did not override every other consideration in Burke's mind. He stated his final position on Anglo-Irish trade shortly before his death, when he foresaw and dreaded an Irish uprising supported by the Jacobin French. "My poor opinion is, that the closest connexion between Great Britain and Ireland, is essential to the well being, I had almost said, to the very being, of the two Kingdoms," with Britain as the seat of the imperial and superior power, and with Ireland "locally, civilly, and commercially independent" but subject to British guidance "in all matters of peace and of War" (*Corr.* 9: 257; cf. 8: 246). As he had explained in 1795, "Ireland, as Ireland, whether it be taken civilly, constitutionally, or commercially, suffers no Grievance. The Catholicks as Catholicks do" (*Corr.* 8: 247; cf. 7: 546). Faced with the danger of Catholics joining forces with the French Revolution because of the blind bigotry of the Ascendancy, Burke thought religious freedom in Ireland more important than commercial equality for England's sister kingdom.

Burke's increasing involvement in the affairs of India from 1780 on was primarily concerned with the East India Company's government there and the British government's failure adequately to supervise it. The chief results of his efforts were Fox's East India Bill, which was defeated in the Lords, and the unsuccessful impeachment of Warren Hastings. Yet he believed that the Company's commercial activities and their negative effect on the welfare of the people of India were intimately involved with its government of that country.

It was, after all, a trading company which had only subsequently become a territorial government and, in Burke's eyes, was doing a bad job of both. "Our Indian government," he said in his speech on the East India Bill, "is in its best state a grievance" (*Works* 4: 42). In a later speech he went so far as to say: "The result of the parliamentary inquiries has been, that the East India company was found totally corrupted, and totally perverted from the purposes of its institution, whether political or commercial" (*Works* 4: 173–174).

In speaking for the East India Bill, he said that the Company operates under a charter that gives it both political power and commercial monopoly, the latter being the right "to exclude their fellow-subjects from the commerce of half the globe." He did not question the existence of the Company's chartered rights: "They belong to the company in the surest manner; and they are secured to that body by every sort of publick sanction" (*Works* 4: 10). But he did question its right to use them as it had been doing.

Burke is the acknowledged author of the Ninth Report of a House of Commons select committee on Indian affairs (*Works* 9: xvii; *W&S* 5: 28). In it he argued that to succeed as a business enterprise, the Company must again be placed "upon a bottom truly commercial." Even before the Company acquired territories and raised revenues from them, it was hampered by mercantilistic regulations which closed the British market to "the most considerable articles" of the Company's trade, namely, "all silk stuffs, and stained and painted cottons," lest they compete with British manufactures. It was also obliged to furnish the Ordnance with a quantity of saltpeter at a set price, without reference to the market price, and to export a certain amount of British manufactured goods, whether or not there was a profitable market for them in India. "The spirit of all these regulations," Burke remarked, "naturally tended to weaken . . . the mainspring of the commercial machine, the *principles of profit and loss*" (*Works* 11: 85–86).

Those principles suffered even more when the Company acquired the rights of sovereignty in certain territories in India, and the right to tax them. The Company then began to invest its surplus revenue in the purchase of goods to be exported. It correspondingly became indifferent to their price and quality: "Merchandise, taken as tribute, or bought in lieu of it, can never long be of a kind, or of a price, fitted to a market, which stands solely on its commercial reputation." Once the Company was able to buy goods with tax revenues, rather than with the profit from the sale of goods it imported into India, its trade moved from showing a profit to an overall loss. But in areas where "the power and dominion of the Company was less, their profit on the goods was greater." This shows the necessity of setting the Company's "commerce upon a commercial basis" (*Works* 11: 86–89).

The same is true of the internal commerce of the Company's main territory in India, Bengal. As it acquired political power there, it obtained for itself exemption from the internal duties on trade in Bengal. Its servants used this exemption for their own benefit in their private trade, as well as for the Company's trade. With this advantage, the Company and its servants began to drive native merchants out of business. One of the native nominal rulers retaliated by announcing that he would abolish all internal duties on trade for natives and foreigners alike. "Never," said Burke, "was a method of defeating the oppressions of monopoly more forcible, more simple, or more equitable." But the Company responded by deposing the impudent ruler and restoring the status quo ante. "The servants, therefore, for themselves, or for their employers, monopolized every article of trade, foreign and domestick," with the result that "the whole trade of the country was either destroyed, or in shackles" (*Works* 11: 90–94).

Monopoly destroys or oppresses not only merchants but primary producers. The monopolist sets a price at which the producer must sell, and it does not favor the producer (*Works* 11: 100–101). Moreover, under pressure from the manufacturing interest in England, the Company adopted a policy "which tended to destroy, or at least essentially to impair, the whole manufacturing interest of Bengal." The policy discouraged the manufacture of wrought silk and diverted producers and laborers to the winding of raw silk to be shipped to England. The Company ordered this to be done even if it required paying higher prices and higher wages, out of the territorial revenues, for winding raw silk. The consequences could have been foreseen: "Whatsoever, by bounties or immunities, is encouraged out of a Landed revenue, has certainly some tendency to lessen the net amount of that Revenue, and to forward a produce, which does not yield to the gross collection rather than one, that does" (*Works* 11: 107–111). The policy therefore sacrificed the interests of both the Company and Bengal to those of British manufacturers.

Subsequent pages of the Ninth Report detail the ill effects of monopolistic practices in the trade of cloths, opium, salt, and saltpeter, and the ineffectiveness of efforts to correct abuses by orders from Company headquarters in London. The remedy, prescribed at the end of the section on cloths, was to allow natives to partake in the trade "on an equal footing with Europeans." But it might do more harm than good to make a sudden change from monopoly to a trade "established upon sound mercantile principles," which on a later page are called "the unerring standard of the publick market." Therefore, while "the revival of trade in the native hands is of absolute necessity, . . . Your Committee is of opinion, that it will rather be the effect of a regular progressive course of endeavours for that purpose, than of any one regulation, however wisely conceived" (*Works* 11: 139–140, 158).

India had prospered under native governments before the English took over, said Burke in his *Speech on the East India Bill*. The invasions by Arabs, Tartars, and Persians were ferocious, but the conquerors had settled in the country and became part of it. Its prosperity thenceforth was their prosperity: "With many disorders, and with few political checks upon power, nature had still fair play; the sources of acquisition were not dried up; and therefore the trade, the manufactures, and the commerce of the country flourished" (*Works* 4: 38–39).

But putting political power in the hands of the East India Company had corrupted it and changed it "beyond all power of reformation [and] the company, in the sense in which it was formerly understood, has no existence." It is no longer a commercial company earning a profit in trade and paying dividends, but an instrument of exploitation. Men in England buy East India stock, not for dividends, but for the power it gives: "The vote is not to protect the stock, but the stock is bought to acquire the vote; and the end of the vote is to cover and support, against justice, some man of power who has made an obnoxious fortune in India; or to maintain in power those who are actually employing it in the acquisition of such a fortune" (*Works* 4: 105–106).

As Burke had written to Henry Dundas, who headed another committee on Indian affairs, the Company's government in India had been ruinous, even to the Company's own interests. When the Company took over the district of Nagore from the Rajah of Tanjore, it had yielded a revenue of £30,000 a year. But "since it has come into English hands, it has yielded *absolutely nothing* to the Company." Therefore, "Native Government can alone combine the prosperity of the Country with the regularity of payments—and this is not only true of Tanjour and Benares, but of every other mediate or immediate dependency in India" (*Corr.* 5: 68–69). Burke did not mean, P. J. Marshall comments, "that the British should now withdraw from Bengal. . . . Ultimate authority would remain in the hands of the British, but they must use it with the utmost restraint. . . . If the British left well alone, regeneration would come from below" (*W&S* 5: 20).

Burke's belief in freedom of trade arose, not only out of his awareness of its material advantages, but also from fear of the combination of commerce with power. Ten years later, while urging the allies in the war against revolutionary France to forgo their usual preoccupation with their own aggrandizement, and to concentrate on destroying, not France (which must be preserved, *Works* 7: 180), but Jacobinism, he recognized the danger of Britain's self-aggrandizement: "I must fairly say, I dread our *own* power, and our *own* ambition; I dread our being too much dreaded." Even Britain's commercial success made him uneasy:

> We are already in possession of almost all the commerce of the world. Our empire in India is an awful thing. If we should come to be in a condition not only to have all this ascendant in commerce, but to be absolutely able, without the least control, to hold the commerce of all other nations totally dependent upon our good pleasure, we may say that we shall not abuse this astonishing and hitherto unheard-of power. But every other nation will think we shall abuse it. It is impossible but that, sooner or later, this state of things must produce a combination against us which may end in our ruin [*Works* 7: 183–184].

Once again, Burke the capitalist turns out to be Burke the Whig, in whom the fear of arbitrary power is stronger then the lust for gain.

If, however, capitalism means the regulation of commercial exchange relations by a market economy, Burke was certainly a capitalist. In his *Thoughts and Details on Scarcity* he sounded like a capitalist *à outrance*, who was willing to deny public relief to poor workers even in time of famine rather violate the laws of the market. But, although *Thoughts and Details* was the nearest approach to a treatise on political economy that he ever wrote, it was in fact a memorandum to Prime Minister William Pitt in response to a particular situation in a year of bad harvests and hardship for farm laborers. It could therefore be taken as something less than a thoroughly thought-out statement of Burke's economics.

Yet he thought well enough of this memorandum that, according to Walker King and French Laurence, who edited the first complete edition of Burke's *Works* (*Corr.* 9: xx), he "proposed afterwards to recast the same matter in a new shape . . . under the title of 'Letters on Rural Œconomicks, addressed to Mr. Arthur Young'" (*Works* 1: xii–xiii). He did not get beyond a bare beginning of this project, however, because by this time he was a sick and dying man.

But since Burke intended to publish the piece, we must give *Thoughts and Details* closer consideration and compare it with other expressions of his economic views. It was occasioned by "Speenhamland," a locality in Berkshire not far from Burke's estate in Buckinghamshire. 1794 and 1795 were years of bad harvests, in which the wages of farm laborers were falling below the subsistence level. To relieve them, the Justices of the Peace in Speenhamland added a subsidy out of the rates to their wages, proportioned to the size of their families and the price of bread. Fearing that this kind of poor relief might become a national policy, Burke wrote his memorandum to Pitt, arguing against it.

Eric Hobsbawm, who was a Communist, and therefore not prejudiced in favor of capitalism, had this to say about the Speenhamland system:

> What the effects of this spontaneously propagated system of social security were has been much argued about. There is little reason to dissent from the traditional view—that they were disastrous. It meant that *all* local ratepayers subsidized the farmers (and especially the large farmers employing much labour) to the extent that they paid low wages. It pauperized, demoralized and immobilized the labourer, who could hope to be kept just above starvation in his own parish, but nowhere else on earth; and it discriminated sharply

against the single or small-family man. . . . It was an attempt—a last, inefficient, ill-considered and unsuccessful attempt—to maintain a traditional rural order in the face of the market economy [pp. 104–105].

Burke also thought that the Speenhamland system was disastrous, but his objection ran along a different line. He wanted to maintain a traditional order which was already a market economy. He regarded "Speenhamland" as a misguided entrance of government into an area that lay beyond its legitimate powers, and as a violation of the natural laws of commerce, the rights of property, and the freedom of contract that belonged to employers and employees alike. Its effects could only be bad, and hard times did not justify it.

Throughout this memorandum Burke was talking about a governmental subsidy to the wages of agricultural laborers in a season of bad harvests, therefore about a transient situation. Yet he reasoned from premises far broader in their scope. "We, the people," he said, "ought to be made sensible, that it is not in breaking the laws of commerce, which are the laws of nature, and consequently the laws of God" that we can relieve the sufferings He chooses to visit upon us (*Works* 7: 404).

Burke here seems to place the laws of commerce on the same level as the natural moral law. More probably, however, he well knew the difference between the physical laws of nature and the laws of moral obligation, both of which can be called laws of God as the Author and Creator of nature. But the first type of law merely describes the ways in which the physical world does and will act, and the other type prescribes the way in which human beings ought to act, in accordance with their nature and therefore with the will of God (see *Works* 15: 346; *Corr.* 7: 474). A man who gives his wife a playful push may be demonstrating affection, but not if she is standing on the edge of the Grand Canyon or the White Cliffs of Dover, where the law of gravity will pull her to her injury or death. Yet that law does not prohibit building airplanes or space rockets, because gravity is only a force to be overcome. It may never safely be ignored, but it is not to be confused with the moral obligation to preserve human life. In like manner, governments must take the laws of commerce into account in promoting the welfare of the people because of the natural ill consequences that follow from attempting to defy them. But they are not laws of God in the same sense as the moral law that binds governments to serve the common good of their peoples.

The several "laws" according to which the world operates constitute "the nature of things," which men must respect—and Burke pushed that respect very far. He did not subscribe, however, to a mechanistic theory of the universe, according to which men could come to understand its laws so thoroughly that they could predict and control the development of their societies on scientifically ascertainable and uniform principles. In many ways, he believed, they must trust "the nature of things," because they could not fully understand and control it.

This was not a new thought that came to him only in 1795. In 1769 he had written: "Men of sense . . . well know, that in the complicated oeconomy of great kingdoms, and immense revenues, which in a length of time, and by a variety of accidents, have coalesced into a sort of body, an attempt towards a compulsory equality in all circumstances . . . is the most dangerous and chimerical of all enterprises" (*Works* 2: 131–132). In 1777 he wrote: "I am, for one, entirely satisfied, that the inequality, which grows out of the *nature of things* by time, custom, succession, accumulation, permutation, and improvement of property, is much nearer that true equality, which is the foundation of equity and just policy, than any thing which can be contrived by the tricks and devices of human skill" (*Corr.* 3: 403). In his *Letter to the Sheriffs of Bristol,* he referred to "the natural operation of things, which left to themselves, generally fall into their proper order" (*Works* 3: 190).

He took the same view of the evolution of constitutions. "The parts of our constitution," he wrote to a member of the National Assembly of France in 1791,

> have gradually, and almost insensibly, in a long course of time, accommodated themselves to each other, and to their common, as well as to their separate purposes. But this adaptation of contending parts, as it has not been in ours, so it can never be in your's [sic], or in any country, the effect of a single instantaneous regulation, and no sound heads could ever think of doing it in that manner [*Works* 6: 62].

He restated this conception of constitutional development in more general terms in 1796: "The states of the Christian world have grown up to their present magnitude in a great length of time, and by a great variety of accidents. They have been improved to what we see them with greater or less degrees of felicity and skill. Not one of them has been formed upon a regular plan or with any unity of design." Burke did not mean here that the constitutions of states have grown like plants, without the exercise of human reason and choice, but only that they have not developed according to any overall plan "directed to any *peculiar* end, eminently distinguished, and superseding every other" (*Works* 8: 251). Constitutions, when they are not the result of strife, with its victories and defeats, are the product of human practical reason prudently providing for present and foreseen needs.

No Christian state, therefore, has had a planned economy. Nor has it needed one because, Burke says in *Thoughts and Details*, "the benign and wise Disposer of all things . . . obliges men, whether they will nor not, in pursuing their own selfish interests, to connect the general good with their own individual success" (*Works* 7: 384–385). Five years earlier, in his *Reflections*, he had denounced the "enthusiasts" of the French Revolution, who

> do not scruple to avow their opinion, that a state can subsist without any religion better than with one; and that they are able to supply the place of any good which may be in it, by a project of their own—namely, by a sort of education they have imagined, founded in a knowledge of the physical wants of men; progressively carried to an enlightened self-interest, which, when well understood, they tell us, will identify with an interest more enlarged and publick" (*Works* 5: 270).

Now, however, he says that in agricultural labor–employer relations enlightened self-interest is enough because, even if a farmer is "excessively avaricious . . . the more he desires to increase his own gains, the more interested is he in the good condition of those, upon whose labour his gains must principally depend" (*Works* 7: 385).

Burke himself did not advocate paying low wages. In 1771, after he had bought his estate at Beaconsfield, he wrote to his cousin Garrett Nagle in Ireland: "I should not even consider the cheapness of Labour in any particular part [of the country] as a very great advantage. It is something without doubt. But then I have always found, that the Labour of men is nearly in proportion to their pay" (*Corr.* 2: 234). In 1778, answering the objection that admitting certain Irish products duty-free into England would give them an unfair advantage because of low wages in Ireland, Burke is reported as saying in the Commons that "the price of labour rises with the growth of manufacture, and is highest when the manufacture is best, . . . [and] where the price of labour is highest, the manufacturer is able to sell his commodity at the lowest price" (*Parl. Hist.* 19: 1122; but see 25: 366, where at a later date Burke spoke on the other side of the Irish trade issue for partisan political reasons).

Burke's point in *Thoughts and Details* was not that wages should be low, but that they should be settled by private contract between employers and employees, and left "entirely to the persons mutually concerned in the matter contracted for" without interference by government (*Works* 7: 380). He repeated the point shortly before his death in a letter to Arthur Young: "My constant opinion was, and is, that all matters relative to labour ought to be left to the conventions of the parties. That the great danger is in Government intermeddling too much" (*Corr.* 9: 361). That proposition implies that wages must ultimately be set by a market in labour:

> Labour is a commodity like every other, and rises or falls according to the demand. This is in the nature of things; however, the nature of things has provided for their [the laborers'] necessities. Wages have been twice raised in my time, and they bear a full proportion, or even a greater than formerly, to the medium of provision during the last bad cycle of twenty years [*Works* 7: 379].

The labor market has provided, on the average, for the needs of workers and has even produced a rising standard of living for them (*Works* 8: 362–366). The market must be respected even in times of temporary hardship. Since labor is a commodity, it is, "as such, an article of trade [and] subject to all the laws and principles of trade" (*Works* 7: 386). Those laws will operate no matter how government tries to counteract them.

If government forces farm wages up, the demand for labor will diminish or the price of food will rise, to the disadvantage of the laborers (*Works* 7: 380). People in towns want fixed prices for food, but they should not be listened to, because they speak in ignorance of the agricultural industry by which they are fed. Nor would they put up with similar price-fixing on what they themselves manufacture (*Works* 7: 391–392).

The just price of commodities is the market price, which alone can properly adjust supply to demand:

> The balance between consumption and production makes price. The market settles, and alone can settle that price. Market is the meeting and conference of the *consumer* and *producer*, when they mutually discover each other's wants. Nobody, I believe, has observed with any reflexion what market is, without being astonished at the truth, the correctness, the celerity, the general equity, with which the balance of wants is settled.

Those who would destroy that balance by arbitrary regulations "directly lay their *axe* to the root of production itself" (*Works* 7: 398). Government therefore should let the market operate by its own inner laws, for "the moment that government appears at market, all the principles of market will be subverted" (*Works* 7: 401).

Since labor is a commodity whose price is set by the market, wages vary with the demand for labor, not with the needs of the laborer. If demand is high, wages will be high; if it is low, wages will be low. That the laborer cannot subsist on the low wages "is totally beside the question in this way of viewing it. The only question is, what is it [his labor] worth to the buyer?" (*Works* 7: 386).

The laws of the market are analogous to the laws of physics rather than to those of morality, but they determine what is just in wage contracts, because they follow from "the nature of things with which we shall in vain contend" (*Works* 7: 386). It is clear that the only kind of justice that Burke recognizes in economic transactions is commutative justice. Because he respected that type of justice, he told his constituents in Bristol, who wanted to maintain imprisonment for debt, that he disagreed with them, for "it is impossible that any thing should be necessary for commerce, which is incompatible with justice" (*Works* 3: 378). But he would not allow government to be concerned with or try to enforce any conception of distributive justice.

We have already quoted a long passage in *Thoughts and Details* on the proper functions of government. Burke later repeated its content in more concise form in his *Third Letter on a Regicide Peace*: "Let government protect and encourage industry, secure property, repress violence, and discountenance fraud, it is all they have to do. In other respects, the less they meddle in these affairs the better" (*Works* 8: 367). The "most momentous of all meddling on the part of authority," he said in *Thoughts and Details*, was "the meddling with the subsistence of the people" (*Works* 7: 419; cf. *Corr.* 9: 361–362). He had earlier criticized the Papal States, where there was, "as I understand a great deal of meddling of Government in the article of provision; an Evil handed down to them from the antient Roman times, by which as the principal men were obliged to court the Roman Inhabitants of the City, they ruined the Agriculture of Italy" (*Corr.* 6: 256). Similar results may be expected in Great Britain: "A greater and more ruinous mistake cannot be fallen into, than that the trades of agriculture and grazing can be conducted upon any other than the common principles of commerce" (*Works* 7: 392).

Burke was willing to push this argument to the point of denying that government should supply food even in time of famine, and to pose the question: "Is the poor labourer to be abandoned to the flinty heart and griping hand of base self-interest, supported by the sword of law, especially when there is reason to suppose that the very avarice of farmers themselves has concurred with the errours of government to bring famine on the land?" His answer was unhesitating: "Whenever it happens that a man can claim nothing according to the rules of commerce, and the principles of justice, he passes out of that department [justice], and comes within the jurisdiction of mercy." Again, justice for Burke is commutative justice alone, and the magistrate has no right to enter the jurisdiction of mercy, because "his interference [in it] is a violation of the property which it is his office to protect." Aid to famished wage earners is a matter of charity and a Christian duty, but it is beyond the right or obligation of government to perform (*Works* 7: 390–391; cf. *Parl. Hist.* 31: 171–175).

There is an apparent difficulty in reconciling this doctrine with Burke's statement in the *Reflections*: "Government is a contrivance of human wisdom to provide for human wants [i.e., needs]. Men have a right that these wants should be provided for by this wisdom" (*Works* 5: 122–123). Since nourishment is undeniably a human need, one might assume that men have a right to have it provided by government in time of famine. Yet it is not clear that Burke meant that, even in this passage of the *Reflections*.

Two pages before, in a passage already cited above in Chapter 4, he had said: "If civil society be made for the advantage of man, all the advantages for which it is made become his right." He then listed these rights in summary terms. Men have a right to live by the rule of law and to do justice, but the only economic rights that Burke mentions are these: "They have a right to the fruits of their industry; and to the means of making their industry fruitful. They have a right to the acquisitions of their parents." That is to say, they have a right to the property they themselves have earned or have inherited. In the most general terms, "Whatever each man can separately do, without trespassing upon others, he has a right to do for himself; and he has a right to a fair portion of all which society, with all its combinations of skill and force, can do in his favour." The "fair portion" may sound like distributionism or even socialism, but in fact it means little more than this: "In this partnership all men have equal rights; but not to equal things. He that has but five shillings in the partnership has as good a right to it, as he that has five hundred pounds has to his larger proportion. But he has not a right to an equal dividend in the product of the joint stock" (*Works* 5: 120–121).

The labor of the working class is their contribution to society's product, and their wages are their dividend: "As to the common people their stock is in their persons and in their earnings" (*Works* 8: 362). They have a right to work and to keep what they earn. Government owes them, as it owes all its productive members, an order of peace, justice, and stability in which they can use their persons and their energies. Burke never tired of insisting that those whose only property was their labor must maintain themselves by that labor.

In his later years he refused to admit that laboring men in good health were, in the proper sense of the word, poor:

> Hitherto the name of poor (in the sense in which it is used to excite compassion) has not been used for those who can, but for those

who cannot labour—for the sick and infirm; for orphan infancy; for languishing and decrepid age: but when we affect to pity as poor, those who must labour or the world cannot exist, we are trifling with the condition of mankind. It is the common doom of man that he must eat his bread by the sweat of his brow [*Works* 8: 368].

This, then, the laborers must be taught: "Patience, labour, sobriety, frugality, and religion should be recommended to them; all the rest is downright fraud" (*Works* 7: 377; cf. 6: 12, *Corr.* 9: 155). We must bear in mind that in *Thoughts and Details* and other writings of the 1790s, Burke addresses himself to the situation in Great Britain, and principally in England, "the most flourishing [country] that exists" (*Corr.* 7: 85), where "the agriculture of the kingdom [is] the first of all its concerns, and the foundation of all its prosperity." In England the landowning or large landrenting class and the laboring class form one people; the interests of the farmer and the laborer "are always the same, and it is absolutely impossible that their free contracts can be onerous to either party" (*Works* 7: 381, 383). We must also remember that he wrote in a season of "comparative scarcity," in which no one, to his knowledge, had died of hunger, and "we have seen no traces of those dreadful exterminating epidemicks, which in consequence of scanty and unwholesome food, in former times, not unfrequently wasted whole nations" (*Works* 7: 415–416). In such a society and at such a time Burke found it possible to believe that the care of unemployed or underpaid farm laborers could be left to private charity.

Nor was he entirely unwilling to have government take some action to get food to the people. In the same month in which he sent *Thoughts and Details* to William Pitt, he praised a committee report which recommended to the House of Commons that the importation of corn from abroad be encouraged by bounties—but government should go no further. A month later he wrote to Henry Dundas strongly supporting the government's efforts in that direction and urging that ships be sent to Africa and Latin America for grain, as well as to Europe and Canada (*Corr.* 8: 344, 354).

One may wonder whether Burke should have repeated the advice he gave in *Thoughts and Details* if he had been born several decades later and had lived to see the Irish famine of 1845–1849. The obvious answer is that he did not live to see that famine, and we do not know what he would have said. The question is worth speculating about, however, even though it has no firm answer.

According to Cecil Woodham-Smith in her book *The Great Hunger*, the Census Commissioners calculated after the famine that "a loss of at least 2 million persons had taken place in Ireland," out of a population of 8 or 9 million. She comments:

> It has frequently been declared, that the parsimony of the British Government during the famine was the main cause of the sufferings of the people, and parsimony was certainly carried to remarkable lengths; but obtuseness, short-sightedness and ignorance probably contributed more. . . . Much of the obtuseness sprang from the fanatical faith of mid-nineteenth-century British politicians in the economic doctrine of laissez-faire, no interference by government, no meddling with the operation of natural causes. Adherence to laissez-faire was carried to such a length that in the midst of one of the major famines of history, the government was perpetually nervous of being too good to Ireland and of corrupting the Irish people by kindness, and so stifling the virtues of self reliance and industry [pp. 407–408].

That passage sounds uncomfortably like the sort of thing Burke was writing in the 1790s. In his last years, though it was not his typical style, he was capable of being, or at least of seeming to be, meanspirited in his attitude toward the poor. So, for example, in 1796 he objected to exempting them from an increased tax on tea: "Why did not Pitt tax the lower teas—a small Duty would not have been felt and surely Tea Drinking, tho' it would be idle to restrain it is not an object of direct encouragement amongst the lower orders of the people." In a letter to another correspondent he asks: "In the name of God what is the meaning of this project of Mr. Pitt concerning the further releif of the Poor. What releif do they want except that which it will be difficult indeed to give to make them more frugal or more industrious" (*Corr.* 9: 152–153, 155).

Nonetheless, if Burke had spoken of the Irish famine in the same terms as *Thoughts and Details,* it would have been a manifestation of the rigid, doctrinaire ideological thinking that he spent his life denouncing. It would not have been characteristic of the practical, prudential cast of his mind, which was always aware both of principles and of the need to apply them to different historical circumstances. "For you know," as he had written to Sir Hercules Langrishe less than four years earlier, "that the decisions of prudence (contrary to the system of the insane reasoners) differ from those of judicature; and that almost all the former are determined on the more or the less, the earlier or the later, and on a balance of advantage and inconvenience, of good and evil" (*Works* 6: 309). Even in *Thoughts and Details* itself, when he drew the distinction between what the state should regulate and what it should leave to private discretion, he said: "Nothing, certainly, can be laid down on the subject that will not admit of exceptions, many permanent, some occasional" (*Works* 7: 416). We should not lightly assume, then, that Burke would have been an insane reasoner in the face of a major famine.

Needless to say, we can prove nothing, one way or the other, about what Burke would have said during the Irish famine had he lived to see it. But what he might have said can perhaps be inferred—though one cannot pretend to any assurance about it—from a passage in his *Speech on the Nabob of Arcot's Debts* in 1785. Having described how the servants of the East India Company had by their injustices provoked an Indian chieftain called Hyder Ali, and how he in return had invaded and utterly laid waste that part of the Carnatic that belonged to the Company (though nominally to the Nabob), Burke reported in amazement that the only problem the Company and the British government could then see was how to collect a revenue from the Carnatic. This, said Burke, was madness: "In order that the people, after a long period of vexation and plunder, may be in a condition to maintain government, government must begin by maintaining them.—Here the road to oeconomy lies not through receipt, but through expence; and in that country nature has given no short cut to your object" (*Works* 4: 264; and see 259–268).

The greatest damage Hyder Ali had done was to destroy the countless reservoirs on which the Carnatic depended for the irrigation of its rice fields. Government's first duty, therefore, was to rebuild them. It would "require a serious attention and much cost to re-establish them, as the means of present subsistence to the people, and of future revenue to the state," but that is what "a virtuous and enlightened ministry" would do (*Works* 4: 267). Burke's faith in laissez-faire, it would seem, was less than fanatical, and recognized that there were situations in which government interference was not only permissible but necessary.

Yet his bias against state action to relieve the poor, and in favor of relief by private charity is obvious and undeniable. He was personally a charitable man. Henry Reed, in a recent history of Beaconsfield, says of Burke:

> To him political principles must be effective. He carried this into effect locally in Beaconsfield with his concern for the community and, particularly, the poor. Several plans for bettering the condition of the poor in the neighbourhood originated at his suggestion. He recommended institutions for mutual support in cases of age and infirmity in the nature of benefit societies. Of one of these he became a patron and a member, subscribing to it as a poor man would do, attending its meetings and visiting those who claimed relief. In 1795 [the year in which he wrote his apparently heartless *Thoughts and Details on Scarcity*] and 1796, when the price of corn was high, Burke had a windmill in the park at Butler's Court grind corn for the poor and the bread made at his own house to sell to the poor at a reduced price ["Edmund Burke: Statesman and Philanthropist," p. 35].

Both as a Member of Parliament and in his private capacity Burke often used his influence and his own money to protect the poor, to mitigate punishments, and to relieve people in need. A few examples must suffice to illustrate the kind of things he did throughout his career.

In the debate on the bill to provide a government for Quebec under British rule, he is reported as saying that, "as to the Noblesse hating juries because it trusted their property to their inferiors, it was a principal reason why he would give the Canadians a jury in order to protect their property from the arbitrary proceedings of the Noblesse, who, in all countries, always wished to have the poor under their control" (*W&S* 2: 473). He praised his original parliamentary patron, Lord Verney, because no other man in England "has been so indulgent humane, and moderate a Landlord on an Estate of considerable Extent, or a greater protector to all the poor within his Reach" (*Corr.* 3: 38). According to Carl Cone, Burke himself was "humane and generous" in his treatment of his own tenants, and "not severe in pressing [them] for their rents" (Cone 1: 139). In a letter to the agent for the Irish estate of which he was the legal owner, Burke complains about the tenants being "very much behind-hand" in paying their rents, but adds: "If they were straitened by any accident, it were but reasonable I should bear part of the loss; but this I do not conceive to be the case; and I am satisfied that they have their farms at a moderate price" (*Corr.* 4: 93).

His correspondence is peppered with requests to help people in need. Thus he writes to the wife of a local Justice of the Peace (with whom Burke was not on good terms), asking her to intercede with her husband so that a poor widow might get her license to run a pub renewed (*Corr.* 4: 21). He replies to a convicted swindler who asked for a mitigation of his sentence, saying he agreed "that the punishment is greater than the offense deserves," and intercedes successfully for him (*Corr.* 4: 134–135). In 1780, two men were sentenced to stand in the pillory on a charge of sodomy, and one of them died as a result of the brutality of the mob. Burke then wrote to the Attorney-General asking that the pillory part of the sentence imposed on two other convicted criminals be remitted, lest they suffer a similar fate at the hands of the mob (*Corr.* 4: 230–231). After the anti-Catholic riots aroused by Lord George Gordon, which were aimed at Burke himself as much as at anyone because of his support of a Catholic Relief Bill, Burke wrote to the Attorney-General, pleading for the executions of convicted rioters to be suspended until emotions died down, and possibly be reduced in number, "especially as they [the offenders] are low in condition, and the managers [of the riots] have had the wicked address not to expose themselves" (*Corr.* 4: 255–256). These and many others cases were ones in which the free market could not function and therefore did not need to be protected from government.

During the French Revolution Burke labored mightily for the relief of French émigrés and, in particular, of refugee Catholic clergy, seeking government as well as private aid for them. A committee he belonged to was instrumental in getting a royal property at Winchester as a residence for these exiled clergy. By the summer of 1793, about 600 priests were housed in the buildings there. In 1795, the government decided to move the priests elsewhere in order to use the buildings as military barracks. Burke wrote to protest this decision, saying: "Charity has its own justice, and its own Rules, as well as any other part of human intercourse; and if I give a Cottage to a poor man to live in I have no more Right to turn him out of it than if I had let it to him for Rent. There is nothing in these things voluntary but the beginning of them" (*Corr.* 8: 265–266).

We must recall that in Burke's time Europe, including England, was emerging from an age in which it was assumed that the Church was a main provider for the needs of the destitute. We find at least hints of this attitude in Burke's writings. In his *Reflections on the Revolution in France* he says that in England the estate of the Church is identified "with the mass of *private property*, of which the state is not the proprietor . . . but the guardian only and the regulator." The English have done this "from their opinion of a duty to make a sure provision for the consolation of the feeble and the instruction of the ignorant" (*Works* 5: 191). In a letter to the Duchesse de Biron in 1791, he excoriated the French nobles who had supported the confiscation of the estates of the Church which were, among other things, "a Provision for the Poor" (*Corr.* 6: 235).

Despite his harsh language in the 1790s, Burke was not simply indifferent to the lot of the poor. His objection to Speenhamland was to government intervention to relieve that lot when it had not reached the stage of pauperism. But he ignored the phenomenon of unemployment and underpaid employment which was to become acute as a result of the Industrial Revolution. In the prosperous England of 1795 he did not see temporary hardship as a problem calling for government action. Society, rather than government, should undertake the task of relieving the sufferings of those who temporarily lacked the means of subsistence. He was confident that private charity was adequate to the task and could perform it with less danger to the country's prosperity and liberty than government could. In particular, he thought that government subsidy of wages was a dangerous infringement of freedom of contract and the rights of property, and an unjustified interference with that best setter of prices, the market.

Hobsbawm was quoted above as saying that Speenhamland was "a last, inefficient, ill-considered and unsuccessful attempt . . . to maintain a traditional rural order in the face of the market economy." Burke's reply to Speenhamland may be seen as an unqualified defense of the market economy, but in the framework of a traditional rural order in which a paternalistic aristocracy would perform the welfare function that the Industrial Revolution would eventually thrust upon government. Although that revolution started during Burke's political lifetime, he did not see that it spelled the end of the traditional rural order. He did see, or thought he saw, that if government assumed the welfare function, England would start down the road that France was already traveling, toward a Jacobin despotism.

Whether Burke was realistic in his assumption about the ability of the traditional order to provide for its own people is open to question. He was, in any case, a man of his age. Writing forty years later in *Democracy in America*, Alexis de Tocqueville remarked:

> The territorial aristocracy of past ages was obliged by law, or thought itself obliged by custom, to come to the help of its servants and relieve their distress. But the industrial aristocracy of our day, when it has impoverished and brutalized the men it uses, abandons them in time of crisis to public charity to feed them. . . . I think that, generally speaking, the manufacturing aristocracy which we see rising before our eyes is one of the hardest that have appeared on earth [vol. 2, part 2, at end, pp. 557–558].

Burke's realism or unrealism is a distinct question, however, from whether he was consistent with his own conception of the nature of society in adopting the view of the labor market and its sheer contractualism in employer–employee relations that he so vigorously advocated in *Thoughts and Details*. Consider, for example, the oft-quoted passage in *Reflections* in which he says:

> Society is indeed a contract. Subordinate contracts for objects of mere occasional interest may be dissolved at pleasure—but the state ought not to be considered as nothing better than a partnership agreement in a trade of pepper and coffee, callico or tabacco, or some other such low concern, to be taken up for a little temporary interest, and to be dissolved by the fancy of the parties. It is to be looked on with other reverence, because it is not a partnership in things subservient only to the gross animal existence of a temporary and perishable nature. It is a partnership in all science; a partnership in all art; a partnership in every virtue, and in all perfection. As the ends of such a partnership cannot be obtained in many generations, it becomes a partnership not only between those who are

living, but between those who are living, those who are dead, and those who are to be born. Each contract of each particular state is but a clause in the great primaeval contract of eternal society, linking the lower with the higher natures, connecting the visible and invisible world, according to a fixed compact sanctioned by the inviolable oath which holds all physical and all moral natures, each in their appointed place [*Works* 5: 183–184].

This passage describes society as contractual to the extent that it is ultimately founded on consent. But it is not a consent that is revocable at pleasure. Burke conceives society in Aristotelian terms as an association in the comprehensive ends of human life on its highest plane: all science, all art, every virtue and all perfection. He is speaking here of the tacit and rightly presumed contract of a society that goes on from generation to generation, and unites the living, the dead, and those yet to be born in a single binding tradition. As such it becomes a contingent but lasting part of the moral order of the created universe that is willed by the Creator. Such a society is a community because it has a common good and a government devoted to protecting and fostering that common good—such a community as Burke believed existed in England but not in Ireland.

This comprehensive order of society is nonetheless compatible with, and indeed depends for the satisfaction of its material needs on, subordinate contracts about such matters as trade in pepper and coffee, calico or tobacco. These contracts are revocable at the will of the contracting parties because they deal with things taken up for a little temporary interest. But Burke does not reduce all the relationships that make up human life to commercial transactions. While he believes that the self-interest of the parties is sufficient in commercial exchanges, he does not propose a narrow self-interest as an organizing principle for all of life. Most fundamentally, the bond that is the contract of a society is modeled on the order of the universe, not on the contracts of the marketplace.

Burke does, however, categorize wage contracts as mere commercial contracts. We can easily understand why he does this as we reflect that when one hires a plumber to repair the kitchen sink, one does not make him a member of the family or assume responsibility for supporting him when he finds work scarce. For Burke, that was sufficient: all that society acting through government owed to its members in respect to their livelihood was the protection of property, enforcement of contracts, and punishment of crimes. The country would flourish economically as a result, and society acting through private charity would take care of the temporary needs of those whose only property was their persons and their labor.

He did not face the question whether society can assume that the otherwise propertyless consent to this arrangement. Yet he had said in his *Tracts Relative to the Laws Against Popery in Ireland*—and his subsequent writings on Ireland show that he never retracted this opinion—that the validity of laws depends on the consent of the people: "For in all forms of Government the people is the true Legislator; and whether the immediate and instrumental cause of the Law be a single person, or many, the remote and efficient cause is the consent of the people, either actual and implied; and such consent is absolutely essential to its validity." This is not an argument for democracy; it applies with equal force to aristocracy and monarchy:

> The people, indeed, are presumed to consent to whatever the Legislature ordains for their benefit; and they are to acquiesce in it, though they do not clearly see into the propriety of the means, by which they are conducted to that desirable end. This they owe as an act of homage and just deference to a reason, which the necessity of Government has made superiour to their own. But though the means, and indeed the nature of a public advantage, may not always be evident to the understanding of the subject, no one is so gross and stupid as not to distinguish between a benefit and an injury. No one can imagine then, an exclusion of a great body of men, not from favours, privileges and trusts, but from the common advantages of society, can ever be a thing intended for their good, or can ever be ratified by any implied consent of theirs [*Works* 9: 348–349].

Burke saw clearly that this argument invalidated the penal laws against Catholics in Ireland. Even in 1795, when the penal laws had been to a large extent repealed, he wrote to a member of the Irish Parliament:

> I cannot hesitate to lay before you my opinion, that whilst any kind of discouragements and disqualifications remain on the Catholicks, an handle will be made by a factious power utterly to defeat the Benefits of any civil rights they may apparently possess. . . . I re-

member but one period in my whole life . . . in which they have been more harshly and more contumeliously treated than since the last partial enlargement—and thus I am convinced it will be . . . whilst they are considered as no better than half Citizens. If they are kept such for any length of time they will be made whole Jacobins. Against this Grand and dreadful Evil of our time . . . I do not know any solid Security whatsoever: But I am quite certain, that what will come nearest to it, is to interest as many as you can in the present order of things, religiously, civilly, politically—by all the ties and principles by which mankind are held [*Corr.* 8: 132; *Works* 9: 406–407].

Burke did not see that an analogous argument might apply to England, and that the landless laborers of that country, too, might reasonably ask why they should consent to a political order that did so little for them in hours of need and over which they had no control. In the following century Disraeli, who was to become a Conservative Prime Minister (and who incidentally got the title, Earl of Beaconsfield, that Burke had chosen for himself if he were made a peer), saw that question and expressed it in *Sybil; or The Two Nations*.

7
The French Revolution

BURKE'S CRITICISM OF THE French Revolution was voluminous and unsparing. Here, however, it will be enough to explain the criticism insofar as it throws light upon his conception of the role of property in society. The purpose will not be to pass judgment on the accuracy of his assessment of the Revolution, but only to present the main themes of Burke's indictment of it.

He had, in a sense, seen it coming, though not in the details of the form it took, when he wrote in 1769 concerning the situation that then existed in France:

> Indeed under such extreme straitness and distraction labours the whole body of their finances, so far does their charge outrun their supply in every particular, that no man, I believe, who has considered their affairs with any degree of attention or information, but must hourly look for some extraordinary convulsion in that whole system; the effect of which on France, and even on all Europe, it is difficult to conjecture [*Works* 2: 86].

When the Revolution came twenty years later, Burke was not quick to make up his mind about it, but had done so by the end of 1789. He was provoked into taking a public stand on it when, in January 1790, he read Dr. Richard Price's sermon in praise of the Revolution, and began making notes for what was published in the following November as *Reflections on the Revolution in France*. In the meantime, in February, Charles James Fox's speech in the Commons in praise of the Revolution had aroused Burke to a reply openly condemning it. He published it later in that month as the *Substance of Mr. Burke's Speech in the Debate on the Army Estimates* (*Works* 5: 3–24). By the end of his life Burke sarcastically claimed: "I confess, I was always blind enough to regard the French Revolution, in the act, and much more in the example, as one of the greatest calamities that had ever fallen upon mankind" (*Works* 9: 31).

In the course of viewing the French Revolution, Burke's judgment on the French monarchy shifted. In the *Speech on the Army Estimates* he said that in the preceding century, Louis XIV had established "a perfect despotism" in France, which was "nothing better than a painted and gilded tyranny," and that "the same character of despotism insinuated itself into every court of Europe." (Today, however, he said the danger from the example of France was that of being led to imitate a "tyrannical democracy" [*Works* 5: 8–9]). By 1794, if we can trust the *Parliamentary History*'s report of a speech he gave in the Commons, Burke thought better of the monarchy in France:

> France must pass through many severe trials, must swallow many a bitter pill, before she could be restored to that happy despotism under which he once saw her flourish. That mild, temperate, chastised government which they experienced under the monarchy, he was afraid, would be very long before it would return; if indeed it were probable that it would ever return again [31: 378–379].

In 1796 he went so far as to claim that, not only pre-revolutionary France, but "the states of the Christian world" were in many ways free countries:

> In all these old countries the state has been made to the people, and not the people conformed to the state. Every state has pursued, not only every sort of social advantage, but it has cultivated the welfare of every individual. His wants, his wishes, even his tastes have been consulted. This comprehensive scheme, virtually produced a degree of personal liberty in forms the most adverse to it. That liberty was found, under monarchies stiled absolute, in a degree unknown to the ancient commonwealths [*Works* 8: 251].

Yet Burke did not propose absolute monarchy as an ideal or deny that it had needed reform in France. On the contrary, he argued that monarchy, "when reformed and balanced, for a great country, . . . is the best of all governments" (*Works* 6: 129). Louis XVI had tried to give his country such a monarchy when he convened the Estates-General in 1789 and "called together the states of his kingdom, to reform abuses, to establish a free government, and to strengthen his throne." If he must be blamed for sinning against his people, blame him for attempting "to give them a free constitution" (*Works* 6: 22–23; cf. *Corr.* 6: 399–400).

When he convened the Estates-General, his plan was admirable—"nothing better could be imagined"—but its execution was rash and without proper preparation, and opened the way for the seizure of power by the Third Estate (*Works* 6: 54–57). The French ended with a bad constitution "when they were absolutely in possession of a good one . . . the day the states met in separate orders." Their mistake was to merge the three orders of nobles, clergy, and commoners into one, by doing which they "destroyed all the balances and counterpoises which serve to fix the state" (*Works* 5: 13).

Burke did not advocate that the French or any other people should slavishly copy the British constitution. Rather, since the French had a constitution comprising a monarchy and the three estates, and thus based on principles similar to those of the British constitution, they should have developed those principles, as the British had done, "conforming them to the state and exigencies of the time, and the condition of property" in their country (*Works* 6: 58). Instead, however, they rejected the old constitution which Louis XVI had tried to revive, and started down the road to an uncontrolled revolution.

If Burke did not advocate slavish imitation of the British constitution, neither did he suggest a simple return to the French monarchy as it had been before the calling of the Estates-General. France, he believed, must be a monarchy, but a reformed one. In 1791, he wrote to a French émigré correspondent:

> My poor opinion is that you mean to establish what you call 'L'ancien Regime', If any one means that system of Court Intrigue miscalled a Government as it stood, at Versailles before the present confusions as the thing to be establishd, that I beleive will be found absolutely impossible. . . . If it were even possible to lay things down exactly as they stood, before the series of experimental politicks began, I am quite sure that they could not long continue in that situation. In one Sense of L'Ancien Regime I am clear that nothing else can reasonably be done. France to be anything must be a Monarchy; and a very strong Monarchy too [*Corr.* 6: 479–480].

But reform of the monarchy did not require the French Revolution. That the latter had done some good, Burke was willing to grant, but it did not follow "that the same things could not have been accomplished without producing such a revolution" (*Works* 5: 435).

The French Revolution was to Burke "a subject of awful meditation," the first "*complete* revolution" in history, one that "extended even to the constitution of the mind of man" (*Works* 8: 5). It was a total revolution that aimed at changing society in all its basic aspects: property, money, social structure, law, government, religion, and morals. It could not be a partial and purely political revolution, as the Revolution of 1688 in Great Britain had been, which changed only the person of the monarch, with the least possible deviation from the line of succession. The French Revolution was an attack on French society that could not stop short of its radical transformation, because all the fundamental features of society were united in a single, compact, corporate whole, to change one of which meant changing all.

First was the attack on property. In his *Speech on the Army Estimates*, Burke said that after the Third Estate had forced the other estates of the realm to merge with it into one National Assembly, and had thereby "destroyed all the balances and counterpoises" of the state, its members next "laid the axe to the root of all property, and consequently of all national prosperity, by the principles they established, and the example they set, in confiscating all the possessions of the church" (*Works* 5: 13–14). This confiscation, said Burke in *Reflections*, could not be regarded as directed only at the Church. It was an "outrage on all the rights of property" (*Works* 5: 201). In fact, from the beginning of the Revolution, and even before the National Assembly took action to legalize what the peasants were doing, the latter were rising up and seizing lands from the landlords. In his *Speech on the Army Estimates* Burke called the attention of the Commons to what was happening to lay property in France:

> He wished the house to consider how the members would like to have their mansions pulled down and pillaged, their persons abused, insulted, and destroyed, their title deeds brought out and burned before their faces and themselves and their families driven to seek refuge in every nation throughout Europe, for no other reason than this; that without any fault of theirs, they were born gentlemen, and men of property, and were suspected of a desire to preserve their consideration and their estates [*Works* 5: 16].

The confiscation of the Church's property could not be justified by the alleged necessity of paying those who had lent money to the state. The men of the National Assembly should have known that "it is to the property of the citizen, and not to the demands of the creditor of the state, that the first and original faith of civil society is pledged" (*Works* 5: 201–202; cf. 283). Nor could they justify expropriating the Church by arguing that its property really belonged to the state: "They say that ecclesiaticks are fictitious persons, creatures of the state whom at pleasure they may destroy, and of course limit and modify in every particular; that the goods they possess are not properly theirs, but belong to the state which created the fiction" (*Works* 5: 200). But this argument threatened all property of every kind in every country:

> It is not the confiscation of our church property from this example in France that I dread, though I think this would be no trifling evil. The great source of my solicitude is, lest it should ever be considered in England as the policy of a state to seek a resource in confiscations of any kind; or that any one description of citizens should be brought to regard any of the others as their proper prey [*Works* 5: 280].

The attack on the property of the Church, therefore, opens the way to an attack on all property and on civil society as such:

> People who . . . could endure even to hear of a maxim that the goods of any one Citizen possessed by a long acknowledged legal title belong to the State, and that those who assume the exercise of sovereign Authority are free to take it from him and to make such a distribution of it as they please, such a People . . . despise the very foundation of social Union [*Corr.* 6: 108].

A people forms itself into a civil society in order to protect its liberty and its property, not to surrender them to a government.

The expropriation of Church lands was also a devaluation of money, because the substitution of the assignats for metallic money was part of the confiscatory scheme: "So that this legislative assembly of a free nation sits, not for the security, but for the destruction of property, and not of property only, but of every rule and maxim which can give it stability, and of those instruments [money] which can alone give it circulation" (*Works* 5: 278). It was all very well for the members of the National Assembly to make speeches declaring that there was no difference between metallic money and the assignats. No one believed it, and the government began to experience difficulties with cash flow as people paid it in devalued paper money (*Works* 5: 425–427).

The Revolution's assault on property, and in particular on landed property, was of necessity and by design an effort to overthrow the society and government founded on that kind of property. Revolutionary France's war on its neighbors, said Burke in his *Third Letter on a Regicide Peace*, "is, above all others, (of which we have heard or read) a war against landed property. That description of property is in its nature the firm base of every stable government" (*Works* 8: 400). The destruction of property and the leveling of society went together in the minds of the revolutionists, "whose object it was . . . to level all ranks, orders, and distinctions in the state; and utterly to destroy property" (*Works* 6: 127). They wanted "to oppress, degrade, impoverish, confiscate and extinguish the original gentlemen, and landed property of a whole nation" (*Works* 6: 4).

More than monarchy, the object of their enmity was the intermediate orders of the nobility and gentry, on which the monarchy necessarily depended. In Burke's mind, property and the social and political order were one, and could not be separated:

> I hope no one can be so very blind as to imagine that monarchy can be acknowledged and supported in France upon any other basis than that of its property, *corporate and individual*, or that it can enjoy a moment's permanence or security upon any scheme of things, which sets aside all the antient corporate capacities and distinctions of the kingdom, and subverts the whole fabrick of its antient laws and usages, political, civil and religious, to introduce a system founded on the supposed *rights of man, and the absolute equality of the human race* [*Works* 7: 129].

Acceptance of the revolutionary political philosophy would destroy the continuity not only of the government: "The whole chain and continuity of the commonwealth would be broken. No one generation could link with the other. Men would become little better than the flies of a summer" (*Works* 5: 181; cf. *Corr.* 6: 173).

In France, revolutionary ideology had already removed the possibility of government by the country's natural governing class. Burke had expressed his fears on this point as early as September 1789 in a letter to William Windham: "I should doubt, whether in the End France is susceptible of the Democracy that is the Spirit, and in a good measure too, the form, of the constitution they have in hand: It is except the Idea of the Crowns being hereditary much more truly democratical than that of North America" (*Corr.* 6: 25). In his *Reflections* Burke claimed to have noticed from the beginning that the deputies of the Third Estate in the Estates-General were equal in number to the other two orders together. In itself, that was not very important until the three orders were merged into one. When that happened, "a very small desertion from either of the other two orders must throw the power of both into the hands of the third. In fact, the whole power of the state was soon resolved into that body" (*Works* 5: 92).

The majority of the deputies of the Third Estate were lawyers, not the leading and distinguished lights of the law, but "inferiour, unlearned, mechanical, merely instrumental members of the profession." They were joined by minor merchants, general practitioners of medicine, dealers in stocks and bonds, and "men of other descriptions, from whom as little knowledge of or attention to the interests of a great state was to be expected." Among them there was "scarcely to be perceived the slightest traces of what we call the natural landed interest of the country" (*Works* 5: 92–96). Such, too, was the government of France under the National Assembly: "The assembly has not fifty men in it . . . who are possessed of an hundred pound a year in any description of property whatsoever" (*Corr.* 7: 61). But that does not make it a government of the poor. "It affects to be a pure democracy," said Burke, "though I think it in a direct train of becoming shortly a mischievous and ignoble oligarchy" (*Works* 5: 230).

Such men were not capable of governing their country well, but, as Burke came to see more and more clearly, they could govern it with enormous energy and zeal. One of the objects of their zeal was the extirpation of Christianity, which Burke believed was the common religion of Europe, divided only by denominational differences which to him were not substantial, and certainly not worth quarreling about in the face of a massive assault on religion as such.

This anti-religious zeal he attributed primarily to the philosophes of the Enlightenment:

> In the Revolution of France two sorts of men were principally concerned in giving a character and determination to its pursuits; the

philosophers and the politicians. They took different ways, but they met in the same end. The philosophers had one predominant object, which they pursued with a fanatical fury, that is, the utter extirpation of religion. To that every question of empire was subordinate. . . .

They who have made but superficial studies in the natural history of the human mind, have been taught to look on religious opinions as the only cause of enthusiastick zeal, and sectarian propagation. But there is no doctrine whatever, on which men can warm, that is not capable of the very same effect. The social nature of man impels him to propagate his principles, as much as physical impulses urge him to propagate his kind. The passions give zeal and vehemence. The understanding bestows design and system. The whole man moves under the discipline of his opinions [*Works* 8: 236–237].

Burke wrote those words in 1796, when he was urging the necessity of keeping up a war for the extirpation of Jacobinism. But from 1790 onward, he had seen the Revolution's attack on Christianity as inherent in its intention radically to reform European civilization. By the French Revolution, he wrote to Lord Fitzwilliam, "the very being and principle of the Christian Religion in every Nation, the existence of Monarchy in every state in the world, and the whole body of the Laws, institutions, manners and morals, as well as the very groundwork of the publick Law, which held all States, as well as all Societies together are attacked at once." The French victims of the Revolution are "those who suffer for their fidelity to the Christian religion, which we have in common, for their attachment to their Lawful and benign Sovereign, and to the antient Laws, orders, and institutions of their Country, *substantially*, as well as their religion, the same as ours" (*Corr.* 7: 232; cf. 6: 103; *Works* 7: 174–175, 9: 433).

In 1792 Burke wrote to his son, who was then in Ireland working for the Catholic cause, that "there should be a reconciliation between the Catholics and Protestants in Ireland." Cunning efforts to bribe the Catholic clergy by giving them some share in the establishment of the Church, however, would only lead to the destruction of both religions, and therefore to the destruction of all religion; "and when that is destroyed, nothing can be saved, or is worth saving" (*Corr.* 7: 298).

In another letter to his son, however, written probably in the same month as the preceding one, he took a more political view of the Established Church in England and Ireland:

> It is a great link towards holding fast the connexion of Religion with the State; and for keeping these two Islands, in their present critical independence of Constitution, in a close connexion of *opinion* and *affection*. I wish it well, as the Religion of the greater number of the primary land proprietors of the Kingdom, with whom all Establishments of Church and State, for strong political reasons, ought in my opinion to be firmly connected. I wish it well, because it is more closely combined than any other of the Church systems with the *Crown*, which is the stay of the mixed Constitution; because it is, as things now stand, the sole connecting *political* principle between the Constitutions of the two independent Kingdoms. I have another, and infinitely a stronger, reason for wishing it well; it is, that in the present time I consider it as one of the main pillars of the Christian Religion itself. The body and substance of every Religion I regard much more than any of the forms and dogmas of the particular sects [*Works* 9: 436–437].

Burke's opinion of the French Church was not much different. In his *Remarks on the Policy of the Allies* he referred to "the king of France, to whom as the protector and governor, and in substance the head of the Gallican church, the nomination to the bishopricks belonged." But, he added, "the catholick religion, which is fundamentally the religion of France, must go with the monarchy of France," and without it the monarchy cannot survive (*Works* 7: 173, 176). He also applauded the royal policy of staffing the French episcopate with noblemen. As he wrote to the Archbishop of Aix:

> One thing I see distinctly, because the Bishops of France have proved it by their example; and that is, that they have made known to all the orders and all the classes of citizens, the advantages which even religion can derive from the alliance of its own proper dignity with the character which illustrious birth and the sentiment of honour gives to man.
>
> It is with good reason that in France, the Noblesse should be proud of the Clergy, and the Clergy of the Noblesse, although those two classes be for the present condemned to passive courage, which gives so much glory to the one and the other [*Corr.* 6: 294; cf. *Works* 5: 206].

Whether this identification of the Church with the royalist and aristocratic cause benefited religion was to be the subject of bitter disputes in France for more than a century to come, but Burke had no doubt about it. It was not, however, that he regarded Christianity as an instrument of politics (on which point see Canavan, *Prescription and Providence*, chap. 3), but that he conceived of Christian societies as single and, to use a somewhat misleading term, organic wholes, living on some necessarily denominational form of the common Christian religion of Europe.

Finally, Burke saw in the Revolution a rejection of Christian morality. Perhaps the most succinct expression of his thought on this matter is found in a letter he wrote in 1791 to the Chevalier de Rivarol, an émigré who had made some "enlightened" remarks on religious life in a letter to Burke. In a lengthy reply Burke said:

> I have observed that the [Parisian] Philosophers in order to insinuate their polluted Atheism into young minds, systematically flatter all their passions natural and unnatural. They explode or render odious or contemptible that class of virtues which restrain the appetite. These are at least nine out of ten of the virtues. In the place of all these they substitute a virtue which they call humanity or benevolence. By these means, their morality has no idea in it of restraint, or indeed of a distinct settled principle of any kind [*Corr.* 6: 270].

In the same year, in his *Letter to a Member of the National Assembly*, Burke said that this philosophy was visible in the Revolution's "scheme of educating the rising generation, the principles which they intend to instil, and the sympathies which they wish to form in the mind." Their policy would corrupt the youth of France:

> Nothing ought to be more weighed than the nature of books recommended by public authority. So recommended, they soon form the character of the age. Uncertain indeed is the efficacy, limited indeed is the extent of a virtuous institution. But if education takes in *vice* as any part of its system, there is no doubt but that it will operate with abundant energy, and to an extent indefinite [*Works* 6: 29].

The chief malignant influence on the minds of the members of the National Assembly is Rousseau: "Him they study; him they meditate; him they turn over in all the time they can spare from the laborious mischief of the day, or the debauches of the night." His is the debased morality they mean to inculcate in the young:

"Rousseau is a moralist, or he is nothing. It is impossible, therefore, putting the circumstances together, to mistake their design in choosing the author, with whom they have begun to recommend a course of studies" (*Works* 6: 30–31).

The vice in Rousseau that wins the favor of the National Assembly, and which it intends to put "in the place of plain duty," is the "selfish, flattering, seductive, ostentatious vice" of vanity: "True humility, the basis of the christian system, is the low, but deep and firm foundation of all real virtue. But this, as very painful in the practice, and little imposing in the appearance, they have totally discarded. Their object is to merge all natural and all social sentiment in inordinate vanity" (*Works* 6: 31).

This vice led Rousseau "constantly to exhaust the stores of his powerful rhetorick in the expression of universal benevolence; whilst his heart was incapable of harbouring one spark of common parental affection." It has become the revolutionary government's "new invented virtue" and the substance of its educational philosophy: "Benevolence to the whole species, and want of feeling for every individual with whom the professors come in contact, form the character of the new philosophy" (*Works* 6: 33). In this way, "they dispose of all the family relations of parents and children, husbands and wives" and remove the virtue of chastity from the hearts of the young (*Works* 6: 36–38). By weakening the family and the social structures founded on it in traditional society, they rid themselves of the kingdom's landed proprietors: "The great object of your tyrants, is to destroy the gentlemen of France; and for that purpose they destroy, to the best of their power, all the effect of those relations which may render considerable men powerful or even safe" (*Works* 6: 40). The Revolution's assault on religion, morals, and property was all of one piece.

Toward the end of this *Letter to a Member of the National Assembly* Burke makes a statement that is essential to understanding his social philosophy:

> Men are qualified for civil liberty, in exact proportion to their disposition to put moral chains upon their own appetites; in proportion as their love to justice is above their rapacity; in proportion as their soundness and sobriety of understanding is above their vanity and presumption; in proportion as they are more disposed to listen to the counsels of the wise and the good, in preference to the flattery

of knaves. Society cannot exist unless a controlling power upon will and appetite be placed somewhere, and the less of it there is within, the more there must be without. It is ordained in the eternal constitution of things that men of intemperate minds cannot be free. Their passions forge their fetters [*Works* 6: 64].

As Burke saw it, the deepest sin of the Revolution was to take the chains off the appetites. One of those chains is respect for other people's property.

Yet although, as was remarked above, Revolutionary France's war with Europe was "a war against landed property," Burke did not regard Britain's resistance to France as a war for landed property alone. He was well aware of other kinds of property, commercial and financial, which were also important and legitimate British interests.

The "financial revolution" of the 1690s, as we have noted, had established the Bank of England, and had created a national debt and a "monied interest." The national debt did not worry Burke as it did his friend Adam Smith, who decried "the progress of the enormous debts which at present oppress, and will in the long-run probably ruin, all the great nations of Europe." The British national debt, said Smith, was never reduced in time of peace in proportion to its growth during wars: "It was in the war which began in 1688, and was concluded by the treaty of Ryswick in 1697, that the foundation of the present enormous debt of Great Britain was first laid" (*Wealth of Nations*, V, 3, 10 and 41; 2: 911, 921). But, whether Burke was consciously disagreeing with Smith or not, he wrote in 1796: "Public credit, . . . which has so often been predicted as the cause of our certain ruin, . . . for a century has been the constant companion, and often the means of our prosperity and greatness" (*Works* 8: 152). Two decades earlier he had referred to accumulation of "a debt of near 140 millions in this country" as a sign of Britain's ability to raise "so mighty a revenue" that it could support that debt (*Works* 3: 121; cf. 7: 260–261, 8: 357).

"Money," Burke believed, "is a productive thing; and when the usual time of its demand can be tolerably calculated, it may, with prudence, be safely laid out to the profit of the holder. It is on this calculation that the business of banking proceeds" (*Works* 3: 295). The owners of money, he said in 1796, must be allowed to make a profit on the use of their money; otherwise there could be no public credit. Furthermore, monied men must be free to lend their money to government at their discretion, without being pressured to lend it by appeals to their patriotism, and the public should remember that much of the profit they make on their loans will go back to government in the form of taxes (*Works* 8: 354–362).

As was noted above, as early as 1769 Burke had foreseen that the excess of expenditure over revenue in France would produce "some extraordinary confusion" in its "whole system." Now that the Revolution had come, in his *Reflections* he blamed it in large part on the public debt and the monied interest. "Nations," he said, "are wading deeper and deeper into an ocean of boundless debt." Great Britain was an exception, because her revenues were great enough to support a national debt which in its own way was useful. But it was not so in France:

> Public debts which at first were a security to governments, by interesting many in the publick tranquillity, are likely in their excess to become the means of their subversion. If governments provide for these debts by heavy impositions, they perish by becoming odious to the people. If they do not provide for them, they will be undone by the efforts of the most dangerous of all parties; I mean an extensive discontented monied interest, injured and not destroyed. The men who compose this interest look for their security, in the first instance, to the fidelity of government; in the second, to its power. If they find the old governments effete, worn out, and with their springs relaxed, so as not to be of sufficient vigour for their purposes, they may seek new ones that shall be possessed of more energy; and this energy will be derived, not from an acquisition of resources, but from a contempt of justice.

The injustice, of course, was the expropriation of the lands of the Church in order to pay the national debt, but it would not stop there: "Revolutions are favourable to confiscation; and it is impossible to know under what obnoxious names the next confiscations will be authorized" (*Works* 5: 281–282).

Earlier in the *Reflections* he had explained why the National Assembly had judged the payment of the public debt more important than respect for private property: "By the vast debt of France a great monied interest has insensibly grown up, and with it a great power." Certain features of pre-Revolutionary French society had made the conversion of money into land and of land into money more difficult in France than in England. This had kept the monied interest more separated from the landed interest than in Britain, and had made "the owners of the two distinct species of property not so well disposed to each other as they are in this country." The monied interest particularly resented the disrespect it felt it got from the old aristocracy (*Works* 5: 204–206; cf. 253).

In this "real, though not always perceived warfare between the noble ancient landed interest, and the new monied interest, the greatest because the most applicable strength was in the hands of the latter." Its wealth was more mobile, and it was by nature more disposed to adventure, novelty, and change. When the Revolution came, therefore, the monied interest got its chance and "struck at the nobility through the crown and the church" (*Works* 5: 206–207; cf. 7: 21). Here we see a reason for Burke's insistence that landed property must be overrepresented in the legislature and must govern.

We have already remarked that in 1796 Burke attributed the character of the Revolution to an alliance between the politicians and the philosophes of the Enlightenment. In the *Reflections*, he attributes it to "a close and marked union" between the monied interest and "the political men of letters," i.e., the philosophes, who "had some years ago formed something like a regular plan for the destruction of the christian religion" (*Works* 5: 207–208). For reasons that will be given below, he later replaced the monied interest with the politicians. But in this, his original criticism of the Revolution, the monied interest is a principal moving force in the revolt against the French government and social order.

In a republic founded on confiscated lands and paper money, Burke predicted:

> The whole of the power obtained by this revolution will settle in the towns among the burghers and the monied directors who lead them. The landed gentleman, the yeoman, and the peasant, have, none of them, habits, or inclinations, or experience, which can lead them to any share in this the sole source of power and influence now left in France. . . . It is obvious, that in the towns, all the things which conspire against the country gentlemen, combine in favour of the money manager and director [*Works* 5: 347–349].

This is the mischievous and ignoble oligarchy toward which Burke had earlier said the National Assembly was tending.

From early on in the Revolution Burke had serious doubts about the ability of the revolutionary government to subsist on a paper currency made legal tender but backed mainly by the credit of the state (*Corr.* 6: 50–54). "The revenue will not be trifled with," he said in the *Reflections.* "The prattling about the rights of men will not be accepted in payment of a biscuit or a pound of gun-powder" (*Works* 5: 429). The revolutionists deceive themselves in comparing their paper money with England's:

> They imagine that our flourishing state in England is owing to that bank-paper, and not the bank-paper to the flourishing condition of our commerce, to the solidity of our credit, and to the total exclusion of all idea of power from any part of the transaction. They forget that, in England, not one shilling of paper-money of any description is received but of choice; that the whole has had its origin in cash actually deposited; and that it is convertible, at pleasure, in an instant, and without the smallest loss, into cash again. Our paper is of value in commerce, because in law it is of none [*Works* 5: 411–412].

Even in England, as Burke, shortly before his death, told George Canning, "if a low Paper Currency [i.e., bank notes of low denominations, such as one guinea] is once admitted, the Market will be overloaded, Gold and silver will be more and more withheld and if Guinea Notes, or any thing resembling them, are once put into currency, you will never see a Guinea" (*Corr.* 9: 269; cf. 271–272, 276, 299–300). Paper money is a form of credit, and when property takes the form of credit, it tends to become simply unreal. Burke did not trust it, certainly not in comparison with that most real kind of property, real estate. Nor did he fully trust the English monied power; in 1796 he wrote to Earl Fitzwilliam: "I dread Attornies and provincial bankers who in my time are grown to a number and consideration which will inevitably at some time or other subvert, what are called the natural interests of the Kingdom" (*Corr.* 8: 373; cf. 9: 145–146, 148–149).

By the end of 1791, however, Burke had written off the monied interest as a major power in France, and now saw a new phenomenon in Europe, a government that could exist and operate in independence of any kind of property. Those people, he said, delude themselves who think that "the assembly must be bankrupt, and that this bankruptcy will totally destroy that system." The bankruptcy indeed has happened: "As soon as a nation compels a creditor to take paper currency in discharge of his debt, there is a bankruptcy." But as long as the lands confiscated from the Church, the Crown, and the royal princes can be purchased with the paper money at its par value, the system will be able to go on, "till that fund of confiscation begins to fail" and there ensues "a *total depreciation*" (*Works* 7: 46–50).

But in any event, "all consideration of publick credit in France is of little avail at present," and a new power has arisen in place of the monied men:

> The action indeed of the monied interest was of absolute necessity at the beginning of this revolution; but the French republick can stand without any assistance itself from that description of men, which as things are now circumstanced, rather stands in need of assistance from the power which alone substantially exists in France; I mean the several districts and municipal republicks, and the several clubs which direct all their affairs and appoint all their magistrates. This is the power now paramount to every thing, even to the assembly itself called national, and that to which tribunals, priesthood, laws, finances, and both descriptions of military power are wholly subservient, so far as the military power of either description yields obedience to any name of authority.

The present fact is *"that the political and civil power of France is wholly separated from its property of every description*; and of course that neither the landed nor the monied interest possesses the smallest weight or consideration in the direction of any publick concern" (*Works* 7: 50–51).

The government of France has become something previously almost undreamed of, a government of unpropertied politicians and writers:

> Very few . . . could have imagined that property, which has been taken for natural dominion, should, through the whole of a vast kingdom, lose all its importance and even its influence. . . . How many could have thought, that the most complete and formidable revolution in a great empire should be made by men of letters, not as subordinate instruments and trumpeters of sedition, but as the

chief contrivers and managers, and in a short time as the open administrators and sovereign rulers [*Works* 7: 198; cf. 8: 52–53]?

How do these men succeed in governing without the natural supports of property and rank? They do it by force and fear, said Burke, in a piece written during the Jacobin Terror:

> I believe very few were able to enter into the effects of mere *terrour*, as a principle not only for the support of power in given hands or forms, but in those things in which the soundest political speculators were of opinion, that the least appearance of force would be totally destructive—such is the market, whether of money, provision, or commodities of any kind. Yet for four years we have seen loans made, treasuries supplied, and armies levied and maintained, more numerous than France ever shewed in the field, by the *effects of fear alone* [*Works* 7: 199].

These were the men whom Burke called Jacobins, following his tendency to identify all of the revolutionaries with their most extreme and *exalté* wing. Even after the fall of Robespierre in July 1794 and the subsequent dissolution of the Jacobin clubs, he continued to call the leaders of the revolutionary government, and all who supported or sympathized with them, Jacobins. For him, the members of the Directory which succeeded the Jacobin dictatorship were Jacobins in knee-breeches, but were not otherwise different: "Are they not the very same Ruffians, Thieves, Assassins, and Regicides, that they were from the beginning?" (*Works* 9: 46). For Burke, the principles of the Revolution were and continued to be simply Jacobinism.

Jacobinism, in one view of it, is the theory of a radically democratic republic, such as the French formed in 1790–1791 "under the name of a Democracie Royale" (*Works* 7: 128). But the adjective, royale, meant nothing:

> Jacobinism does not consist in the having or not having, a certain pageant under the name of a king, but 'in taking the people as equal individuals, without any corporate name or description, without attention to property, without division of powers, and forming the government of delegates from a number of men so constituted, in destroying or confiscating property, and bribing the publick creditors, or the poor, with the spoils, now of one part of the community, now of another, without regard to prescription or profession' [*Works* 7: 128–129; no reference given for the inner quotation].

As far as Burke was concerned, "some sober and sensible form of a republick, in which there was no mention at all of a king, but which held out some reasonable security to property, life, and personal freedom," would be preferable to "this democracie royale" (*Works* 7: 130).

But even the democratic theory is illusory. The real goal of Jacobinism is to put power in the hands of the enlightened few:

> What is Jacobinism? It is an attempt (hitherto but too successful) to eradicate prejudice out of the minds of men, for the purpose of putting all power and authority into the hands of the persons capable of occasionally enlightening the minds of the people. For this purpose the Jacobins have resolved to destroy the whole frame and fabrick of the old societies of the world, and to regenerate them after their fashion. To obtain an army for this purpose, they every where engage the poor, by holding out to them as a bribe the spoils of the rich. . . . As the grand prejudice, and that, which holds all the other prejudices together, the first, last, and middle object of their hostility is Religion [*Corr.* 8: 129–130 and *Works* 9: 402].

Despite his low opinion of the deputies of the Third Estate in the Estates-General, and his continuing belief that the Jacobins were thieves and murderers, Burke had to admit that they did have talent. "Jacobinism," he said in 1795, "is the Vice of men of Parts; and, in this age, it is the Channel in which all discontents will run" (*Corr.* 8: 242–243). A year later he said: "Jacobinism is the revolt of the enterprising talents of a country against its property" (*Works* 8: 170). He pointed out in one of his *Letters on a Regicide Peace* how far their enterprise and ability could carry them:

> Material resources never have supplied, nor ever can supply the want of unity in design and constancy in pursuit. But unity in design, and perseverance, and boldness in pursuit, have never wanted resources, and never will. We have not considered as we ought the dreadful energy of a state, in which the property has nothing to do with the government. Reflect, my dear sir, reflect again and again on a government, in which the property is in complete subjection, and where nothing rules but the mind of desperate men [*Works* 8: 255].

These desperate men, the Jacobins, were themselves the product of "a silent revolution in the moral world," which preceded the political revolution and prepared it. The moral revolution included the rise and growth of energetic and wealthy middle classes, increasingly discontented with their lot. "There were all the talents which assert their pretensions, and are impatient of the place which settled society prescribes to them." Their influence, interposed "between the great and the populace," was exercised through "the correspondence of the monied and the mercantile world, the literary intercourse of academies; but, above all, the press, of which they had in a manner entire possession" (*Works* 8: 259–260). Out of this bourgeoisie emerged the ambitious men who seized control of the great Revolution when it came.

The nobility and gentry of pre-revolutionary France had nursed these vipers in their bosoms, thinking them harmless because of the philosophy of "*douce humanité*" that they preached, yet "all this while they meditated the confiscations and massacres we have seen" (*Works* 8: 53–54). "I may speak it upon an assurance almost approaching to absolute knowledge," said Burke in 1791, "that nothing has been done [in France] that has not been contrived from the beginning, even before the states had assembled" (*Works* 6: 7). A letter that Burke received from Thomas Paine in January 1790, quoting one that the latter had received from Thomas Jefferson in Paris the previous July, could well have given Burke this impression (*Corr.* 6: 70–72). But if the nobles and gentlemen did not see before the Revolution, they should certainly see now that "the great object of the Jacobin system is to excite the lowest description of the people to range themselves under ambitious men, for the pillage and destruction of the more eminent orders and classes of the community" (*Works* 7: 263).

It is not force and fear alone that enable the Jacobins to govern a bankrupt state. It is also the ability of clever, ambitious, and unscrupulous men to excite the envy and resentment of the lower orders of society against their natural rulers, to make the poor see the interests of the rich as hostile to their own, and so to turn the populace into a revolutionary army that threatens all Europe. "The poison of other states," Burke wrote in 1796, "is the food of the new republick. That bankruptcy, the very apprehension of which is one of the causes assigned for the fall of the monarchy, was the capital on which she opened her traffick with the world." Revolutionary fervor, to be exported throughout Europe, is the secret of Jacobin success:

> The republick of regicide with an annihilated revenue, with defaced manufactures, with a ruined commerce, with an uncultivated and half-depopulated country, with a discontented, distressed, enslaved, and famished people, passing with a rapid, eccentrick, incalculable course, from the wildest anarchy to the sternest despotism, has actually conquered the finest parts of Europe, . . . and so subdued the minds of the rulers in every nation, that hardly any resource presents itself to them, except that of entitling themselves to a contemptuous mercy by a display of their imbecility and meanness [*Works* 8: 83].

Revolutionary France, having begun in the radical individualism of democratic ideology, thus ends in sheer statism:

> In that country, entirely to cut off a branch of commerce, to extinguish a manufacture, to destroy the circulation of money, to violate credit, to suspend the course of agriculture, even to burn a city, or to lay waste a province of their own, does not cost them a moment's anxiety. To them the will, the wish, the want, the liberty, the toil, the blood of individuals is as nothing. Individuality is left out of their scheme of government. The state is all in all. Every thing is referred to the production of force; afterwards, every thing is trusted to the use of it [*Works* 8: 253–254].

As Burke was aware, the transition from a democracy founded on radical individualism to a centralized despotism is neither impossible nor even illogical. All it requires is a theory of civil society as a collection of originally sovereign individual wills, the emergence from those wills of a general will, and a party that embodies and expresses it. The French monarchy had contributed to the process that left nothing between the individuals and the state by weakening intermediate institutions and concentrating power in itself: "To strengthen itself the Monarchy had weakend every other force: To unite the Nation to itself, it had dissolved all other ties. When the chain, which held the people to the Prince was once broken, the whole frame of the commonwealth was found in a State of disconnection" (*Corr.* 6: 242; cf. *Works* 7: 54). The success of the Revolution consisted in transferring the power of the monarchy, with all customary and traditional checks removed, to the

National Assembly: "That assembly, since the destruction of the orders, has no fundamental law, no strict convention, no respected usage to restrain it" (*Works* 5: 98).

Even before the Jacobins came to power, Burke was convinced that the French Revolution and its principles were incompatible with peace, security, and civilization in Europe. "Never shall I think any country in Europe to be secure," he said in 1791, "whilst there is established, in the very centre of it, a state (if so it may be called) founded on principles of anarchy, and which is, in reality, a college of armed fanaticks, for the propagation of the principles of assassination, robbery, rebellion, fraud, faction, oppression, and impiety" (*Works* 6: 20). To a French noblewoman he wrote in the same year:

> I feel, as an Englishman, great dread and apprehension from the contagious nature of these abominable principles and vile manners, which threaten the worst and most degrading barbarism to every adjacent country. No argument can persuade me, that if they are suffered finally to triumph in France, they will want more than the occasion of some domestic trouble or disturbance (against which no government can be insured) to extend themselves to us, and to blast all the health and vigour of that happy constitution which we enjoy, by acting upon other principles and in another spirit [*Corr.* 6: 211].

Or, as he wrote a few months later to Lord Fitzwilliam, "if the powers of Europe, from a Sense of their own danger, do not destroy the seminary from whence are propagated all these Evil principles, their prevalence here is a thing, not of contingency or speculation, but of absolute certainty" (*Corr.* 6: 416). This was a conviction that he repeated incessantly for the rest of his life (see, e.g., *Corr.* 6: 418–421; 7: 177–178, 218–219; 8: 134, 300, 331, 335; *Works* 6: 252; 7: 235, 244, 255–256; 8: 215). Concern for Britain and the British constitution, he said, was uppermost in his mind. A week before the publication of his *Reflections*, he wrote to Calonne, the émigré former Controller-General of Finance, saying that his object in writing the book "was not France, in the first instance, but this Country" (*Corr.* 6: 141).

Burke had never been in favor of parliamentary reform, i.e., extending the right to vote in elections to the Commons and eliminating rotten and decayed boroughs. But with the advent of the

French Revolution, he saw petitions for such reform as attempts to introduce the principles of the Revolution into Great Britain. Many of the changes in the representation proposed in earlier decades, and "by a great misnomer called parliamentary reforms," he said, were undoubtedly well-intentioned, but would have led to "the death-dance of democratick revolution," and "a gate would have been opened, through which all property might be sacked and ravaged" (*Works* 8: 13–14, 19).

Once the French Revolution had arrived, it was the overriding issue of European and British politics, according to Burke, because it had as its "great aim not only to change the government, but to make an entire revolution in the whole of the social order in every country" (*Works* 7: 244; cf. 255–256). Burke regarded this aim as thoroughly evil because it was "the subversion of that order of things under which our part of the world has so long flourished, and indeed been in a progressive State of improvement, the Limits of which, if it had not been thus rudely stopped, it would not have been easy for the imagination to fix" (*Corr.* 7: 387; cf. 276, 381, 474, 518–519; 9: 317, 357; *Works* 7: 292, 362). The French Revolution, therefore, was "the common enemy of the human race," and all factions in Europe should drop their quarrels and unite against it (*Corr.* 7: 298; cf. 312; 8: 44, 332; 9: 133–134; *Works* 8: 166, 169, 183–189, 214–217; 9: 68).

When the French Republic declared war on Great Britian in 1793, Burke insisted and never ceased to insist that it should be waged as an all-out war, and prosecuted to the final extinction of Jacobinism. This was the thesis of his four *Letters on a Regicide Peace*, succinctly expressed in a line in one of them: "That this new system of robbery in France, cannot be rendered safe by any art; that it *must* be destroyed, or that it will destroy all Europe" (*Works* 8: 256). The cause of his despair in his final years was that the powers of Europe, including Britain, would not wage the war in that spirit and to that end.

At the same time, however, he argued that if the war were carried through successfully, it would have to result in a restoration of the whole social order of France. When the Emperor Joseph II (Marie Antoinette's brother) and the King of Prussia, in their Pillnitz Declaration in 1792, put the persons of the King and Queen of France above the monarchy and the intermediate orders of the state, they made a grave mistake. It would be foolish, said Burke,

> to imagine that monarchy can be acknowledged and supported in France upon any other basis than that of its property, *corporate and individual*, or that it can enjoy a moment's permanence or security upon any scheme of things, which sets aside all the antient corporate capacities and distinctions of the kingdom, and subverts the whole fabrick of its antient laws and usages, political, civil and religious [*Works* 7: 129; cf. *Corr.* 6: 268; 7: 262].

The restoration, therefore, must re-establish not only the monarchy, but property, the social order, and the Church as they were in France before the calling of the Estates-General. First, then, the revolutionaries "must make restitution of all stolen goods whatsoever" (*Works* 5: 275; cf. 6: 51). That includes emphatically the property of the Church. The émigré leaders in Coblentz, Burke wrote to his son, must not promise to confirm the confiscation of Church lands, for "they may be assured that such a mass of property cannot be dispersed as it has been, without leaving the monarchy and aristocracy nothing upon which they *can* stand. . . . They who can dispose or hold such a confiscation, must be masters of the country" (*Corr.* 6: 334). Speaking more generally: "if the old proprietors (of whatever name) be not restored, an immense mass of Possession will be thrown into hands who have been enriched by the subversion of the Monarchy, and who never can be trusted for its support" (*Corr.* 7: 388; cf. 262, *Works* 7: 130). The common people, therefore, "must be made to see; their Leaders must be made to feel, that such Spoil is no sure possession—and that when they shake the property of Others, they can never convert it to property in their own favor" (*Corr.* 7: 383–384).

With restitution of property would go the restoration of the old French constitution, by which Burke of course did not mean a document, but the social order which constituted France as a nation. The French constitution (like the British) was not a document but the basic structure of society:

> The body politick of France existed in the majesty of its throne; in the dignity of its nobility; in the honour of its gentry; in the sanctity of its clergy; in the reverence of its magistracy; in the weight and consideration due to its landed property in the several

bailliages; in the respect due to its moveable [i.e., trading] substance represented by the corporations [i.e., boroughs] of the kingdom. All these particular *moleculae* united, form the great mass of what is truly the body politick in all countries [*Works* 8: 191].

These were the property-owning classes of France, and they were France as a nation, because "the property of the nation is the nation." Even after the fall of the monarchy and the emigration of the princes of the blood royal, along with so many of the nobility and gentry, they continued to be the French nation: "Nation is a moral essence, not a geographical arrangement." France still exists in exile, because "the proprietary, and the government to which the proprietary adheres, exists and claims" (*Works* 8: 190–191; cf. 7: 126–127, 154; *Corr.* 6: 359–360).

This was the order that must be restored, and it was not an arbitrary despotism. In 1791, while Louis XVI was still on the throne, but very much in the shadow of the National Assembly, Burke insisted that "the Monarchy of France is not in the disposal of any one of its Kings and that he cannot even by his freest consent destroy his Throne, his Nobility, His church, his Tribunals, his corporations, His orders, and the general Tenure of property among his Subjects" (*Corr.* 6: 361–362).

As we have already seen above, Burke included Catholicism in the restoration of the old order because "the catholick religion, which is fundamentally the religion of France, must go with the monarchy of France." He went on to say that "we know that the monarchy did not survive the hierarchy, no not even in appearance, for many months; in substance, not for a single hour. As little can it exist in future, if that pillar is taken away, or even shattered and impaired." If it should please God to restore peace and order through the success of the war against Jacobinism, the first step the victorious allies should take would be to reinstate all the "old clergy," who had not conformed to the revolutionary regime, "because we have proof more than sufficient, that whether they err or not in the scholastick disputes with us, they are not tainted with atheism, the great political evil of the time." Then he felt it necessary to add:

> I hope I need not apologize for this phrase, as if I thought religion nothing but policy; it is far from my thoughts; and I hope it is not

to be inferred from my expressions. But in the light of policy alone I am here considering the question. I speak of policy too in a large light; in which large light, policy too is a sacred thing [*Works* 7: 176].

Burke, however, as has already been remarked, did not advocate a simple return to the ancien régime. In August 1791, when his son was in Coblentz with the émigré princes, he wrote to make some suggestions about items to be included in a manifesto that the princes intended to publish. Among them were the following:

> The manifesto certainly ought, as you observe, to turn much more upon the Benefit of the people, on good order, religion, morality, security, and property, than upon the Rights of sovereigns. . . . That France had been always taken and understood as a Monarchy—. . . That certain orders and Ranks were in the essence of the French constitution, and highly beneficial to the Nation—That a certain established Religion—with certain legal possessions— were the old common Law of France—A judicature arising from the authority [of the] Throne—also of immemorial usage, of great Benefit—. . . An assurance that they mean nothing against the *true* antient Rights, Liberties, and priveleges of the people, or any thing which the publick wisdom acting without restraint, may contrive for their further Benefit. That it is for *that very purpose*, the Restoration of the King and Monarchy is desired [*Corr.* 6: 359–360].

In the following month he wrote again to this son, commenting on what the princes had published, and sketching a reform program they ought to follow:

> I have read the declaration of the Bourbon Princes. . . . I think it well penned, and in many points very right, and proper. . . . But the Ton is not just what one would wish in all points. They ought to promise, distinctly, and without ambiguity, that they mean, 1 when the Monarchy as the essential Basis shall be restored, to secure with it, a free constitution, 2 and that for this purpose they will cause at a meeting of the States freely chosen according to the antient Legal order, to vote by orders—3 All Lettres de Cachet and other means of arbitrary imprisonment to be abolished. 4 That all Taxation shall be by the said States conjointly with the King. 5. That responsibility shall be established; and the publick Revenue put out of the power of abuse and malversation; 6. a canonical 'synod of the Gallican Church to reform all abuses' and (as unfortunately the K has lost all reputation) they should pledge themselves,

with their Lives and fortunes, to support, along with their King those conditions and that wise order, which can alone support a free and vigorous Government [*Corr.* 6: 413–414].

Even as Burke wrote these words, he had come to the conclusion "that no counter-revolution is to be expected in France from internal causes solely," and "that the longer the present system exists, the greater will be its strength; the greater its power to destroy discontents at home, and to resist all foreign attempts in favour of these discontents" (*Works* 7: 56; cf. *Corr.* 6: 242). Only a foreign invasion in force could overthrow the revolutionary republic, but the princes who were to be restored by that invasion needed to offer the French people a program of reform. The one that Burke proposed was in effect to go back to 1789 and start over again, but this time to do it right on the model of the British constitution.

Though he admitted that many of the old feudal tenures in France badly needed to be changed, he wanted to believe, and made some efforts to get information to assure himself, that conditions there and relations between the great landlords and the peasants had not been so bad as the partisans of the Revolution alleged (*Works* 5: 251–252, 263–264; *Corr.* 6: 207–208). On the other hand, during the same years in which he was attacking Jacobinism in increasingly unmeasured language, Burke wrote: "All the miseries of Ireland have originated, in what has produced all the miseries of India, a servile patience under oppression, by the greatest of all misnomers called prudence" (*Corr.* 8: 147). The miseries of Ireland and India were on his mind almost as much as the evils of the French Revolution.

That he was able simultaneously to hold these apparently contradictory positions may be due to his faith in the British Empire. The imperial government could err badly, as it had done in America, and continued to do in Ireland and India, but the British constitution was a sound one. Under that constitution, Burke hoped, the government could be brought to recognize its mistakes and amend the way in which its outlying dominions were governed. The government's faults were not irremediable. In France, however, the Revolution was a destructive and expansive force. It had become a menace to the traditional and fundamentally good social order of all Europe. Therefore, as Cato of old had said of Carthage, so Burke said of Jacobinism: it must be destroyed.

His indictment of the Revolution and its ideology contained several closely connected counts. The Revolution concentrated all legal power in the National Assembly. It rendered private property ineffective as a check on the power of the state. It leveled all ranks and classes in civil society, and thereby eliminated the intermediate orders that stood between individuals and the state. Consequently, it weakened monarchy (a consequence that monarchs were often too blind to see), and eventually abolished it. By destroying the natural ruling class of great landlords, it put an end to limited constitutional government. Finally, and not accidentally, it sought to drive from men's minds the Christian religion, which was the inspirational source and unifying bond of European civilization, and to substitute for it a purely secular enlightenment.

In the success of the Revolution, which Burke dreaded but feared was possibly the mysterious design of Divine Providence, he saw the end of a world that he genuinely and deeply loved: "There is the hand of God in this business, and there is an end of the system of Europe, taking in laws, manners, religion and politics, in which I delighted so much" (*Corr.* 9: 307; cf. 6: 453; 8: 35–36, 412; *Works* 6: 267; 7: 84–85). As one reads his correspondence during the revolutionary years, it is hard to believe that he loved that system solely or primarily for the sake of property simply as such or of wealth merely as wealth.

It is equally difficult to ascribe to greed and ambition his devotion to the aristocratic world he so fiercely defended. If he had had his eye on the main chance, he would have played his economic and political cards quite differently. At Beaconsfield he lived the life of an English country gentlemen, beyond his modest means and always heavily in debt and dependent on subsidies from Lords Rockingham and Fitzwilliam. But except for whatever part he had in the stock speculations of Richard and Will Burke, he made no serious effort to get rich. He wanted a peerage, but knew that his chances of getting one were slim (*Corr.* 7: 60), having given King George III so little reason to love him. When it became evident that he would not get a peerage, and when the death of his son removed his reason for wanting it, he nevertheless spent the remaining years of his life in trying to arouse the monarchs and aristocrats to their need to make more vigorous efforts to defend themselves and their society. Merely personal motives, it seems clear, did not make Burke the aristocrat he was in principle, even though, as he said, in situation God knew nothing less.

The world that Burke loved was, in words that he used in the *Reflections*, "this world of reason, and order, and peace, and virtue, and fruitful penitence," from which a revolution chosen for any cause less than unavoidable and compelling necessity casts society "into the antagonist world of madness, discord, vice, confusion, and unavailing sorrow" (*Works* 5: 185). The stakes, for Burke, were very high.

Many think, perhaps rightly, that he set them too high. He was doubtless right in rejecting the radically individualistic political theory on the basis of which democracy was proposed and defended in his age. But democracy could be based on another and better theory which could learn something of value even from Edmund Burke. Most important, as the present writer said in an earlier work, "The authority of the state derives from the rational and moral ends that it is intended to serve," and, therefore, "in Burke's thought purpose and obligations are more fundamental than rights and consent" (*Prescription and Providence*, p. 112).

On the other hand, Burke was doubtless mistaken in making the cause of Western civilization depend so entirely on the particular political and economic system that prevailed in his time. It would be a highly optimistic liberal who would think that the culture of the West has only improved since Burke's time, but surely in a number of ways life has become better for the greater part of the people.

Alfred Cobban comments in his *Edmund Burke and the Revolt Against the Eighteenth Century*: "As a school of statesmanship, Burke's constitutional theory remains of permanent value; as a working system it was dead almost before it was expounded" (p. 71). That would have been true even if the French Revolution had not occurred. The Industrial Revolution reduced the importance of landed property and thereby undermined the political position of the aristocracy. Technological and financial developments have significantly changed the nature of property itself, even of agricultural property (think of agribusiness), and have created a world vastly different from the one that Burke knew. There is now no elite on the political scene that one can regard as an aristocracy, and no form of property to give an elite the stable and assured position that the British aristocracy once had.

Yet some features of a society must be permanent, even though they assume changing forms, if it is to be a free and good society. We may still find them expounded and defended in Burke's thought. That, no doubt, is why, to this day, there is a small but steady stream of books on the thought of Edmund Burke. More than any British statesman of his generation, he speaks to our concerns.

In our post-Communist world, private property is as important as ever. Property and the freedom to acquire it remain essential to a nation's welfare, because, as has been said, the energies of society spring from below and are not generated from above. Individuals and private institutions must therefore be guaranteed the right to deploy their energies in the creation of wealth within an order of law which the state maintains. Government will harm them and society at large if it tries to take their place and to do what it should leave them free to do. Properly administered, private property serves the good of the whole community. Where the line between liberty and regulation should be drawn in any particular set of historical circumstances is, of course, a matter of continuing political debate.

Property is still a bulwark of the people's liberty, both individual and social. It sustains individual independence and self-respect, supports intermediate institutions, and checks the expansive power of the state. It is also a protection against the rise of a class which dominates the economic order through its possession of public office and control of the state's instruments of coercion.

As Burke's writings on Ireland show, he was aware that those who have neither property nor access to it are not truly free. We may judge him to have been naïvely certain about the freedom of the lower classes of the people in Great Britain and about the mutuality of the interests of the rich and the poor there. Yet fostering that mutuality remains a necessity for the societies that we like to call free.

Burke saw landed property as a firm foundation for the continuity and stability of society and society's tradition. Land can no longer perform that role. On the other hand, our present-day capitalist system generates constant flux, not only economic, but social, political, and moral. It does not of itself generate internalized restraints on greed, lust, and the drive for power. It is not, therefore, a self-sufficient and self-regulating system, as the economic liberals called conservatives like to believe. It needs to be checked from sources other than competition and the free market, useful though these are as a mechanism for setting prices. We may still heed Burke's warning that society cannot exist unless a controlling power upon will and appetite be placed somewhere, and the less of it there is within, the more there must be without.

Robert N. Bellah has remarked in the *New Oxford Review*: "At the moment our public discourse is divided between conservative liberals who believe only in the free market and liberal liberals who believe only in individual rights" (June 1992, p. 18). That is an oversimplification, of course, but accurate enough. To escape from that sterile dichotomy, we shall need, among other things, to rethink the role of property in producing and sustaining the institutions of a good society. It will be a process to which Burke's thought, despite its obvious historical limitations, can make a contribution.

WORKS CITED

Primary Sources

The Correspondence of Edmund Burke. Ed. Thomas W. Copeland. 10 vols. Cambridge: Cambridge University Press; Chicago: The University of Chicago Press, 1958–1978.
Correspondence of the Right Honourable Edmund Burke. Ed. Charles William, Earl Fitzwilliam, and Sir Richard Bourke. 4 vols. London: Francis & John Rivington, 1844.
Samuels, Arthur P. I. *The Early Life, Correspondence, and Writings of the Right Honourable Edmund Burke*. Cambridge: Cambridge University Press, 1923.
The Parliamentary History of England from the Earliest Period to the Year 1803. Ed. William Cobbett. 36 vols. London: Longmans, Hurst, Rees, etc., 1806–1820.
The Works of the Right Honourable Edmund Burke. 16 vols. London: F. C. & J. Rivington, 1808–1827.
The Writings and Speeches of Edmund Burke. Ed. Paul Langford. 9 vols. to date. Oxford: Clarendon, 1981—.

Secondary Literature

Bellah, Robert N. "Small Face-to Face Christian Communities in a Mean-Spirited and Polarized Society." *New Oxford Review* 59.5 (June 1992): 17–21.
Berman, Harold J. *Law and Revolution: The Formation of the Western Legal Tradition*. Cambridge and London: Harvard University Press, 1983.
Bisset, Robert. *The Life of Edmund Burke*. 2 vols. London: Cawthorn, Richardson, Symonds, etc., 1800.
Bush, M. L. *The English Aristocracy: A Comparative Synthesis*. Manchester: Manchester University Press, 1984.

Canavan, Francis. *Edmund Burke: Prescription and Providence.* Durham, N.C.: Carolina Academic Press, 1987.
Cannon, John. *Aristocratic Century: The Peerage of Eighteenth-Century England.* Cambridge: Cambridge University Press, 1984.
Cobban, Alfred. *Edmund Burke and the Revolt Against the Eighteenth Century.* 2nd. ed. New York: Barnes & Noble, 1961.
Cone, Carl B. *Burke and the Nature of Politics.* I. *The Age of the American Revolution.* II. *The Age of the French Revolution.* Lexington: University of Kentucky Press, 1957, 1964.
Curtis, Edmund. *A History of Ireland.* 6th ed. London: Methuen; New York: Barnes & Noble, 1961.
Fasel, George. "'The Soul That Animated': The Role of Property in Burke's Thought." *Studies in Burke and His Time* 17 (1976): 27–41.
The Federalist, any edition.
Gandy, Clara, and Stanlis, Peter J. *Edmund Burke: A Bibliography of Secondary Studies to 1983.* New York and London: Garland Publishing, 1983.
Hill, Christopher. *Reformation to Industrial Revolution: The Making of Modern English Society.* I. *1530–1780.* New York: Random House, 1967.
Himmelfarb, Gertrude. *The Idea of Poverty: England in the Early Industrial Age.* New York: Alfred A. Knopf, 1984.
Hobsbawm, E. J. *Industry and Empire: From 1750 to the Present Day.* Harmondsworth: Penguin Books, 1986.
Jones, E. L., ed. *Agriculture and Economic Growth in England, 1650–1815.* London: Methuen, 1967.
Laslett, Peter. *The World We Have Lost, Further Explored.* London: Methuen, 1983.
Lucas, Paul. "On Edmund Burke's Doctrine of Prescription." *Historical Journal* 11 (1968): 35–63.
McIlwain, Charles H. "Medieval Estates." *The Cambridge Medieval History* 7 (1958): 665–713.
Macpherson, C. B. *The Political Theory of Possessive Individualism.* Oxford: Oxford University Press, 1970.
———. *Burke.* Oxford: Oxford University Press, 1980.
Mahoney, Thomas H. D. *Edmund Burke and Ireland.* Cambridge: Harvard University Press, 1960.
Marshall, Dorothy. *Eighteenth-Century England.* New York: D. McKay, 1962.

Marshall, P. J. *The Impeachment of Warren Hastings.* Oxford: Oxford University Press, 1965.
Mingay, G. E. *English Landed Society in the Eighteenth Century.* London: Routledge & Kegan Paul; Toronto: University of Toronto Press, 1963.
———. *The Gentry: The Rise and Fall of a Ruling Class.* London and New York: Longman, 1976.
Morley, John. *Burke.* English Men of Letters Series. New York: Harper & Bros., n.d.
Namier, L. B. *England in the Age of the American Revolution.* London: Macmillan, 1930.
Pares, Richard. *King George III and the Politicians.* Oxford: Clarendon, 1953.
Plumb, J. H. *England in the Eighteenth Century.* London: Penguin Books, 1950.
Pocock, J. G. A. *Virtue, Commerce, and History: Essays on Political Thought and History, Chiefly in the Eighteenth Century.* Cambridge: Cambridge University Press, 1985.
Reed, Henry. "Edmund Burke: Statesman and Philanthropist." In *The History of Beaconsfield.* Ed. A. W. Taylor, C.B.. Rev. ed. Beaconsfield: The Beaconsfield and District Historical Society, 1983.
Smith, Adam. *An Inquiry into the Nature and Causes of the Wealth of Nations.* 2 vols. Oxford: Oxford University Press, 1976, 1979. Repr. Indianapolis: Liberty Press/Liberty Classics, 1981.
Stanlis, Peter J. *Edmund Burke and the Natural Law.* Ann Arbor: University of Michigan Press, 1958.
———. *Edmund Burke: The Enlightenment and Revolution.* New Brunswick, N.J.: Transaction Books, 1991.
Tocqueville, Alexis de. *Democracy in America.* New York: Harper & Row, 1988.
Veitch, George Stead. *The Genesis of Parliamentary Reform.* London: Constable & Co., 1913. Repr. Hamden, Conn.: Shoe String Press, 1965.
Warburton, William. *The Alliance Between Church and State.* 4th ed. London: Fletcher Gyles, 1766.
Wecter, Dixon. "Adam Smith and Burke." *Notes and Queries* 174 (January-June 1938): 311.
Woodham-Smith, Cecil. *The Great Hunger.* London: New English Library, 1970.

INDEX

agriculture: major part of British economy, 6, 15, 18, 39, 137; revolution in, and effects of, 6–7, 16; progress of, 13–15; 174

America: British policy toward, 36, 64, 106, 117, 120–21, 172; Revolution, 109; independent republic, 110–11

aristocracy, aristocrats: glorious age of, 2; composition of, 3–4, 8; ideals, 12; virtues and vices, 22–23, 86–87, 102–107; wealth, 3, 7–9, 12, 14–15; power, 5, 12, 15, 18–20, 23, 40, 46, 77, 174; Burke's attitude toward, ix, 2, 79, 86–87; check on capitalism, 13; on royal absolutism, 18–19, 100–102, 104, 113; on democratic tyranny, 20, 102, 113; natural governing class, 6, 21–23, 46, 77, 81–88, 95, 104, 106, 152; for good of the people, 40, 80, 95, 108–109, 143; prop of monarchy, 152, 169; in Ireland, 89, 91, 95; revolutionary assault on, 152, 159–60; disappearance from today's world, 175

Ascendancy, Protestant, 88–90, 94–96, 98, 124

Beaconsfield, 78, 109, 132, 140, 146, 173
Bedford, Duke of, 79, 86
Bellah, Robert, 176
Berman, Harold, 9–10
Bisset, Robert, 116–17
bourgeois, -ie, 8–9, 12, 14, 18, 23, 165
Bristol, 32–33, 81, 100, 103, 122, 134
Burke, Edmund: family, 1, 40, 58–59, 65, 86, 171, 173; early life and education, 1–2; pre-parliamentary career, 2; parliamentary career, 2, 32–33, 59–60; member of gentry, 58, 78, 173; estate owner, 13, 63, 78, 129; never rich or ennobled, 58–59, 78–79, 86, 116, 173; aristocrat in principle only, 79, 174; *royaliste raisonné*, 114; economist, ix, 116–17, 129
Bush, M. L., 4, 10–12, 14, 18–19, 20, 22–23

Canavan, Francis, 48, 174
Cannon, John, 3, 5–9, 13, 18, 20, 22
capital, -ism, -ist, 7, 9–13, 15–16, 23, 42–45, 87, 118, 120, 128–29, 175–76
Catholic, -s, -ism, 1, 11, 65–66, 72, 75, 98, 124, 141, 155, 170; penal laws against, 29–30, 90–93, 145; need a propertied Catholic aristocracy, 91, 95; and right to vote, 37–38, 92–94
Catholic Relief Acts, 32, 38, 49, 74, 92, 94, 141
charter, -s, 41, 125
Christian, -ity, Christendom, 9, 31, 45, 74–75, 80, 82, 97, 132, 135, 153–57, 160
Church, 1, 5, 43, 50–51, 62, 74, 81, 88–89, 114, 142, 150–51, 154–56, 159, 169
class, -es: lower than aristocracy, 4–5; divisions, 5–7, 80; mobility among, 5–6; conflicts, 9, necessity of, 80, mutuality of interests, 26, 39, 41–42, 82, 92–93, 137, 175; danger of merely political class, 38, 46, 84
Cloots, Anacharsis, 109
Cobban, Alfred, 174
commerce: revolution in, 6–7, 10, 15–16; England a commercial nation, 28; perhaps too dominant a one, 128; principles of, 117–18, 125–27, 135; natural laws of, 130, 133–35; and of justice, 134–35; de-

pendent on aristocratic, Christian order, 81–82; flourishes in liberty, 117–19, 127–28, 145; ruinous effects of combining with political power, 124–28, 135
Cone, Carl, 7, 20, 98, 101, 116–17, 140
Copeland, Thomas, x, 99
credit, public, 17, 38, 158–59, 161–62
Curtis, Edmund, 88–89

democracy: danger of becoming tyrannical, 38, 48, 56, 65, 68, 98, 110, 113, 148, 165–67; radical theory of, 112, 163–64, 166, 174; in French Revolution, 152–53, 163–64, 166–67
Depont, Charles-Jean-François, 34
Disraeli, Benjamin, 146
Dundas, Henry, 30, 38, 65, 89, 93, 137

"economical reform," 103–104
empire, Burke's view of, 95–86, 119–28, 172
enclosure, -s, 11, 14, 118–19
engrossment of land holdings, 11, 13
Enlightenment, the, 153, 160, 164
entail, -ed, -ment, 5–6, 12–13, 40, 55, 81
equality, natural, 25, 131

farmer, -s, 4, 11, 25, 32, 129, 132
Fasel, George, 24
feudal, -ism, 9–10, 12, 14, 67, 172
financial revolution, 16–17, 158–59
Fitzwilliam, Earl, 79, 94–95, 107, 110–13, 161, 173
Fox, Charles James, 40, 72, 106, 108–12, 114, 147
Francis, Philip, 54
freehold, -er, -s, 4, 20, 30, 32, 37, 89, 93
free trade, 32–34, 117–19, 122–24, 128
Furber, Holden, 124

gentry, tentlemen, 3–5, 11, 14, 20–21, 23–25, 56, 58, 77, 83, 92–93, 105, 113, 152, 157, 160, 165

George III, 65, 99, 101, 103, 105, 109–10, 114, 173
government: duties of, 19, 56–57, 77, 130, 129–40, 143–44; a trust, 72, 79, 90; by party, Burke's theory of, 94–101, 108; *see* "society, civil" and "state"

Hastings, Warren, 27, 35–36, 40, 54–55, 59, 71, 104, 124
Hill, Christopher, 8, 14–18, 23
Himmelfarb, Gertrude, 16
Hobsbawm, Eric, 2, 7–8, 10–11, 15–16, 23, 129–30
Hussey, Thomas, 72, 94

India, East India Company, 27, 35, 40, 53–55, 72–75, 102–103, 124–28, 139–40, 172
Industrial Revolution, 10, 16, 142–43, 174
intermediary orders and institutions, 76, 80–81, 152, 166, 169–70
Ireland: economy, 11, 24–25; miseries, 172; government, 24, 41, 88–90, 95; commercial relations with Britain, 121–24; famine in, 137–39

Jacobin, -s, -ism, 91, 94–95, 97, 124, 143, 146, 154, 163–68, 173
Jefferson, Thomas, 85, 165
job, -bers, -bing, 41, 89, 95
John, A. H., 7
Jones, E. L., 4, 6, 15
Joseph II, 168
Junto, the, 89, 96

King, Walker, x, 98, 129

labor, a commodity, 133
laborer, -s, 4–5, 10–11, 14, 25, 75, 87, 129–30, 132, 134, 136–37, 146
laissez-faire, 23, 39, 132–39, 143
landlord, -s, 3, 10–15, 21, 25, 30, 39, 137, 140, 157
Langford, x
Laslett, Peter, 3, 5–6, 8–9, 14, 16, 19–22
Laurence, French, x, 94, 129

INDEX
183

law: natural, 47, 57, 60–63, 66–69, 130; and convention, 50–3; made for good of community, 70–71, depends on consent, 145–46
lease, -s, -holders, lessees, 4, 10, 30, 32
Leopold II, 114
liberty: defined, 107–108; dependence on property, 7, 36–37, 46, 82, 107, 115; not found in abstract, 36–37; economic: freedom of contract, 130, 133–37, 142–44; duty of government to, 34, 62, 76, 118, 130–31, 133–37; source of prosperity, 34, 76, 127–28; found in all Christian states, 148
Locke, John, 70
Louis XVI, 148, 170
Lucas, Paul, 61

McDowell, R. B., 35
McIlwain, C. H., 18
Macpherson, C. B., 8, 10, 23, 26
Mahoney, Thomas, 30, 32, 38, 99, 123–24
Mandeville, Bernard, 29
Marie Antoinette, 114, 168
market, market economy, 6, 8, 10–11, 13, 17, 23, 128, 130, 133–34, 142–44, 163, 176
Marshall, Dorothy, 4, 6, 16
Marshall, P. J., 54, 59, 128
Marx, -ism, -ist, 8–9, 12, 26
Mercer, Capt. Thomas, 64–65, 110
Merchants: as class, 5, 80–81, 91, 165; relations with aristocracy, 5, 6, 15, 17, 22, 81, 93; mercantilism, 32–33
Mingay, G. E., 3–8, 10–15, 17–22
Mitchell, L. G., 59–60
monarchy: limited, 18–20, 24–25, 36–37, 57, 98, 100–104, 114–15, 148–49, 170; absolute, 18, 37, 62, 97–98, 100, 110, 113–15, 148, 166, 170; reform and restoration of, in France, 115, 149, 152–55, 168–72; dependence on property and intermediary orders, 152, 169
money: market in, 17, 158; devaluation of, 151, 159–61, 165–66;

monied interest, men, 17–18, 27, 158–62, 165
monopoly, 73, 118, 120, 125–27
Morley, John, 115

Nagle, -s (Burke's cousins), 1–2, 32, 63, 132
Namier, Sir Lewis, 11–12, 18, 22
natural: moral order, 143–44; unplanned order ("nature" or "course of things"), 44–45, 131–35
nature: human (corruptible), 27; teleology of, 51–52; rights derived from goals of, 47–48; and convention, 50–53
nobles, nobility, 3, 5–6, 19–21, 62, 80–81, 83, 86, 92, 101–102, 105, 113, 155, 165
North, Lord, 109, 122–23
Nullum Tempus Acts, 61–62

Paine, Thomas, 109, 112, 165
Pares, Richard, 99
Parliament: aristocratic control of, 18–21, 85; independence from Crown, 18, 37, 62; representation in, 4, 22, 93; reform of representation, 22–23, 98, 104, 167–69
Parliamentary History, defects of, x
philosophes, -ers, 153–54, 156, 160, 164–65
Pitt, William, the Younger, 30, 59, 78, 104, 107, 123–24, 129, 137–38
Plumb, J. H., 11
Pocock, J. G. A., 9, 16–17
poor, pauper, -s, ism, poverty, 1, 4–5, 7, 14, 23–24, 39–40, 42, 45, 58, 76, 79, 93, 118–19, 129, 136–38, 140–42
poor laws, 19, 23
Portland, Duke of, 26, 61, 78, 83, 107, 113
power, political: a trust from and for the people, 39–41, 54, 72, 79, 83–84, 112; qualifications for exercising, 82–88, 101–102, 104–105, 107–109; open to new men, 77, 84, 107; ruinous effects of joining with commerce, 124–28, 135; dreadful when independent of property and

rank, 161–64; arbitrary, Burke's hatred of, 98, 110, 128, 170
prescription, 47, 60–70, 92, 163
Price, Dr. Richard, 147
primogeniture, 12–13, 81
property: right, -s to and of, 28, 34, 48–54, 56–57, 67, 130, 142; subject to regulation, 49–50, 56, 142, 175; access to, 29–32, 46, 92; means of acquiring, 32, 80; division of, 13; distribution of, 3, 11, 25, 29, 42–45; privatization of Crown lands, 119; effect of laws upon, 29, 32, 38, 90–91; a trust held for the people, 21–22, 24–26, 39–41, 44, 46, 85, 95, 175; landed, 6–7, 10–13, 17–18, 29–30, 32, 38, 40, 42, 48, 55, 61–62, 77, 82–84, 88, 95, 98, 107, 152, 159–61, 169, 174–75; new forms of, 9–10, 17–18, 158–61, 174–75; of the poor is their labor, 136, 145; material base of civilization, 12, 29, 46, 58, 85, 88, 92; goal of civil society, 28, 47–49, 70–72, 91–92; subordinate to higher goals, 17, 28–29, 46, 77, 87, 173; bulwark of liberty, 7, 18–20, 32, 35–37, 46, 48, 107, 150, 175; spur to industry, 26, 29, 32, 42, 46, 58; forms long views, 30; supports the family, 12–13, 40, 88; and personal dignity, 35–36, 175; generates ruling class, 87; large protects smaller property, 85; society and government must protect, 28, 34, 43–46, 49, 52–53, 55–58, 69, 71–72, 87, 95, 135–36, 140, 150–52, 169; poor must respect, 58, 95, 169; is the nation, 170; is power, 37–38, 101; but this not universally true, 38, 161–64; checks power of government, 37, 98, 104, 175; also supports it, 152, 169; must share in political power, 37–38, 92–93; must govern, 77, 82–84, 115; danger of separating from power, 38–39, 46, 56, 175; confiscation of, 35, 43–45, 50, 55–57, 61, 65, 68, 142, 150–51, 159, 163, 169; enduring importance of, 175

prosperity, 13–14, 24–25, 29, 38, 58, 76, 87
public, the British, 87

Reed, Henry, 140
religion, 42, 45, 74–75, 81, 93, 95, 132, 150, 154–56, 160, 170–71
rent, -ed, -er, -s, 4–5, 10–11, 25, 30, 42, 91, 137, 140–42
revolution, sometimes, but rarely, justified, 64, 98, 149, 174
Revolution, French, 2, 23, 34–35, 37, 40, 42–43, 59, 61, 67, 78, 80–81, 87, 97–98, 107–11, 113–14, 124, 141, 147–74; foreseen by Burke, 147; unnecessary, 149; total, 150–52, 161–68, 172; anti-property, 150–53, 157–58, 161–63; anti-sound money, 152–53, 160–61, 165–66; anti-monarchy, 152; anti-aristocracy, 152, 157; anti-religion, 153–54; anti-Christian morality, 156–58, 164–65; a menace to Europe, 152, 154, 167–68, 172–73; summary of Burke's indictment of, 173
Revolution, Glorious, 97–98, 110
Richmond, Duke of, 82, 104, 106
rights: of men, 47–48, 67, 73, 161; to political power not among them, 47; natural, 47–54, 70, 72; conventional, 36, 47–53, 145; chartered, 41, 53, 72–73, 125; to advantages of society, 48, 79, 135–36, 145; to property, *see* "property"
Rockingham, Marquis of, 2, 59, 81–82, 98, 100, 102, 105–107, 121, 173
Rousseau, Jean-Jacques, 156–57

Samuels, Arthur, 24
self-interest, sufficiency of, 132, 144
slavery: reform of, 30–32; feudalism as, 67; condition of Irish Catholics as, 75, 90; poor law as, 118
Smith, Adam: references to *Wealth of Nations* explained, x; cited, 6, 13–15, 158; acquaintance with Burke, ix, 116–17
society, civil: defects of, 26; both natural and conventional, 52–53,

69, 80; goals of 47–48, 72–75, 77, 79, 142, 144–45; must protect property, 28, 53, 151; generates a natural aristocracy, 85–86

Speenhamland, 23, 129–30, 142

Stanlis, Peter, ix, xi, 47, 98

state, the: a natural entity, 5; broad definition of, 143–44, 174; narrower definition of and of its functions, 75–77, 135, 139, 142–44; exists to protect proerty, 71–72; not the owner of private property, 56–57, 68, 142, 151

statism, 161–67, 172; *see* "democracy"

strict settlement, *see* "entail"

Sutherland, Lucy, 77

tenant, -cy, 4, 10–12, 14, 25, 140–41

Trinity College, 2, 88

Veitch, George, 22

wage, -s, 4–5, 7–8, 14, 129–30, 132–36, 142, 144

Warburton, William, 60

wealth: distribution of, 24, 42; differentials in, 7; circulation of, 39, 44–45; lust for, 24–27; object of lawful pursuit, 27–30; not highest goal of life, 28–29, 173; old landed leads to large views of general welfare, 39, 82, 107; a trust for the people, 39, 43–44; true nature of, 57–58; new wealth should not govern, 81, 104, 160; depends on a free, legal order, 175

Wecter, Dixon, 117

Whig, -s, ism, 2, 7–8, 18, 20, 40, 53, 59–61, 75, 81, 83, 95, 97–115, 128

Windham, William, 78, 90, 110–11, 152

Woodham-Smith, Cecil, 138–39

yeoman, 4

Young, Arthur, 129, 133

www.ingramcontent.com/pod-product-compliance
Lightning Source LLC
Chambersburg PA
CBHW031246290426
44109CB00012B/465